wholefood

For my daughter Nessie:
the sweetest sugar roughie pineapple of them all.

First published in the United States in 2007 by Running Press Book Publishers

Printed in the United States

9 8 7 6 5 4 3 2 1
Digit on the right indicates the number of this printing.

Library of Congress Control Number: 2006931040

ISBN-13: 978-0-7624-3074-1
ISBN-10: 0-7624-3074-5

American Edition Editor: Diana C. von Glahn
Cover design by Amanda Richmond

This book may be ordered by mail from the publisher.
Please include $2.50 for postage and handling.
But try your bookstore first!

Running Press Book Publishers
2300 Chestnut Street
Philadelphia, PA 19103-4371

Visit us on the web!
www.runningpresscooks.com

wholefood

heal ... nourish ... delight

JUDE BLEREAU

RUNNING PRESS
PHILADELPHIA • LONDON

Acknowledgments

This book is the product of far more than just one person. Many angels, friends and midwives have helped to shape and bring this book to be. I am indebted and eternally grateful to all who follow. Blessings, the deepest of thank yous, armfuls of love to you all.

The biggest thanks of all must go to my daughter, Nessie, who endured much when she was young. I was in my extreme left phase of what constituted good/bad food...it was recently on one Mother's Day she said how much she loved to go to her Nonna's, because she could have meat. She has been one of my greatest teachers, helping me realize we are all individual, and what is healthy for one, may not be for another. To my Mom, who truly has a great sense of beauty in all things and surrounded her family with it. She always put her children first, cooked great food and sewed us the most exquisite clothes. Thank you, thank you for that beauty. To my family, who in their many differing ways supported me throughout my journey. While at many times they thought I was crazy, they stuck by me—thank you from the bottom of my heart.

There are many who have shone light on my path and helped shape who I am. Anne Marie Colbin, who changed my path when I came across her book *Food and Healing* in New Orleans, 1986. I had been studying nutrition at that time, and I truly felt much of it was not right. Her words were so refreshing and made so much sense—she is a visionary, and we owe much of the current natural food movement to her. Alice Waters, who stood out there on a limb, unashamed to want true, beautiful food. She gave birth to the organic food industry because of that passion. Deborah Madison and the entire Greens' cast over the years, who insisted that vegetarian food be delicious and beautiful...rabbit food and fads had no place at their tables or in their books, just good technique and excellent results. To Elyse who helped my true self shine through.

To my Australian publisher Kay Scarlett—who saw the manuscript and immediately understood—another visionary. I am deeply grateful, not only for that, but for the enthusiasm and style you bring to it all. Many blessings and thank yous.

To my editor, Emma Hutchinson. Always calm, softly spoken, always ever so firmly and gently keeping me on track, and always finding the best way for my voice to come through. The task was huge, and I am in awe of the way you worked it all out, made it whole and enabled it to be what I wanted it to be. I am deeply grateful.

To my food editor, Katy Holder, who listened to what I wanted, helped me find better ways to achieve it and cared and watched over it all as if it was her own—the best fairy godmother that ever existed. Without Katy, this book would not have been what I wanted—something of value, easy to use and excellent. I am deeply grateful and will endeavour to write a better recipe format from now on.

To gifted designer, Katie Mitchell, who clothed my words with so much beauty and photographer, Natasha Milne, for such gorgeous photos. To all at Murdoch Books, for your passion for excellence, style, enthusiasm and support. Blessings and thank yous.

To Julia Collingwood and Theresa Pitt, thank you for the belief and support.

Big armfuls of thank yous and blessings, to all who I count as friends, all angels in disguise who have helped me bring this book to birth in your own various ways: my dear friend Jeanie, who always knew what I was on about, taught me much, and continues to inspire me. Michael, for just being the beautiful person he was. I'm so very sorry you're not here to see the end result, dear friend, you are missed. To each and every one of my clients and students for giving me the opportunity to cook and teach—it brings me so much joy. Thank you for all the questions you ask, and feedback you give…it keeps me reaching further and always learning more. Maria, Rene and Jane, for giving so freely of yourselves to help me when the going got tough. I could not have done this without you all. Brendan for stepping in and saving the day, you are my computer guardian angel. Julie, Denise and Peter—for the love, support, the meals—for it all. Tracie, for her unfailing support for me during The Earth Market days. Dean, for The Earth Market and the lessons learned. Rowley, for the friendship and support—above and beyond, Tess, Nola and Kerri, for just being who you are, beautiful, and for always being there if I needed you.

To each and every organic and biodynamic farmer—I know how hard it has been for you. Your work has not gone unnoticed and unvalued. Thank you.

Jude Blereau

contents

the wholefood kitchen

PERSINWARE
0 1 2 3 4 5 6 7 8 9 10 11 12 13 14
TRADE MARK

When my daughter was little and, even now, when she is not so little, I would ask her, as a parent does, was there anything she needed? 'Love me, feed me and hug me' was her reply, and still is. And here, in this simple wisdom, lie the fundamentals of life. Food is not something that simply keeps us from feeling hungry. It is exactly the same as love—an elemental human need. Together, they sustain and nourish us, providing fuel for our bodies and hearts to grow and our lives to fulfill their potential. But for food to do these things, it must be authentic and real.

It seems that we have forgotten what good food really is, where it comes from (not plastic-wrapped from the supermarket) and what it should taste like. One look in a school cafeteria, hospital, workplace cafeteria, bakery or corner shop will show you exactly what I am talking about: food with little flavor, loaded with refined sugar and damaged fat (see pages 24 to 25) to give taste. It is manufactured with the cheapest of compromised ingredients. Today, even fresh produce is grown to last—superficial and tasteless. And you have to ask yourself, how can this be in this day and age, when we have so much knowledge and have so much available to us? Refined and processed foods give nothing to your body: in fact, they take away as your body tries to digest them. These foods cannot sustain you; they cannot nourish you. Your body knows this: you can eat and still be malnourished. Your soul knows this: you can eat and still be hungry. It is absolutely no coincidence that our children, raised on these foods, are lost and angry, hungry and searching for something they do not understand: for on a cellular level, they are starving.

We are not machines; we are the most amazing of beings. We live, sing, create, laugh, sigh, make love and do much, much more. We, like our food, are wondrous things, and to not care about the quality and growing of our food is to not care about ourselves. To pay no attention to the source of our food and the way in which it is farmed, stored and sold is to be disconnected from the earth in a most fundamental sense. That humankind as a whole has been so willing to use (and continue to use) poisonous products on our produce (often simply for profitability's sake) is a damning indictment of our attitude toward the food we feed ourselves. To pursue technologies and practices such as refining, genetic engineering and food irradiation and to use herbicides and pesticides is to absolutely ignore the integrity of our food, and demonstrates the profound misunderstanding of our relationship with it. While it would be naive to discount the great advances and tremendous opportunities that exist for us now, thanks to science and technology, we often find ourselves adapting to it, rather than it adapting and finding ways to work with us. The profound work at hand for the 21st century will be to bring heart and soul to much of what science and technology has to offer.

You can begin this work today by considering your living, shopping and cooking habits. And that is really what this book is all about—appreciating food that is real and seeking out food that is compatible with your body. Real food tastes great and has the ability to contribute to your health rather than harm it, and this goodness needs to be available to your body every single day.

You won't find lots of recipes for meat, fish or dairy in this book, but that's not because I feel that they don't fit the category of everyday goodness, but rather that I believe other people do them much better than me. The recipes here are for the times you want something different. Most are vegetarian, many are dairy- and wheat-free and some are vegan and gluten-free. What you will find are recipes for everyday cooking to heal, nourish and delight.

My fondest hope is that you will see how easy it is to cook something real and that you can learn that it is simply a matter of developing an understanding of some basic principles. I teach people wholefood cooking, and I see this time and time again in my classes: with knowledge and a little practice, comes capability. Then when you are walking along and you are feeling hungry, and see something pretending to be apple pie, for example, you won't want it. Because you'll know that if you eat it, not only will it taste gluey and sickly sweet, but it will also do nothing to leave you feeling satisfied, nourished and strengthened.

When you cook for family or friends, you are providing more nourishment than packaged food ever could. I assure you that those meals you make contain powerful medicine—love medicine. Go into your kitchen; let the flour fly and the knife chop. Next time you're tempted to go and get a take-out chicken, stop; know that when you make the effort to cook, your work is of value. Instead, grab a real chicken (one that is not loaded with antibiotics, growth stimulants, hormones and bleach), take a few minutes to season it with thyme, a little salt and garlic and throw it in the oven. Grab a handful of vegetables that are bursting with life and take 10 minutes to organize them in a salad, or put them in the oven to roast with the chicken—infinitely yummier and far more potent and fulfilling than anything store-bought.

Making changes can be overwhelming and learning new ways to cook can be confusing. And to look around and identify the huge amount of processed foods can be scary. What is there left to eat? Lots! But changes will have to be made. The most important thing I can say to you is to take it one step at a time. Don't try and do it all at once—it won't work that way and you will end up disheartened. Start with one thing, such as beans. Get to know them, use them and see how they react. Learn their rules and how they work best, and then move on to the next thing. Accept that there will be failures. When I first started on this path, some 15 years ago, I had many. These disasters are now the center of many a hilarious conversation within my family. Like love and life itself, it will be a learning process.

You are about to embark on a journey down a new path. And here's my advice. Never, ever accept mediocrity posing as convenience. Never, ever accept glitter over substance. Care about what you eat: absolutely insist that it be delicious and true; and never, ever accept anything less. When you sit down to a real meal, with real food, the body is fed and, having been fed and delighted, the soul is nourished. And only then are you able to become the amazing being you were born to be...

How this book works

Labeling a diet, be it vegetarian, vegan or gluten-free, is no guarantee that it is healthy. Wholefood cooking is a broader perspective that acknowledges the integrity of food, the basic rule being that, the more food is refined and processed, the more its integrity and its inherent ability to nourish are lost. Below are some simple rules for healthy eating.

Food should be good enough to eat

Good food starts in a field's rich soil: farmed sustainably, in harmony with nature, without the use of chemical fertilizers, pesticides or herbicides, and without genetic engineering. Once harvested, good food has nothing toxic added to it. Food grown in this manner is usually referred to as 'organic,' which is how all food used to be grown, before big business got hold of it. Organic foods include meat and dairy products as well as vegetables. When the forces of the cosmos are also used (planting and harvesting by the moon, for example) these foods are called 'biodynamic'. Just as there is a noticeable difference (in taste) between organic and 'conventional' food, so there is between biodynamic and organic.

In buying organic or biodynamic food, we seek to live within an ecosystem rather than control it. The important thing to realize is that every single thing we do has an impact on the environment. Every time we use plastic bags for shopping we have an impact; every time we buy compromised or processed food we are supporting an industry that does not care what is damaged or destroyed in the growing, or how incompatible some components of that food will be with our bodies (for instance, additives, preservatives, flavorings, colorings, pesticides and herbicides). What we do or do not buy has become a powerful way to send a message to the big food companies and, sadly, the only way left that makes any impression. Companies may not make changes out of concern for the rapidly declining health of our soils, but they will when it comes to their profit line.

Unfortunately, many people believe that organic foods are less attractive and more expensive than their conventional counterparts. Yet organic produce and the way it is created is a beautiful thing, and, depending on the grower, can be perfect and stunning. The higher price charged for a lot of organic produce reflects the true cost of producing food, but when a product is in season, organic is often cheaper than, or at least equal in price to, its conventional counterpart; if bought in bulk, it becomes cheaper still. Canned organic produce, it must be admitted, is often more expensive than food bought fresh, and this is usually because most of it is imported. Organic meat, dairy and eggs are usually more expensive as well, but given the large amounts of hormones, growth stimulants, antibiotics and morally bankrupt practices used in the conventional production of these foods, choosing them is a decision that I find easy to make.

Seek out farmers' (growers') markets. Not only are they a wonderful way to source well-priced, local and fresh organic produce, they also offer community—giving urban dwellers the opportunity to get closer to the source of food itself. Most of us live in a world that is profoundly disconnected from the natural world, a suburban life where families and the people who grow our food rarely interrelate, and one in which food is something that simply comes off a shelf. It is this disconnection that makes it easy for us to buy cheap, packaged meat from a supermarket, produced from animals that live and die in terrible and unnatural conditions. It is this distance that allows us to buy vegetables and produce with no concern for how they are grown and the impact this is having on our environment and our health.

We are now in the fortunate position of having farmers' markets becoming a familiar part of our urban life: it is there that we can find a balance between the need to grow and produce food that can sustain and support life and the need to respect our environment. At a farmers' market we can come together, respecting and connecting with each other and forming a vibrant and rich community.

Food should be real

Processed and refined ingredients are, fundamentally, incompatible with our bodies. For example, some ingredients in commercially produced ice cream: diethyl glycol is a chemical used in place of eggs, and is also used as antifreeze in radiators and paint remover; banana flavor is from amyl acetate, an oil paint solvent; strawberry flavor is from benzyl acetate, a nitrate solvent; and vanilla flavor is from piperonal, which is used to kill lice. This is fake food. Its only attraction is that it is cheaper than the real thing.

Focus on the quality of the food

Virtually every day, you will read or hear some new discovery that tells you what you should or should not be eating. What concerns me is that I rarely see people questioning this information. The crucial question is, 'what is it that actually makes this food good or bad?'

If you want to eat less fat, for example, focus on eating a smaller amount of quality fat rather than substituting it with one of the 'low-fat' products. Take apricot pie as an example. For a short time each year these fruits come into season. We can eat them in many healthful ways, but nothing quite compares with the comforting effects of a freshly cooked pie. You are far better off with a slice of organic apricot pie made with butter or unrefined coconut oil pastry than you are with a piece of pie made with highly-refined ingredients. Good food is real, wholesome and intact.

Eat in balance

If you are having that slice of special occasion apricot pie and treating yourself to a little ice cream, don't overload your body. Balance your food intake with vegetables, whole grains, and added fruit and protein. You could also consider saving the pie until a Sunday lunch, the digestive system being most active during the middle of the day. Have a light breakfast, then the big meal, followed by something light for dinner, such as soup.

Eat what suits your body

Many people have allergies to foods, for example, to the lactose in dairy and the gluten in some grains. But beyond this, it is important to understand that we are all individuals, and react to foods differently. No one diet is right for everyone. Some will thrive on meat and dairy, others not. Some will do well with soy, others not.

Eat a wide range of foods

There are many diets around, each with their own prescription, which often contradict one another, that it is no wonder so much confusion abounds. I believe that, beyond every diet, there are some fundamentals that are being overlooked. Include lots of vegetables, and then support this with whole grains and good-quality protein (legumes, meat, fish and eggs). Include good quality fat (saturated, unsaturated and essential fatty acids)—from meat, eggs, fish, butter, yogurt, cheese, cream, milk, seeds, nuts, whole grains and sea vegetables (for a list, see page 302). Include fruit also. Foods that you can ignore are refined products, such as white flour, white sugar and processed fats.

Remember, your body needs a range of nutrients from the main food groups: proteins, complex carbohydrates and fats, as well as fruit and vegetables. It also needs a balance of vitamins, minerals and enzymes, among many other things. You cannot eat a lot of one thing and expect to retain balance, even on the 'healthiest' of diets. For example, it is not uncommon for vegetarians to rely too heavily on dairy products and pasta (refined grain) and end up severely out of balance.

Eat seasonally and locally

To eat in season is to be attuned to nature's wisdom. As the seasons change, the way we cook will change also, with hearty stews and warm desserts sustaining and warming us in winter, while lightly cooked or raw vegetables help to refresh us in summer.

When we eat locally, we are truly embracing the 'whole'—because good food, healthy food, links us directly with the riches that the ecosystem has to offer. Eating organically and locally is to denounce—on a profound level—the generation of pollution and wasted energy involved in bringing foods to us by truck, train, ship or plane. I would much prefer to give snow peas (mangetout) a miss than eat those flown in from Africa because, in buying them, I am not only accepting the huge amount of energy involved, but am endorsing the unregulated use of herbicides and pesticides in many third world countries to produce our foodstuffs.

Don't stress

It is important to realize that you can only do the best you can at any given time. On one occasion this may mean buying organic bread, made from organic sour dough, on another the most decent one you can find, with the least amount of additives. With each opportunity you take to buy organic produce you are having a profound effect on your life and that of the planet.

How to cook

Cooking is a matter of developing some basic knowledge. The most important step as a cook is to become familiar with ingredients: to learn how they behave, and then apply that knowledge. Another skill is to actively involve all of the senses. Listen. A gentle sizzle in a frying pan, for example, means that other tasks can happily be attended to without too much fear of frying or burning. With touch we determine texture—is it too soft, too firm, does it feel like it should? Smell can alert us to pivotal moments, such as burning, toasting or roasting. And sight can confirm all these things.

Buffing and shining

The most important of all the senses in cooking is, of course, taste. With taste, a recipe becomes a guideline only, and what you cook becomes its own creation. In tasting the dish you are assessing the flavors, and are being asked to balance them to give the dish depth, fullness and roundness. I call this process 'buffing and shining.'

Some ingredients that give sweetness are: apple juice concentrate, green peas, mirin, orange sweet potato and pear juice concentrate.

Some ingredients that give groundness are: genmai miso, Kelpamare and tamari.

Salt throws 'light' on the finished product and makes flavor fully available.

The single biggest mistake people make when cooking, especially with vegetarian and vegan food, is to give it one dimension only—that is, not adding texture or flavor or added interest (such as pre-roasting). One-dimensional food is boring, and will leave you unsatisfied, even though you may have eaten a lot. Each time we make a dish it will require different degrees of balancing. For example, one winter squash may be sweet, with a well-ripened depth to it, reflecting the fullness of the soil it was grown in. Another may lack that sweetness and depth, requiring a touch of pear juice concentrate to deepen the flavor. (As a general rule, I consistently find organic vegetables need less buffing and shining.)

Different dishes need different approaches to balance them. Tamari, which is a dark sauce made from soybeans, will 'ground' winter squash, yet be too harsh for asparagus—a well-developed stock and fresh thyme would be the better choice for this delicate vegetable. Some dishes may only need a little grounding, some only a little sweetening, while others may require both.

The role of fat in cooking

Fat is one of the mediums most heavily relied upon to contribute, carry and deliver flavor. Dairy products such as butter, cheese and milk all do this easily and brilliantly, while olive oil contributes fabulous flavor as well.

Cooking at high temperatures can damage fats, making them less chemically stable, contributing towards rancidity and turning them into harmful substances. Therefore, it is important when heating fats to choose the ones that are the most stable: saturated fats and mono-unsaturated fats. It is also important to heat fats gently, as smoking will not only damage the fat but affect the taste as well.

Saturated fats

These are solid at room temperature, and are the most stable fats in the presence of heat, oxygen and light. Ghee (clarified butter) is a saturated fat, and is one of the oldest and simplest forms of fat for cooking. It has a high burning point and delivers superb flavor.

Palm and coconut oils are both extremely stable fats and have been used in cooking for centuries. Unrefined palm oil is among the richest sources of beta carotene (which helps prevent cancer and heart disease) and has a high content of vitamin E (a powerful antioxidant). Unrefined coconut oil is an extremely rich source of lauric acid (a fatty acid believed to have strong anti-fungal, anti-microbial and anti-tumor properties).

Mono-unsaturated and unsaturated fats

These fats are liquid at room temperature (therefore, oils) and are unstable in the presence of heat, oxygen and light. The most stable oil for heating is olive oil, a mono-unsaturated oil with a high content of oleic acid.

Unrefined sesame oil has the antioxidant 'sesamin' and, while not as stable as olive oil, can be gently heated, for use in sautéing, for example. In recent years, both sunflower and safflower oils have been developed to a high oleic formula, which makes them far more stable to heat. The problem with sautéing or frying food in good-quality high-oleic sunflower oil, however, is its strong flavor and color, which profoundly influences the flavor of the food. High-oleic safflower oil may be a better choice as it is naturally light in color and flavor.

The more unsaturated oils (and therefore the more fragile oils), such as flaxseed oil, should never be heated and are best used at room temperature, for example, in salad dressings.

Good oil should reflect the source from which it came—many will be strongly scented and brightly colored. Look for terms 'cold pressed' or 'expeller pressed' when shopping and only ever buy good quality oils. Oils should be stored in a cool dark place and the most fragile oils kept in the fridge.

TIPS

Ways to achieve flavor and mouthfeel without relying on fats are to:

- Use organic or biodynamic ingredients.
- Add flavor wherever possible (such as using stock instead of water).
- Build flavor into the finished dish (such as topping a dish with pesto).
- Cook gently—a low and gentle heat allows for much better development of flavor.
- Encourage reduction—a thicker consistency will create a deeper and more substantial flavor.

Basics and assumptions

To cook well, you will need to start with a few standard pieces of equipment and learn some simple rules and terminology to help set you on the right track. Here are some basic facts and assumptions that are used throughout the book.

Measurements and temperatures

Tablespoon measure

The tablespoon measure used is 4 teaspoons.

Cup measure

A cup measurement is 9 fluid ounces.

Oven temperatures

A low oven temperature is 235 to 275°F, a moderate oven temperature is 350°F and a hot oven is 400°F. Fan-forced ovens (gas or electricity) cook hotter and quicker, and generally a low oven temperature for a fan-forced oven is 200°F, a moderate temperature is 275 to 300°F and a hot oven temperature is 325 to 350°F.

Food goes into a pre-heated oven. Specified temperatures in this book are for a conventional, non-fan-forced oven.

Organic ingredients

Organic ingredients have a more powerful taste than non-organic produce. This needs to be taken into account when using recipes; for example, an organic maple syrup will have far more sweetening power than its conventional counterpart. If you are unable to find organic produce then you will need to factor this in.

Techniques

To blanch

Put the vegetables into a saucepan of salted boiling water for 1 to 3 minutes (depending on the size of the vegetables) or until just tender. Drain well, run under cold water then leave to cool completely in a bowl of cold water.

To cut julienne

Finely slice vegetables or fruit into pieces similar in length and size to a matchstick.

Add to taste

Start off with a little and build up. This is especially relevant when dealing with pepper or chiles.

To sauté

Literally meaning 'to jump,' sautéing traditionally encourages a quickish browning of ingredients in a rather hot pan, while shaking and stirring regularly. The term is applied rather loosely in this book, and describes a more gentle heat than is traditionally used, to encourage development of flavor.

Fat should never be so hot that it is smoking. To check the temperature, simply pinch a bit of flour or food into the oil—if it sizzles gently it is ready.

To shallow fry

The oil should cover the bottom of the pan well, usually by about ¼ inch when shallow frying. For large items (such as rice balls) a depth of about ½ inch will ensure that some of the side is sealed also. If frying large amounts, clear the oil (or at least the debris) every couple of batches. The oil should always be hot before you put the food in, so as to seal the food and brown it quickly. If the heat is too low, the food will stick and absorb the fat.

To simmer

This is to cook over a gentle heat, with just a few bubbles coming to the surface. Simmering encourages flavors to mingle and come together; too many bubbles and you will get loss of liquid through evaporation.

Roasting seeds and nuts

Roasting seeds and nuts enhances flavor and can be done in the oven or in a frying pan on top of the stove. To roast the seeds, simply put the seeds in a pan over a low heat, shaking gently. Do not let the seeds smoke, as this indicates that the fragile oils in the seeds are burning. If the pan gets too hot, remove from the heat and continue to gently shake the pan. When ready, the seeds should be lightly colored with a distinct aroma. Pour them into a bowl immediately.

To roast nuts, preheat the oven to 350°F. Put the nuts on a baking tray and bake for 10 to 20 minutes, or until they are lightly colored.

The use of lids

Having a lid on or off makes a great difference. With the lid on, moisture is trapped and returned to the pot or pan. Keeping the lid on is useful when cooking with a little liquid for a long period of time. It is also useful when you need to cook, but not fry, a mixture of ingredients rather than using a large amount of oil to stop things from sticking, and also aids the cooking process.

Cooking without the lid enables evaporation and, hence reduction, to take place. As well as starting with good-quality organic produce, reducing over a long period of time (at a low simmer) is an invaluable way to boost the flavor of a dish, concentrating the flavors.

Cookware

There are many facets to cooking and the quality of ingredients is one thing that will obviously have an impact on the end result. But equally important is the mode of heat transfer you decide to use. Cooking on top of the heat source (such as the stove top) delivers the quickest transfer of heat; however, this results in less concentration of flavor. Cooking in the oven is slower, with a diffused transfer of heat, and the result is more depth of flavor. For a faster cooking time while still achieving an intensity of flavor, a good-quality cast-iron pot, casserole dish or 'French oven' is invaluable.

Authentic French ovens (also known as Dutch ovens) can be expensive, but will last a lifetime and reward you time and time again. They are useful to brown base ingredients (onions and herbs, for example) on top of the stove; the other ingredients can then be added to the pot, the lid put in place and the pot put in the oven to finish off the cooking process. Unless you have extremely good quality stainless steel cookware, it tends to transfer heat too quickly and too directly and gives a poorer end result, and I prefer to use French ovens in a lot of my cooking.

When I refer to a heavy-based saucepan in recipes, a French oven would be ideal.

Heat diffusers

A heat diffuser is a cheap and invaluable tool for slow cooking on the stove top. It is a circular metal implement with a handle that sits under your pan. It diffuses the heat so that it is more evenly distributed across the whole bottom surface of the pan, allowing you to cook considerably more slowly. They are widely available.

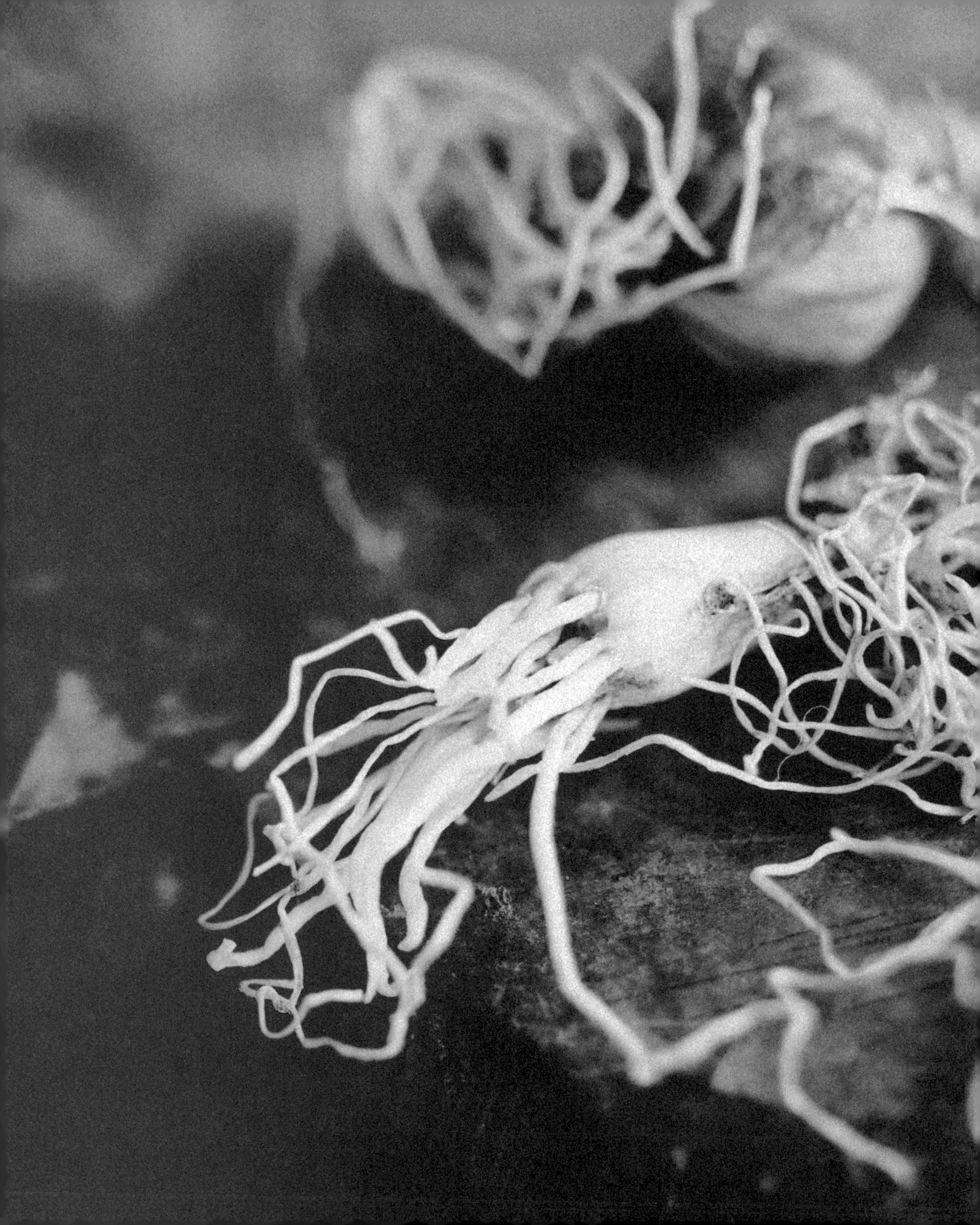

Foundations

A well-flavored stock, some slow-roasted tomatoes or a fiery salsa can turn an ordinary recipe into an outstanding one. This section contains a few basic recipes that are used throughout the book to add that extra touch.

Chipotle chile

These are dried, smoked jalapeño chiles. They are fiery and hot, and add a delicious smokiness to a dish. They are available whole, *en adobo* (reconstituted in a can) or ground.

To use, simply roughly tear the jalapeño chile and put in a saucepan with a little water. Gently simmer for 20 minutes until the chiles are soft and moist. Be careful not to breathe in the steam as it can easily 'burn' your lungs. Use in this form, or allow to cool, and then blend with a little of the cooking water to make a purée.

Chipotle chile will keep in a sealed container in the fridge for a few weeks.

Tamari seeds

DAIRY FREE / VEGAN

Salty, crunchy and delicious, these add immediate flavor and wonder to salads and many other dishes.

Stored in an airtight container, tamari seeds will keep in the fridge for 1 week.

- 1/4 cup hulled sunflower seeds
- 1/4 cup pepitas (pumpkin seeds)
- 1/4 cup sesame seeds
- 1 tablespoon tamari

Put the seeds in a frying pan and cook over a gentle heat for 5 to 8 minutes, until fragrant and lightly golden. Shake and stir often to prevent burning. Immediately after they begin to color, take them off the heat and add the tamari. Stir with a spoon and turn them into a bowl to cool.

Roasted garlic purée

Roasted garlic is delicious, with the very assertive flavor of garlic softened and almost caramelized.

Try adding some rosemary and thyme to the roasting garlic—it adds a gentle and delicious flavor.

Preheat the oven to 350°F.

Take the garlic and break the cloves apart. Put them in a square of baking paper, drizzle with a little good olive oil and sprinkle with fresh herbs. Twist the paper together to form a bag and cook in the oven for 20 minutes or until the bulbs are soft. Be careful not to overcook—they can still burn, even through paper. Allow to cool, then snip the tops off the cloves and squeeze out the soft purée.

VARIATION

To make a large amount of roasted garlic, take a whole head of garlic and snip the top off, exposing some of the inner flesh. Put in an ovenproof dish, sprinkle with fresh herbs, drizzle with a little good olive oil and add a little stock (enough to come 1/2 to 1 inch up the side of the dish). Cover with either foil or baking paper, and bake for 1 hour, until the bulb is soft when you squeeze it lightly. Remove from the oven and allow to cool before squeezing out the soft flesh.

Oven-baked tomatoes

Not quite dried, these are tomatoes that have been slowly baked, allowing the heat to concentrate the moisture content and intensify the flavor. What results is a soft yet deeply flavored tomato with a variety of uses.

The best tomatoes to use are those that are well-ripened.

Preheat the oven to 235 to 275°F. Wash the tomatoes and cut in half.

Lay the tomatoes in a roasting tin. Sprinkle with a little salt and pepper. Drizzle with olive oil. Top with roughly chopped fresh basil (not absolutely necessary).

Cook for about 1½ hours, or until the tomatoes are soft to the touch but becoming firm. As the moisture in the tomato reduces, the tomato will darken in color—cook it too long and it will become very dark and leathery in appearance. The cooking time will vary depending upon the size and moisture content of the tomatoes.

As their flavor is concentrated and developed, oven-baked tomatoes can be used to enrich the flavor in a stew or sauce or in a salad. They will keep for a few days in the fridge.

Roasted peppers

Roasted peppers can be used to add flavor to many dishes. They are great added to salads. Red pepper is used because it provides vibrant color to dishes and a lovely sweet taste.

Preheat the oven to 350°F. Wash the pepper well and cut the top off close to the stem. Remove the inside core and seeds. Stand upside down in a baking dish and rub well with olive oil. Bake for 1 hour, or until the skin is well wrinkled and the top begins to blacken. Remove and put into a bowl and top with a plate to cool. Remove the skins.

These will keep covered in the fridge for 2 to 3 days. Covered well in olive oil, roasted pepper will keep for 1 to 2 weeks.

Caramelized onions

GLUTEN FREE / VEGAN

These add a fabulous depth of flavor to savory dishes, such as tarts.

Heat 1 tablespoon of olive oil in a frying pan. Add 3 thinly sliced onions and cook over a gentle heat, stirring often, for 15 minutes, or until the onions are very soft. Add 1 to 2 tablespoons of mirin and continue to cook over a gentle heat (a heat diffuser is useful here) for 10 to 15 minutes, stirring often. The end result should be beautifully soft, richly flavored and lightly colored onions.

These can be stored, covered, in the fridge for up to 5 days.

Fresh tomato sauce

GLUTEN FREE / VEGETARIAN

The best-flavored tomato sauces are generally made from well-ripened, organic tomatoes, preferably roma (plum). They can be peeled and seeded first, although this is not absolutely essential. The keys to developing a deeply flavored sauce are a good length of time to sauté the onion and herbs, using well-ripened tomatoes, and a long, slow reduction time. Canned tomatoes can be used to make a good sauce, particularly in winter, but when tomatoes are in season fresh ones make a far superior sauce.

Fresh basil or oregano gives a more fragrant sauce, with dried herbs giving an earthier, more savory flavor.

MAKES 2 TO 3 CUPS

10 large, well-ripened roma (plum) tomatoes (or 14 ounces canned tomatoes)
olive oil (or ghee), for frying
1 onion, finely diced
1 to 2 garlic cloves, crushed
7 to 10 fresh basil leaves, finely chopped
1 sprig fresh oregano (optional)
2 to 3 teaspoons apple juice concentrate (or to taste)
sea salt, to taste
freshly ground black pepper, to taste

The consistency of your sauce will be determined by its use—for pasta that is uncooked (especially dried pasta sheets, such as dried lasagne) it will need to be quite watery, allowing the pasta to absorb liquid while cooking in the oven. Fresh pasta sheets will absorb little liquid and the sauce will need to be quite thick.

If using fresh tomatoes, cut an X at the bottom of each tomato, to pierce the skin. Bring a large saucepan of water to the boil. Put 2 to 3 tomatoes at a time in the water for 15 to 20 seconds. Remove and allow to cool just a little. Using a sharp knife, peel off the skins. Cut the tomatoes into quarters—if you prefer to remove the seeds, simply remove them with your fingers, into a bowl, and then dice the flesh into another. Put all skins and seeds into one bowl (this is later squeezed, or put through a sieve, to extract all the remaining liquid. Some tomatoes will have a lot of liquid, others virtually none). If retaining the seeds, simply cut the tomato quarters into dice and add to a bowl.

Heat 1 tablespoon of olive oil in a frying pan. Add the onion and sauté for 5 minutes over a very low heat (a heat diffuser is useful here), stirring occasionally. Add the garlic and continue to cook for 5 minutes. Add all the other ingredients (with 2 teaspoons of apple juice concentrate to start). If using fresh tomatoes, include all the liquid squeezed from the tomato skins and seeds, cover with a lid and simmer slowly for 30 to 40 minutes (to release the juices). If using canned tomatoes, break them up and cook, covered, at a gentle simmer for approximately 15 minutes. A slow reduction will take place as the flavors come together.

Remove the lid and check for taste—depending on the tomatoes, you may need to add a little more apple juice concentrate or salt and pepper. Continue to cook over a moderate to high heat for 10 to 15 minutes, encouraging evaporation and stirring occasionally, until desired consistency is achieved. (The longer and slower the reduction stage, the richer the end result.)

VARIATIONS

- Add 1/4 to 1/2 cup of red wine when simmering the tomatoes.
- Add 1 tablespoon of tomato paste (concentrated purée) when simmering the tomatoes—choose an organic one if you can find it.
- Add vegetables for a heartier sauce. Pepper, carrot, mushroom, celery, baby (pattypan) squash or zucchini all work well. Dice fairly small and add to the onions after a few minutes of sautéing.
- Add cooked cannellini beans to the raw tomato.

Fresh salsa

GLUTEN FREE / VEGAN

This is the classic and most versatile salsa, and is quick and easy to make. Leftover salsa is a great addition to dal and pairs well with corn fritters. In summer try adding diced mango to this. It is excellent with fish, Thai dishes, chicken, tofu cakes and rice paper rolls.

SERVES 3 TO 4

2 to 3 ripe tomatoes (if making by hand use 3, if making in a food processor use 2)
1 fresh chile, seeded (or to taste)
¼ to ½ small red onion (or green onion (scallion) to equal)
½ red pepper
1 to 2 tablespoons fresh cilantro leaves
juice of 1 lime (2 to 3 tablespoons)
freshly ground black pepper, to taste

This can be made in two ways: in the food processor or by hand (by hand looks more attractive).

With a food processor

Roughly chop 2 tomatoes, chile, onion and pepper. Put in a food processor and pulse until just finely chopped. Do not over-chop, it should be slightly chunky, not a mushed-together sauce. Add the finely chopped cilantro, lime juice and black pepper, and stir it through.

If you find the salsa is not hot enough, try adding a little ready-made chile sauce to taste.

By hand

Cut the 3 tomatoes into small dice, cut the chile into very fine dice, roughly cut the onion and the pepper and chop the cilantro. Mix all the ingredients together.

Blackened tomato and chipotle salsa

GLUTEN FREE / VEGAN

This is an extremely simple yet very effective salsa—a true favorite. When you blacken a fresh chile you end up with a softer flavor and a pronounced, rounder and deeper heat than fresh chile.

MAKES 2 CUPS

6 ripe tomatoes (the best you can find)
1 to 2 fresh red jalapeño chiles
3 to 4 garlic cloves, roughly chopped
1 to 2 teaspoons puréed chipotle chile (see page 32)
1 to 2 teaspoons apple juice concentrate

Put a simple flameproof rack (such as a cake cooler) over the flame on your stove. If you don't have a gas stove, blacken them under the broiler, turning to blacken the skins evenly. Put the tomatoes on top in batches and cook over a full flame until the skin is blackened, but not cooked. Turn occasionally to evenly blacken the skin. Remove to a bowl and cover with a plate.

Cut down one side of the chile and open so it lies flat. Remove the seeds. Put on the frame skin side down and blacken over a slightly lower heat, or under the broiler, so the flesh has a little time to cook before the skin is blackened. Add the chile to the bowl with tomatoes, and allow to cool. Roughly peel the tomatoes and chile. If you find the chiles too difficult to peel, use a small knife to scrape the flesh from the skin.

Put the tomatoes and chile in a food processor with the garlic and process until puréed, adding a little black pepper if desired. Turn the mix into a frying pan. Add 1 teaspoon each of the chipotle chile purée and apple juice concentrate and simmer gently for 15 to 20 minutes, stirring occasionally until the salsa thickens slightly. (A low heat will enable the flavors to come together, without reducing too much.) After this time, the salsa should have taken on a darker color, with a thicker and less-watery appearance, and have reduced by approximately one-third—check for taste, adding more chipotle purée and apple juice concentrate if desired and reducing further if needed. Turn into a bowl.

Salsa ranchera

GLUTEN FREE / VEGAN

This is the Mexican version of a simple tomato sauce. It is excellent to use for enchiladas and other oven-baked dishes.

MAKES APPROXIMATELY 28 FLUID OUNCES

olive oil, for frying
1 onion, finely chopped
2 garlic cloves, finely chopped
1 teaspoon ground cumin
pinch cayenne pepper (or to taste)
pinch freshly ground black pepper
pinch chilli powder (or dried or reconstituted chipotle chile) (or to taste)
28 ounces canned tomatoes (or fresh tomatoes, roughly chopped, to equal)
1 to 2 tablespoons chopped fresh cilantro leaves

It is the cayenne pepper that gives the hot bite, the chilli powder, chipotle chile and black pepper the deeper heat. You can play with the kind of heat by varying the peppers used.

Heat 1 teaspoon of oil in a frying pan. Add the onion and garlic and sauté over a gentle heat for approximately 3 minutes. Add the spices and cook for 1 minute.

Add the tomatoes and cilantro. Cover and cook for 30 minutes over a gentle heat. Remove the lid, and continue to cook over a low heat until thick. If you are using fresh tomatoes, it is especially important to keep the heat low, allowing time for the tomatoes to sweat their juices out. Stir occasionally.

Tofu sour cream

GLUTEN FREE / VEGAN

This is quick and easy to put together and works wonderfully with Mexican dishes.

MAKES APPROXIMATELY 5 OUNCES

5½ ounces silken tofu
2 teaspoons lemon (or lime) juice
1 teaspoon shiro miso
sea salt, to taste
freshly ground black pepper, to taste
2 tablespoons finely chopped fresh chives (or cilantro leaves)

¼ cup of ricotta added to this makes a delicious low-fat topping for potatoes.

Combine all of the ingredients together in a blender or food processor and blend until smooth and creamy. Turn into a bowl.

VARIATIONS

- Add more herbs, such as 1 tablespoon of finely chopped fresh basil, parsley or dill.
- Add 1 to 2 crushed garlic cloves, or 2 to 3 teaspoons roasted garlic purée (see page 33).

Tofu 'ricotta'

GLUTEN FREE / VEGAN

Very easy to put together, this makes an excellent replacement for ricotta cheese in lasagne, cannelloni and other Italian-style dishes.

MAKES APPROXIMATELY 1 CUP

10 ½ ounces silken tofu
large handful fresh basil leaves
¼ cup pine nuts
2 to 3 garlic cloves, crushed

Put all the ingredients in a food processor and blend until just smooth.

Béchamel—dairy version

A good white sauce can be indispensable. The classic béchamel is made with butter, flour to thicken and dairy milk, and it is a superb sauce with a sweet and rich flavor. It is especially good in winter, when the high fat level warms the body.

MAKES 2 CUPS

2 to 2½ tablespoons unsalted butter
2 tablespoons unbleached all-purpose wheat or spelt flour
2 cups whole milk (preferably non-homogenized)
Herbamare (or sea salt), to taste
freshly ground black pepper, to taste

Melt the butter in a saucepan over a low heat. Remove from the heat and add the flour, and mix to a smooth paste with a wooden spoon. Slowly add the milk, using a whisk to bring it to a smooth, lump-free consistency. Continue to whisk gently until it just comes to the boil. (Heavy boiling will only cause the milk to separate.) Immediately remove from the heat and season to taste. Extra milk can be added at this stage to thin the consistency of the béchamel.

VARIATIONS

Infusing the milk before use with fresh herbs (such as sprigs of parsley, thyme and a few bay leaves) and a clove of thinly sliced garlic adds a great amount of flavor, helping to earth the sweet flavors of whole organic milk. Simply add the herbs to the saucepan with the milk and gently heat—until it just begins to steam. Immediately take the milk off the heat and sit for 10 to 20 minutes. Strain the milk (removing the herbs and garlic), then use.

Adding cheddar cheese is another great way to add flavor. It can be a little too rich when using whole non-homogenized organic milk, but the richness can be balanced out by using a smaller amount of butter. Add the desired amount of cheese after the sauce has boiled and stir through.

Béchamel—non-dairy version

GLUTEN FREE / VEGAN

The quality of a good dairy-free béchamel depends greatly on the quality of soy milk used. It also depends upon sources of flavor other than the milk. The easiest and most successful way is to steep fresh herbs in the soy milk before use. This adds an enormous range of flavor to the end result.

Many non-dairy béchamel sauces are made using oil as the initial fat medium added to the flours; however, this usually results in a sauce with heavy olive oil overtones, dominating the béchamel flavors.

MAKES 2 CUPS

2 cups soy milk
2 sprigs fresh flat-leaf (Italian) parsley
1 to 2 sprigs fresh thyme
1 to 2 fresh bay leaves
1 garlic clove, finely sliced

1½ tablespoons rice flour
1 tablespoon cornstarch
Herbamare (or sea salt), to taste
freshly ground black pepper, to taste

Put the milk, parsley, thyme, bay leaves and garlic in a saucepan and gently heat until it just begins to steam. Immediately remove from the heat and allow it to sit for 10 to 20 minutes. Strain the milk, removing the herbs and garlic—the garlic can be mashed into the milk for extra flavor.

Put the flour and cornstarch into a saucepan and add a small amount of the milk. Mix with a wooden spoon until a smooth paste is formed, then gradually add the rest, whisking to bring it to a smooth consistency. Put over a gentle heat and continue to gently whisk until just boiling. (Heavy boiling will only cause the milk to separate.) Immediately remove from the heat and season to taste. Extra milk can be added at this point to thin the consistency of the sauce.

VARIATIONS

- Add 2 to 3 teaspoons of roasted garlic purée (see page 33) to the cooked sauce.
- Add finely chopped flat-leaf (Italian) parsley to taste after the sauce is cooked.

Shiitake mushroom gravy

DAIRY FREE / VEGAN

This is a wonderful gravy, rich with immune-boosting shiitake mushrooms—great over mashed potatoes and baked dishes during the colder months. Kudzu flour can be found in Asian markets.

Prized for centuries, shiitake mushrooms are considered to be rich in nutrients that help to control cancers and strengthen the immune system.

MAKES APPROXIMATELY 1¾ CUPS

8 to 10 small to medium dried shiitake mushrooms
1½ tablespoons kudzu powder (or cornstarch or arrowroot)
olive oil, for frying
1 onion, finely sliced lengthways
1 to 2 small garlic cloves, crushed
1 to 2 sprigs fresh thyme

1½ tablespoons mirin
1 teaspoon Kelpamare (or sea salt) (or to taste)
1 to 2 tablespoons tamari
freshly ground black pepper (optional)

Soak the mushrooms in 2½ cups of hot water for 20 minutes. Remove the mushrooms and discard the tough stems. Slice the caps thinly. Reserve the liquid and allow to cool.

Mix the kudzu powder with a small amount of the reserved, cool liquid to a smooth paste. Add the rest of the liquid and set aside.

Heat 1 teaspoon of olive oil in a frying pan. Add the onion and sauté over a low heat for 4 minutes. Add the garlic, thyme, mushrooms and mirin. Continue to cook, stirring occasionally until the onion is soft and translucent. Add the Kelpamare and 1 tablespoon tamari, then the kudzu liquid. Stirring, bring the mixture to a boil. Test for flavor; add pepper or the extra tamari if desired. Continue to cook over a gentle heat for 10 minutes, stirring frequently, until it reduces to a gravy consistency of your liking.

Barbecue sauce

DAIRY FREE

Quick and delicious, this is an easy sauce to make for burgers.

Finely chopped fresh cilantro and chile are great additions to this sauce.

MAKES 1 CUP

olive oil, for frying
1 small onion, finely chopped
2 garlic cloves, finely chopped
½ cup tomato paste (concentrated purée)
½ cup apple juice
1 teaspoon dry mustard
pinch ground cinnamon
freshly ground black pepper, to taste
3 teaspoons tamari
3 teaspoons apple cider vinegar
3 teaspoons honey

This recipe will be gluten-free if wheat-free tamari is used.

Heat 1 tablespoon of olive oil in a small saucepan over low heat. Add the onion and garlic, cover with a lid and cook gently for 3 to 5 minutes, or until soft (a heat diffuser is useful here). Add all the other ingredients. Cover again with the lid and continue to cook over a low heat for 15 to 20 minutes. Blend in a food processor or blender until smooth.

VARIATIONS

Adding chipotle chile (see page 32) gives the dish a delicious, smoky heat.

Sweet ginger sauce

GLUTEN FREE / VEGAN

This sauce is something a little different to use as a dipping sauce or poured over steamed vegetables.

MAKES APPROXIMATELY 12 FLUID OUNCES

roasted sesame oil, for frying
3 teaspoons grated ginger
2 garlic cloves, crushed
1½ tablespoons brown rice vinegar
1½ tablespoons lemon juice
1½ tablespoons rice syrup
3 teaspoons kudzu powder (or cornstarch or arrowroot)

Heat 1 teaspoon of sesame oil gently in a saucepan and add the ginger and garlic, cover with a lid and cook over a low heat for 2 minutes, until just soft. Add the brown rice vinegar, lemon juice and rice syrup.

Dissolve the kudzu powder in 1 cup of water and add to the pan. Over a low heat, stir continuously until thick and clear. Allow to cool a little before serving.

Carrot and ginger sauce

DAIRY FREE / VEGAN

With a bright orange color and vibrant flavor, this is a wonderful sauce for vegetables and is great served with fried rice.

MAKES 1 CUP

2 teaspoons kudzu powder (or cornstarch or arrowroot)
1 cup carrot juice (preferably freshly juiced)
1 teaspoon ginger juice
1 teaspoon chopped fresh cilantro leaves

To make ginger juice, peel the ginger and then roughly grate using a grater, microplane, or a specialist ginger grater. Gather up and squeeze out the juice.

Put the kudzu powder in a saucepan. Pour in a little of the carrot juice and mix to a paste. Add the rest of the carrot juice, together with the ginger juice.

Put the saucepan over a gentle heat and bring to the boil, stirring. As the mixture boils, it will thicken. Immediately after it begins to boil, remove from the heat. Add the cilantro. Taste and add more ginger juice if required.

Pesto

GLUTEN FREE

To make a good pesto you need good ingredients. It is important to buy fresh parmesan cheese and fresh garlic, and the olive oil you use should be the absolutely best quality—unrefined and unfiltered.

MAKES APPROXIMATELY 1 CUP

2 handfuls fresh basil leaves
½ cup grated parmesan cheese
¼ cup pine nuts
3 garlic cloves, crushed
⅓ cup olive oil

Put all the ingredients in a food processor and pulse until well incorporated. Try not to blend for too long; it should be chunky, not a smooth, homogeneous blend.

Pesto will keep in the fridge for about 2 weeks, and can be used in so many wonderful ways—dolloped on top of minestrone soup, spread on toast, or as a topping for a quick pasta meal.

Tomato jam

DAIRY FREE / GLUTEN FREE

A spicy, fragrant, savory tomato jam—this is especially good with chickpea fritters, but it goes with so many other things as well.

MAKES 1 CUP

olive oil, for frying
¼ cup crushed ginger (you will need a piece about 3½ inches long)
3 garlic cloves, crushed
¼ cup apple cider vinegar
2 cinnamon sticks
4 large tomatoes, peeled, seeded and finely chopped
¼ cup brown sugar
1 teaspoon ground cumin
pinch ground cloves
¼ cup honey

Heat 2 tablespoons of olive oil in a saucepan over a gentle heat. Add the ginger and garlic, and cook for 2 to 3 minutes. Add the vinegar and cinnamon sticks and cook until reduced by half. Add the tomatoes, brown sugar, cumin and cloves. Cover with a lid and cook over a very gentle heat for 4 to 5 minutes, stirring occasionally and checking it has not run dry. Remove the lid, add the honey and continue to cook over a gentle heat until thick.

Tomato jam can be kept in the fridge for up to 4 weeks.

Tahini, yogurt and cilantro sauce

GLUTEN FREE / VEGETARIAN

Wonderfully versatile, this sauce works especially well with Middle Eastern inspired dishes, but could also be used as a dressing for a salad.

MAKES APPROXIMATELY 1½ CUPS

½ cup tahini
1 cup plain yogurt
2 tablespoons lemon juice
1 large handful fresh cilantro leaves, chopped
2 garlic cloves, crushed
sea salt, to taste
freshly ground black pepper, to taste

Mix all the ingredients together well in a bowl.

Stock

Stock has a reputation as being something that requires a lot of work, but it only takes a few minutes to put together, then you just leave it on the stove to do its thing. This is a great Sunday job, done every couple of weeks; the stock can be frozen in portions to use in the time between. Stocks are an invaluable source of nutrients and goodness, and are one of the easiest ways to deliver flavor.

Stocks made from animal bones: Throughout the centuries, stocks made from bones have been considered to be crucial foods for health. Meat stocks, particularly when cooked with a little wine or vinegar, draw out the minerals, amino acids and cartilage in the bone, making them more freely available. As a component of stock made from animal bones, gelatine is of particular value. Gelatine enables the easy digestion of cooked foods—in particular protein, and it also allows the body to utilize more fully the complete proteins that are eaten.

Stocks made from fish heads and bones: As with animal stocks, fish stocks are rich in minerals, particularly iodine. Fish stock is revered in East Asia as a restorer of 'Chi'—life force.

Vegetarian and vegan stocks: When making stock without relying on animal bones to give nutrients and depth of flavor, you need to give extra thought to the ingredients used. The addition of dried shiitake mushrooms provides both nutrients and depth of flavor while kombu and agar (agar-agar) flakes add desirable nutrients and minerals. A dash of Kelpamare will also add flavor, nutrients and depth. Avoid using vegetables from the brassica family, such as broccoli, cabbage, cauliflower and brussels sprouts, which can adversely flavor the stock.

Stock cubes: These should generally be avoided, as many (even the 'healthy' ones) are overly salty and contain lactose, hydrolized vegetable protein and other additives.

Vegetable stock

GLUTEN FREE / VEGAN

This is great standard stock. It works and it is easy. Because the quality of the ingredients is so important for this recipe, try to use organic vegetables where possible.

Increase flavor by chopping the vegetables into smaller roughly cut chunks and sautéing them in a little olive oil for 10 minutes before adding to the stock. Do so over a gentle heat—as the vegetables sauté and begin to lightly color, so will the flavor develop.

MAKES APPROXIMATELY 6 CUPS

1 large onion (unpeeled), quartered
1 leek, well rinsed, roughly cut (if not in season, simply omit)
5 medium carrots (unpeeled), roughly cut
1 large sweet potato (unpeeled), roughly chopped (essential for its subtle sweetness)
2 to 3 celery stalks, roughly chopped
5 dried shiitake mushrooms
3 to 4 sprigs fresh flat-leaf (Italian) parsley
1 fresh bay leaf (fresh or dried)
2 sprigs fresh thyme

Put all the ingredients in a large heavy-based saucepan, add 12 cups of water and bring to the boil. Continue to cook over a low heat for 1 to 1½ hours. (It is important to cook over a low heat, so as not to encourage rapid boiling, and thus evaporation.) Strain to remove all vegetable matter and discard this. You now have a basic stock. At this stage, you can either use it as is, or continue to cook it over a fairly high heat, reducing it and thus concentrating the flavor.

MUSHROOM VEGETABLE STOCK VARIATION

To make mushroom vegetable stock add an extra 6 dried shiitake mushrooms.

OTHER VARIATIONS

- Add 1 strip kombu (or 2 teaspoons of agar (agar-agar) flakes or ¼ teaspoon powder) to the stock for added nutrients.
- Add kernels from 1 corn cob to add sweetness to the stock.
- Add a handful of strongly flavored mushrooms (such as porcini) to the stock for a more intense mushroom flavor.
- Add a dash of Kelpamare to the stock to boost the flavor.
- Add a selection of animal bones and 1 tablespoon of either wine or vinegar to draw minerals from the bones. These will take 1 to 5 hours to cook properly at a very low simmer. Chicken will take 1 to 2 hours. Lamb will take 2 to 3 hours. Beef (including marrow bones) will take 3 to 5 hours. When using bones, brown them gently first before adding other ingredients.

breakfast

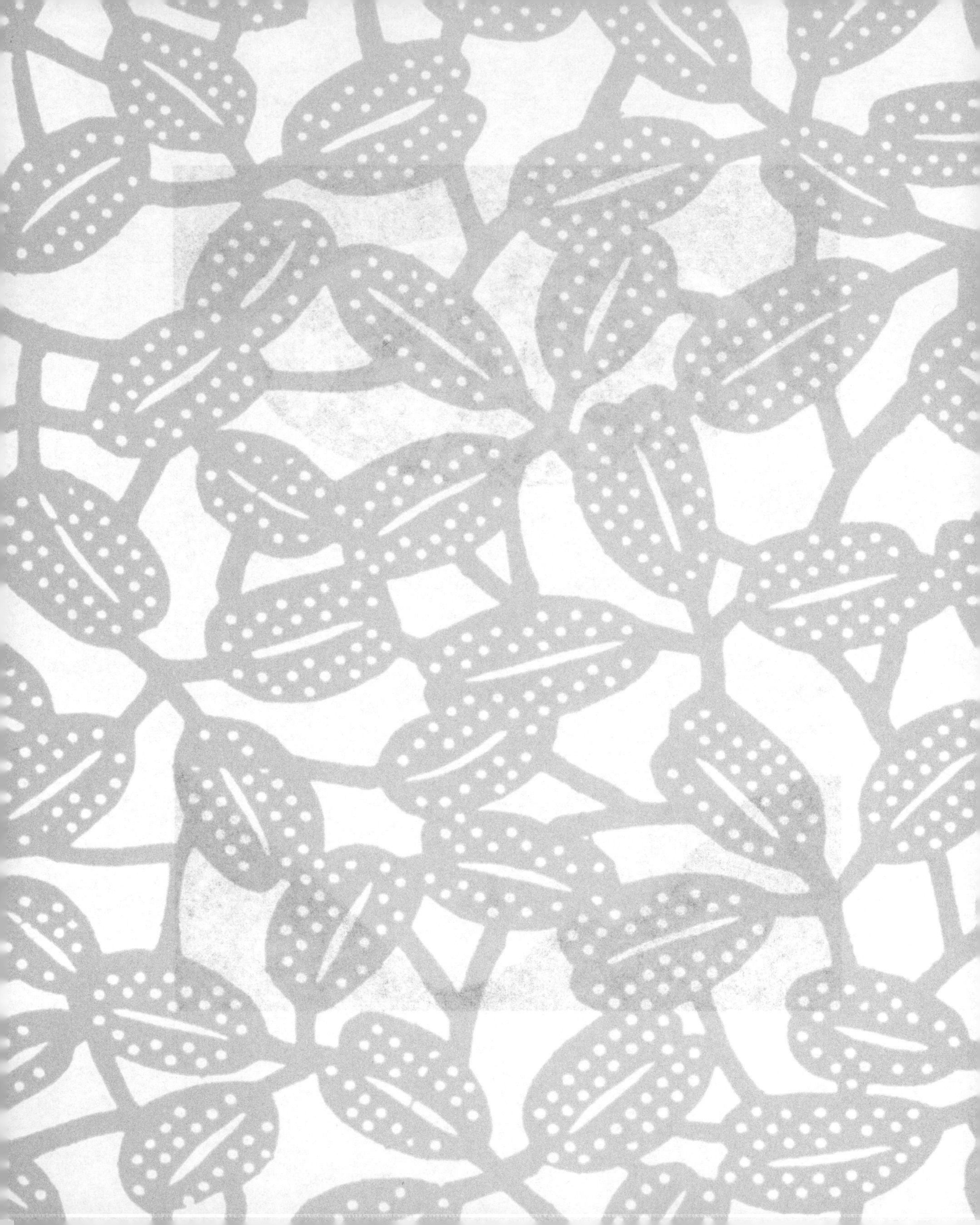

One of the questions I'm most often asked is "What can I eat for breakfast?" While everyone starts the day differently, the fact remains that breakfast is the most important meal of the day and provides the foundation for your daily activities. Walking, thinking and doing all require energy and, when fuel isn't available, low blood sugar reactions such as shaking, confusion, loss of performance, loss of concentration and fatigue set in. There is no 'right' breakfast. Look ahead to your morning, assess your needs and provide yourself with the fuel you require. When you know you have a particularly busy or physically demanding morning, then eating a breakfast based on complex carbohydrates will keep you going. This can simply be in the form of a bowl of grain—like oatmeal or muesli. If you require a little more of a kick-start, then protein (such as eggs, meat, beans, tofu, tempeh or miso) does the job admirably. Fruit is good but, on its own, won't sustain you for very long: by 10 a.m. the sugars will have been burnt up, and you'll be craving something else; and usually the first thing you will find available is a commercial cookie, refined and loaded with damaged fats.

Your morning grain

With its rich store of nutrients and slow-release fuel, grain is an excellent choice for breakfast. Though extremely popular and convenient, commercial breakfast 'cereals' made from puffed grains or grain flakes are highly processed and much of the nutrient content is damaged or destroyed. Grains are great for breakfast, but they need to be real.

Porridge

A nourishing and satisfying breakfast, porridge can be made from any one or a mixture of grains cooked with water to a creamy consistency. In the cooler weather, oats (with their high fat content) provide more warmth; but also good are barley and whole wheat berries (with their high complexity of carbohydrate). In summer, millet, buckwheat or rice make a lighter porridge and are easier to digest.

Different types of grains

Porridge can be made with whole, cracked, ground or rolled grains, with different results. When using the whole grain, the smaller softer grains, such as buckwheat, hulled millet, oats, quinoa and rice are the best choice; hardier grains, such as barley, rye, spelt and wheat require a fair bit of chewing. Cracking or grinding (in a blender or food processor) breaks these hardier grains down into smaller pieces, giving a quicker cooking time and creamier result. Oats, whole millet, rice and quinoa can be cracked, while buckwheat and hulled millet will simply be too floury. As a rolled grain (sometimes called 'flakes') is pre-cooked, any grain in this form is suitable for porridge.

Whole grain porridge topped with butter or cream is not just delicious, but is very beneficial for your body. It is rich in the fat-soluble vitamins A and D, which helps you absorb the other vitamins and minerals in the grain—Grandma was right!

Soaking

Pre-soaking the porridge grains for 6 to 8 hours makes them more digestible, quicker to cook and much creamier.

A useful routine is to soak them overnight in a large bowl with 2 teaspoons of whey, buttermilk or yogurt stirred gently through. Soaking is recommended at room temperature, allowing a little fermentation to occur.

Though beneficial, it is not essential that all grains be soaked overnight. The softer grains, such as polenta, buckwheat and hulled millet, can be simply added to the pot and cooked as required.

TIPS FOR MAKING PORRIDGE

- Add dry-roasted whole grains to bring out a full and robust flavor.
- Use fruit juices and milks (either 100% or cut with water) instead of water when cooking porridge to add depth of flavor, sweetness and creaminess.
- Include spices such as cinnamon and ginger, dried fruits, seeds and nuts, grated fruit, natural vanilla extract or coconut during the cooking process to greatly boost the flavor of porridge.

Basic whole grain porridge

Whole grain porridges are very easy to make and provide a nutritious start to the day. Use one of the following grains and cook in the amount of water suggested for the length of time given.

SERVES 2

½ cup kasha (toasted buckwheat)
  soaked, 1½ to 2 cups liquid, 15 to 30 minutes
  unsoaked, 1¾ to 2¼ cups liquid, 20 to 30 minutes

1 cup oat groats
  soaked, 1¾ to 2 cups liquid, 20 to 25 minutes
  unsoaked, 2¼ to 3 cups liquid, 25 to 30 minutes

½ cup quinoa
  soaked, 1½ to 2 cups liquid, 15 to 20 minutes
  unsoaked, 2 cups liquid, 20 to 25 minutes

½ cup medium/short grain brown rice
  soaked, 1¼ to 1½ cups liquid, 30 to 50 minutes
  unsoaked, 1½ to 2 cups liquid, 45 to 55 minutes

If using soaked grains (see page 55), pour the grains into a sieve, shaking gently (reserving the soaking liquid to use for cooking if desired). If using unsoaked grains, rinse well. Put the grain into a heavy-based saucepan, add the required amount of liquid, cover with a lid and cook over a gentle heat for required length of time (see above), stirring frequently.

Just before the cooking time is up, remove the lid and check consistency. If, after this time, the grain is cooked but too runny, simply continue to cook over a vigorous heat, stirring, to allow evaporation and reduction. If it is too thick, simply add more liquid.

Leftover porridge will set to an almost cake-like consistency—this can be stored in the fridge and used the next morning—just add extra liquid.

Basic cracked and ground whole grain porridge

For a creamier porridge and quicker cooking time, put the whole grains in a food processor or blender and crack (roughly grind) or finely grind. Then mix with liquid and cook. Use one of the following grains.

SERVES 2

½ cup pearled barley
soaked, 2 cups liquid, 40 to 45 minutes
unsoaked, 3 cups liquid, 1 hour

½ cup kasha (toasted buckwheat)
soaked, 1½ cups liquid, 15 to 20 minutes
unsoaked, 2 to 2½ cups liquid, 20 to 25 minutes

½ cup polenta (already ground)
unsoaked, 2½ cups liquid, 30 minutes

½ cup whole millet
soaked, 1½ cups liquid, 45 to 50 minutes
unsoaked, 2 cups liquid, 60 minutes

1 cup steel cut oats (already ground) or oat groats
soaked, 2 to 2½ cups liquid, 20 minutes
unsoaked, 3½ cups liquid, 30 minutes

½ cup quinoa
soaked, 1½ cups liquid, 20 minutes
unsoaked, 2 to 2½ cups liquid, 20 to 25 minutes

½ cup medium/short grain brown rice, ground
soaked, 2 cups liquid, 30 minutes
unsoaked, 3 cups liquid, 40 minutes

½ cup wheat (or spelt) berry
soaked, 2 to 2½ cups liquid, 60 minutes
unsoaked, 3½ cups liquid, 1½ hours

To toast grains, simply dry-fry in a frying pan over a gentle heat for 5 to 10 minutes, or until fragrant and lightly colored, stirring often.

If using soaked grains (see page 55), pour the grains into a sieve, shaking gently (reserve the soaking liquid to use for cooking if desired). If using unsoaked grains, rinse well. Put the grains into a heavy-based saucepan, add the required amount of liquid, cover with a lid and cook over a gentle heat for required length of time (see above), stirring frequently (a heat diffuser is useful here).

Just before the cooking time is up, remove the lid and check the consistency. If the grain is cooked but too runny, simply continue to cook over a vigorous heat, stirring, to allow evaporation and reduction. If it is too thick, simply add more liquid.

Leftover porridge will set to an almost cake-like consistency—this can be stored in the fridge and used the next morning—just add extra liquid.

Basic rolled grain porridge

Using rolled grains to make porridge reduces the cooking time considerably, as they have already been steamed before the rolling process and thus are already partly cooked. Not all grains are available in this form, but barley, oats, rice, rye and spelt are quite common.

SERVES 2

1 cup rolled (flaked) grain (barley, oats, rice, rye or spelt)

If using soaked grains (see page 55), pour the grains into a sieve, shaking gently (reserve the soaking liquid to use for cooking if desired). If using unsoaked grains, rinse well. Put the grain into a heavy-based saucepan and add 1½ to 2 cups of liquid.

Cover with a lid and gently bring to the boil, then simmer over a gentle heat until cooked and creamy, stirring frequently. Oats will take approximately 7 to 10 minutes, with barley, rice, rye and spelt taking 10 to 20 minutes. When it is nearly ready, remove the lid and check consistency. If, after this time, the grain is cooked but too runny, simply continue to cook over a vigorous heat, stirring, to allow evaporation and reduction. If it is too thick, simply add more liquid.

Rice cream

GLUTEN FREE

This is an excellent example of turning cooked rice into a delicious breakfast. It is a simplified version of rice pudding that takes very little time to cook and is excellent any time of the day.

SERVES 2

1 cup cooked brown rice
¾ cup milk (dairy, soy or almond)
zest of ½ small lemon
¼ cup dried apricots (or peach), roughly chopped
¼ cup golden raisins
¼ cup roughly chopped almonds
¼ teaspoon ground cinnamon

Instead of rice, you could also use buckwheat, hulled millet or quinoa.

Place all the ingredients in a saucepan with ½ cup of water and bring gently to a slow simmer. Continue to cook over a very low heat, without a lid, until thick and creamy. This will take approximately 10 minutes. The mixture can stick and burn easily, so stir frequently and keep your eyes on it. If you feel the mixture is too thick, just add more liquid.

VARIATION

You can serve this with stewed fruit as well as or instead of the dried fruit. Stir it through at the end.

Muesli and granola are both incredibly easy to make and are best stored in an airtight container, in a cool dark spot.

Muesli and granola

Muesli is a mixture of rolled (flaked) grain(s), nuts, seeds and dried fruit. Granola is sweeter, usually because of the addition of maple and rice syrup, and is roasted in the oven. Muesli is normally served with milk, but can be cooked (as for porridge) for a delicious winter breakfast, or used as an addition to crumble toppings, muffins, cookies or muesli/granola bars. One of the most wholesome ways to eat muesli is Bircher style. Bircher muesli is soaked overnight in yogurt or a mixture of yogurt and milk—making it much easier to digest.

Basic muesli

WHEAT FREE

MAKES 7 CUPS

4 cups rolled (flaked) grain (barley, oats, rice, rye or spelt)
½ cup hulled sunflower seeds
½ cup pepitas (pumpkin seeds)
½ cup sesame seeds
1 cup roughly chopped almonds
1 cup chopped dried fruit
1 teaspoon ground cinnamon
fresh fruit, to serve
plain yogurt, to serve

Mix all the ingredients together in a large bowl and serve with fruit and yogurt.

See breakfast toppings (pages 68 to 69) for other serving suggestions.

VARIATIONS

- Add roasted seeds and nuts (such as walnuts, hazelnuts and macadamia nuts).
- Store the muesli with a vanilla bean for a subtle vanilla flavor.
- Add flaxseed.
- Add ½ cup (1 ounce) flaked coconut, preferably fresh.

Bircher muesli

WHEAT FREE

SERVES 2 TO 4

1 cup basic muesli (see previous page)
½ cup plain yogurt
1 apple, grated

Combine the muesli with 1 cup of water, the yogurt and apple in a bowl, cover with a plate and refrigerate overnight.

See breakfast toppings (pages 68 to 69) for serving suggestions.

By soaking muesli overnight with yogurt and apple the lactic acid and enzymes help to break down the grain, ensuring easy digestion and maximum absorption of nutrients.

Basic granola

WHEAT FREE

MAKES 7 CUPS

½ cup maple syrup
½ cup rice syrup
4 cups rolled (flaked) grain (barley, oats, rice, rye or spelt)
1 cup roughly chopped almonds
½ cup hulled sunflower seeds
½ cup pepitas (pumpkin seeds)
½ cup sesame seeds
1 cup chopped dried fruit
1 teaspoon ground cinnamon
1 teaspoon natural vanilla extract

Preheat the oven to 350°F. Put the syrups in a saucepan and gently heat to loosen. Remove from the heat and leave to cool slightly.

Put the rolled grain, almonds and seeds in a large bowl and toss through the cooled, but still slightly warm, syrups. Put on a large baking tray and bake for 15 to 20 minutes, stirring occasionally as the sugars, nuts and seeds can easily burn. Remove from the oven and stir through the dried fruits, cinnamon and vanilla essence. Cool.

See breakfast toppings (pages 68 to 69) for serving suggestions.

Pancakes

Pancakes are simple grain cakes, easy to whip up on the spot and deliver quickly. Freshly cooked, topped with seasonal fruit, they make a healthy snack any time of the day. They are particularly suitable for gluten-free grains, because they are not required to hold height or form (which they do not do successfully). By soaking the batter overnight the grain is broken down, which results in a softer and more digestible pancake.

When made with whole grain flours and low levels of fat, pancakes are much denser than traditional ones. Adding fat in the form of melted butter, egg or whole dairy milk will increase the 'softness' factor considerably. In the following recipes, where there are very low levels of fat, toppings play an important role, providing moistness, flavor and mouthfeel.

Brown rice and buckwheat pancakes

GLUTEN FREE

MAKES APPROXIMATELY 6 (4-INCH) PANCAKES

½ cup brown rice flour
½ cup buckwheat flour
1 to 1¼ cups milk (soy, dairy, buttermilk or a mix of rice and coconut)
1 tablespoon and 2 teaspoons natural plain yogurt
½ teaspoon natural vanilla extract (optional)
1 egg (optional)
butter (or light olive oil), for frying

Combine the rice and buckwheat flours in a bowl. Add 1 cup of milk and the yogurt and mix through. Cover and leave out (or in the fridge) to stand overnight.

Add the vanilla, egg and up to an extra ¼ cup of milk gradually if required. Check the texture. Additional milk will make a softer pancake.

Heat 1 teaspoon of butter or oil in a frying pan. Pour about 2 tablespoons of the pancake mixture into the pan. As the batter hits the lightly sizzling fat, lift the pan and tip it on an angle, allowing the batter to spread out, moving the angle to achieve a circle. Cook well on one side for 1 to 2 minutes before turning over (bubbles should appear in the batter as it cooks). Cook on the other side for approximately 1 minute.

See breakfast toppings (pages 68 to 69) for serving suggestions.

Pancakes are often rolled around a filling. Butter- or egg-free pancakes can still be rolled when hot, but will crack as they cool. By replacing brown rice flour with spelt (whole wheat or unbleached) the pancakes will be much lighter, although no longer gluten-free.

Adding 1 egg to this recipe will make a softer and more flexible pancake.

Brown rice, buckwheat and banana pancakes

GLUTEN FREE

Mashed banana is used here to provide moistness and flavor. The pancakes can be lightened by replacing the brown rice flour with spelt flour (or whole wheat or unbleached), but they will not be gluten-free.

MAKES APPROXIMATELY 10 PANCAKES

½ cup brown rice flour
½ cup buckwheat flour
1 to 1¼ cups milk (soy, dairy, buttermilk or a mix of rice and coconut)
1 teaspoon baking powder
2 bananas, roughly mashed

These pancakes will be dairy-free if you choose a non-dairy milk.

Combine the rice and buckwheat flours in a bowl. Add 1 cup of milk and the yogurt and mix through. Cover and leave out (or in the fridge) to stand overnight.

The next morning, add the sifted baking powder, mashed fruit and up to ¼ cup of extra milk if required.

Heat a teaspoon of butter or oil in a frying pan. Pour about 2 tablespoons of the pancake mixture into the pan. Cook well on one side for 1 to 2 minutes before turning over (bubbles should appear in the batter as it cooks). Cook on the other side for approximately 1 minute.

See breakfast toppings (pages 68 to 69) for serving suggestions.

Berry nice pancakes

MAKES APPROXIMATELY 6 (4-INCH) PANCAKES

1 cup all-purpose whole wheat flour
  (wheat or spelt, or combined with some added oat flour)
⅔ cup milk (dairy, soy, rice or rice and coconut)
1½ tablespoons plain yogurt (for soaked version only)
1½ teaspoons baking powder
1 egg, lightly beaten
1⅓ cups fresh blueberries (or other berries)
butter (or light olive oil), for frying

Soaked
Put the flour in a bowl with the milk and yogurt. Cover and leave out (or in the fridge) to stand overnight. Sift in the baking powder, add the beaten egg and mix through. Add the fruit and stir gently.

Unsoaked

Combine the flour and the sifted baking powder in a bowl. Add the egg and a small amount of milk and mix well until smooth, before adding the remaining milk. Let it sit for 5 minutes, allowing the flour to absorb the liquid. Add more milk if necessary. Add the fruit and stir gently.

Using either the soaked or unsoaked pancake mixture, heat a teaspoon of butter or oil in a small to medium sized frying pan. Pour a small amount (approximately 2 tablespoons) of the pancake mixture into the pan. As the batter hits the lightly sizzling fat, lift the pan and tip it on an angle, allowing the batter to spread out, moving the angle to achieve a circle. Cook well on one side for 1 to 2 minutes before turning over (bubbles should appear in the batter as it cooks). Cook on the other side for approximately 1 minute, until ready.

See breakfast toppings (pages 68 to 69) for serving suggestions.

VARIATION

This pancake recipe can easily be made into a savory version by adding one or a mixture of grated vegetables such as zucchini, baby (pattypan) squash or carrot, finely diced pepper, corn kernels, fresh basil or green onions (scallions). Use between 4 to 7 ounces of vegetables and season with pepper and salt.

Other breakfast ideas

And finally, a few slightly different breakfast options; the more traditional favorites like French toast, scrambled eggs and smoothies but with a twist. Baked beans (see page 77) on toast and corn fritters (see page 133) make some other great breakfast ideas.

The green drink

This drink is a breakfast on the run and all-round pick-me-up. A powerhouse of nutrients, it contains spirulina—a blue-green micro-alga, known as one of the world's most potent natural food sources. Also included is flaxseed oil (rich in omega 3 fatty acids) and wheat germ oil (containing vitamin E).

SERVES 2

1 to 2 teaspoons good-quality spirulina
3 teaspoons flaxseed oil
2 teaspoons wheat germ oil
5 almonds

- 1 banana (or blueberries to equal)
- 1½ cups milk (rice, almond, soy or dairy)
- 3 teaspoons plain yogurt
- honey, to taste

Put all the ingredients in a blender and process until smooth.

French toast

This is a somewhat different approach to the traditional egg-based French toast, but it is equally delicious. Eggs are replaced by flaxseed, which is high in omega 3 fatty acids. The sweetness of amasake (see page 306) balances out the slightly bitter taste of the flaxseed.

Use olive oil to make this a dairy-free recipe.

MAKES 4 TO 6 SLICES

- 3 teaspoons flaxseeds
- 1 to 1½ tablespoons amasake
- 2 cups soy milk
- 1 teaspoon ground cinnamon
- ½ teaspoon natural vanilla extract
- 4 to 6 thick slices bread (preferably stale)
- butter (or ghee or light olive oil), for frying

Combine all the ingredients (except the bread and the butter) in a blender and blend until smooth. This may take a couple of minutes—the flaxseeds are quite hard.

Pour the mixture into a flattish dish and lay the bread in this, 2 slices at a time. Soak for 1 minute on each side.

The butter must lightly sizzle without smoking before you add the bread.

Heat the butter in a frying pan over a low to medium heat. Add the bread and cook for approximately 5 minutes on each side, until lightly golden and slightly puffed.

See breakfast toppings (pages 68 to 69) for serving suggestions.

Scrambled tofu

This recipe will be gluten-free if wheat-free tamari is used. To make this suitable for vegans, use olive oil instead of butter when frying.

This is a wonderfully satisfying breakfast. It is quick to make, nutritious and won't leave you going hungry for the rest of the morning.

SERVES 4

1 pound, 5 ounces firm tofu
butter (or light olive oil), for frying
4 tablespoons finely chopped green onions (scallions)
2 tablespoons finely chopped fresh flat-leaf (Italian) parsley
8 fresh basil leaves (optional), finely chopped
1/4 teaspoon ground turmeric
2 tablespoons tamari
sea salt, to taste
freshly ground black pepper, to taste

Loosely crumble the tofu into a bowl.

Any addition of sautéed, finely chopped vegetables at the same time as the green onions and herbs works extremely well. Mushrooms are particularly delicious, but make sure you cook out all the liquid before adding the turmeric and tamari.

Heat 1 teaspoon of butter in a frying pan over a low heat. Add the green onion, parsley and basil and sauté for approximately 3 minutes, or until soft. Add the turmeric and tamari, stirring until combined. Add the crumbled tofu and stir for 1 to 2 minutes. As you stir, the mixture will start to become a little moist as the water leaves the tofu—when this happens the tofu is ready. Do not be tempted to cook it any longer than it takes to just heat through, as it will become dry and tough. Season with salt and pepper and serve.

BREAKFAST TOPPINGS

These are the best of the best—simple, delicious and entirely health-supportive. They can be used to top porridge, muesli and granola, pancakes or anything else you fancy.

Fresh fruit
Seasonal fruit is a simple and delicious way to add extra flavor.

Stewed fruit (fruit compotes)
Unsweetened or lightly sweetened, stewed fruit is a great topping. Don't overlook dried fruit, such as apples, pears, figs, peaches and apricots. When cooked in a little water with the addition of cinnamon and vanilla these make a delicious compote.

Stewed berries

These make great toppings and provide an intense flavor. Lightly stew the berries in a little water over a very gentle heat with a lid. Sweeten to taste.

Yogurt

When made from good whole milk with bacterial cultures intact, yogurt is an excellent topping, and very delicious.

Flaxseed oil

This is high in omega 3 fatty acids although it can be an acquired taste.

Seeds and nuts

With bountiful stores of good-quality fats, seeds and nuts are exceptionally nutritious. Lightly roasted, fresh or soaked, all are good. In particular, flaxseed, hulled sunflower seeds and almonds are a rich source of omega 3 and six essential fatty acids (sesame seeds are also a great addition).

Sweeteners

Maple syrup, honey, rice syrup and barley malt are healthy sweeteners.

Many people are either lactose intolerant or allergic to the protein in milk and other dairy produce. Good-quality yogurt contains live bacteria that breaks down much of the reaction-causing properties and makes it easy to digest.

Always keep seeds and nuts away from light and heat—store in the fridge to protect their good-quality fats.

beans and legumes

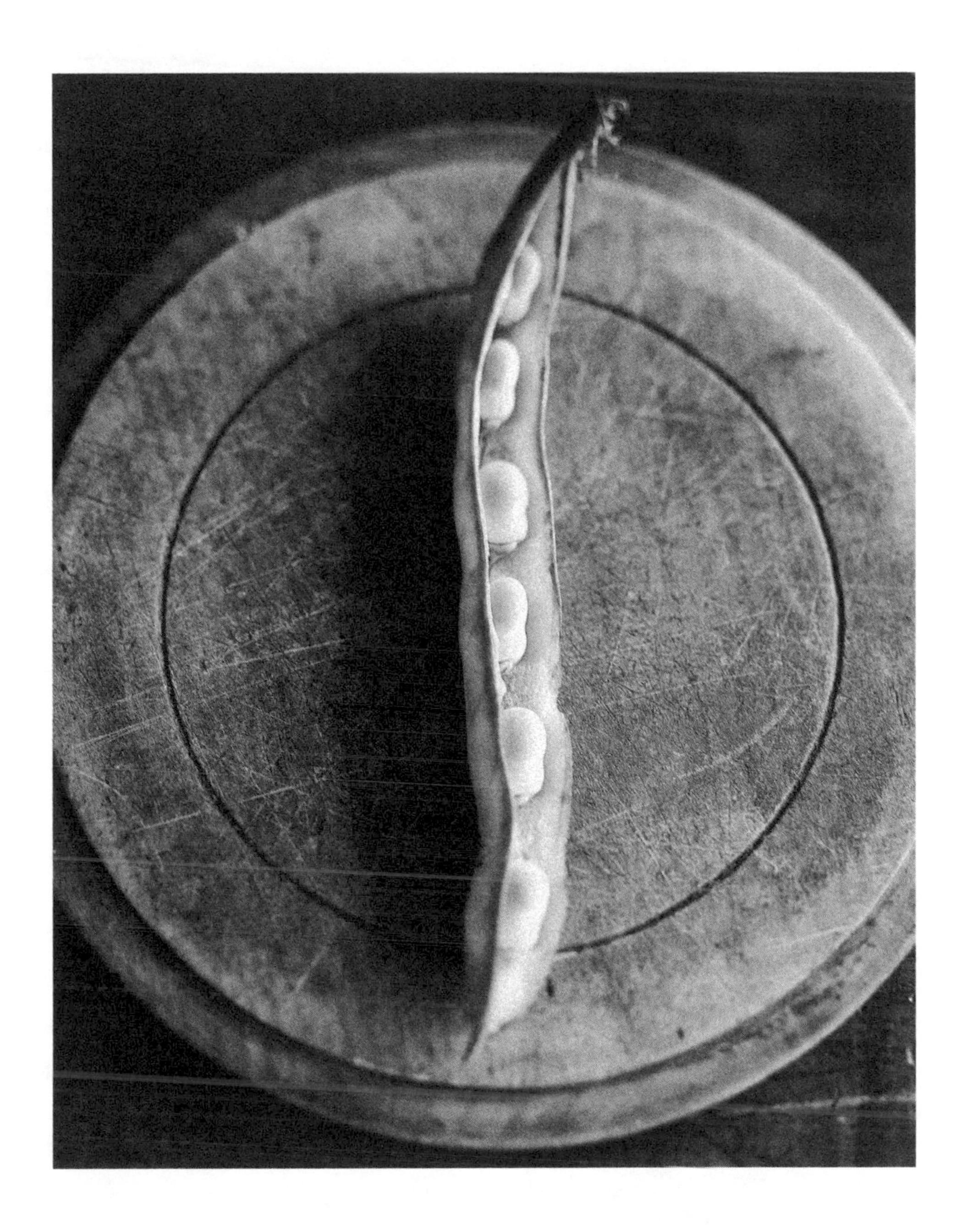

Beans, lentils and split peas belong to the legume family. Cheap and nutritious, they are a great addition to many dishes and are traditionally served with grain. They are a rich source of protein and contain all eight essential amino acids. Legumes are low in fat and are an excellent source of complex carbohydrates, B complex vitamins and minerals including iron, calcium, phosphorus and potassium. It is important to note, however, that the iron in legumes (as with vegetables generally) is of the nonheme variety and is not absorbed as readily as that in meat. Eating legumes in combination with foods rich in vitamin C (such as tomato, pepper and parsley) will dramatically increase the amount of iron absorbed. Legumes are an extremely rich source of fiber, which helps to maintain blood glucose levels and lower blood cholesterol; they also contain omega 3 and 6 fatty acids. The only real problem with legumes occurs with beans, which produce wind. This is due to the complex sugars they contain, known as oligosaccharides, which are extremely difficult for humans to digest. The best way around this is to soak the beans in large amounts of water, allowing much of the oligosaccharides to leach out and dissolve. Soaking also helps to break down phytic acid, ensuring optimum absorption of their minerals.

How to prepare beans

It's true that beans take a long time to cook, but once they are ready, you have either a great meal or the beginnings of one. Beans take planning, that's all. If you are cooking them from scratch, you'll need to organize soaking and cooking time. A good habit is to cook beans in bulk and then freeze them for future use. There are many ways to use beans; as a rule, deeply flavored stews and soups benefit from the addition of uncooked beans, while pre-cooked beans are great for spreads, dips, stir-fries and lighter, quicker cooking stews.

Soaking beans

Pre-soaking beans for 6 to 8 hours makes them more digestible. A useful routine is to soak them overnight in a large pot, covered with water and 2 teaspoons of whey, buttermilk or yogurt stirred gently through. Soaking is recommended at room temperature, allowing a little fermentation to occur.

Cooking beans

Beans must be well cooked to ensure optimum digestion; they can take between 1 and 4 hours to cook on the stove top. They need to be well covered with liquid as they swell considerably. The yields for cooked beans, given below, are approximate; it will vary depending on the age of the beans, length of soaking time and other factors.

If you need to hurry the soaking process, bring the beans to the boil first and then leave them to soak for a couple of hours.

TIPS

Kombu

Adding a small portion of this sea vegetable at the beginning of cooking will soften the beans and improve their digestibility. A 1¼ to 2 inch piece will be adequate for the quantities of beans cooked in the recipes in this chapter.

Do not add salt

Salt only helps to toughen beans. If you must add salt, do it when they have finished cooking. Usually though, the addition of kombu adds a saltiness for you.

Think small

Beans are concentrated and powerful foods—a little goes a long way. A good-sized serving is about ½ cup of cooked beans per person.

Canned beans

These are a great standby and handy to have in the cupboard but shouldn't be the only beans you use. Canned beans are often harder to digest due to the reliance on pressure to create a soft bean rather than long soaking and cooking times. When using, it's best to rinse them as this takes away some of the 'canned' taste.

Cooking beans in the oven creates a better-textured bean, but will take longer to cook (4 to 6 hours). After the soaked beans are drained, transfer them to an ovenproof dish and cover with water up to 1½ inches. Put the pot over a medium heat and bring to the boil, skimming off any foam. Cover with a lid and transfer to a 275 to 350°F heated oven until cooked.

Method for cooking beans

SERVES 4 TO 6

After the beans have soaked, discard the water, drain well and put in a large heavy-based saucepan. Add enough water to cover the beans up to 4 inches and bring to the boil over a medium heat.

As soon as it reaches boiling point, turn the heat down very low (a heat diffuser is useful here). Begin timing from this point, based on the cooking times below.

Beans cook very well in a pressure cooker and need to be covered by approximately 1¼ inches of water. Bring the beans to a boil, skimming off any foam, before beginning to cook under pressure. Cooking times will be radically shorter—20 minutes for the lighter beans such as aduki, pinto, borlotti (cranberry), great northern and cannellini; 45 to 50 minutes for the hardier beans, such as kidney, chickpea and soy.

1 cup dried adzuki beans, 1 to 1½ hours
makes 3 cups

1 cup dried black beans, 1½ to 2 hours
makes 2¼ cups

1 cup dried borlotti (cranberry) beans, 1½ to 2 hours
makes 2¼ cups

1 cup dried cannellini beans, 1½ to 2 hours
makes 2½ cups

1 cup dried chickpeas, 2½ to 4 hours
makes 3 cups

1 cup dried fava beans, 1½ to 2 hours
makes 3 cups

1 cup dried great northern beans, 1½ hours
makes 2¾ cups

1 cup dried kidney beans, 2 to 3 hours
makes 2½ cups

1 cup dried butter (lima) beans, 1 to 1½ hours
makes 2 cups

1 cup dried navy beans, 1 to 1½ hours
makes 2½ cups

1 cup dried pinto beans, 1 to 1½ hours
makes 2⅓ cups

1 cup dried soy beans, 3 to 4 hours
makes 3 cups

Check the beans regularly to ensure that they are always well covered with liquid.

Some beans, particularly chickpeas, produce a large amount of froth, foam and scum—this needs to be removed as they cook. You can tell when they are cooked—they begin to yield their soft, starchy centers to light pressure.

Baked beans

Baked beans are pioneer food—traditionally they were cooked with basic foodstuffs that could survive long journeys and were cheap.

SERVES 4 TO 6

This recipe will be gluten-free depending on the tamari and mustard used, and will also be vegan if water or vegetable stock is used.

1 cup dried navy beans, soaked
olive oil, for frying
1 onion, finely diced
1 teaspoon dried basil
1 garlic clove, finely chopped
2 inch strip kombu (see page 303)
6 cups vegetable stock (see page 48) (or water)
3 teaspoons apple juice concentrate
2 teaspoons molasses sugar
1 tablespoon tamari
½ teaspoon wholegrain mustard
1 teaspoon chipotle chile (dried or reconstituted) (see page 32) (or to taste)
14 ounces canned tomatoes (or fresh to equal)

After the beans have soaked, discard the water and drain well.

Heat 1 teaspoon of oil in a large heavy-based saucepan or flame-proof casserole dish. Add the onion, basil and garlic and gently sauté for 5 minutes, until lightly colored. Add the navy beans and all other ingredients, except for the tomatoes. Cover, leaving a tiny crack for a little steam to escape, and cook over a gentle heat for approximately 1 hour, then add the tomatoes and continue to cook for another 4 to 5 hours (the longer the better). As the cooking time is long, you will need to monitor the pot to ensure the ingredients are always well covered with liquid (a heat diffuser is useful here). Remove the lid, check for taste and adjust as necessary. You should find that the kombu has broken down into the mix, if not, simply use a spoon to do so. Continue to cook without a lid over a gentle heat until the mixture thickens.

Adding the tomatoes after 1 hour of cooking ensures you will end up with soft beans—otherwise their acidity will often inhibit the softening process.

VARIATION

There are infinite variations to this dish. Add extra vegetables to the cooking process, smoked ham bones or hock—all will be good.

This is a great dish to serve for breakfast with toast.

Mexican beans

DAIRY FREE

This recipe will be gluten-free if making nachos.

Tex-Mex meals are healthful, highly flavored and pair naturally with corn— which is gluten-free. The following recipe can be used to make burritos or nachos. The use of chipotle chile adds superb smoky tones to the mix with a deep and powerful heat that a commercial chilli powder will never match.

SERVES 4 TO 6

Preferably, use freshly roasted and ground cumin seed.

Flat bread such as mountain bread or large lavash is ideal. If the bread is less than 10 inches square you will need to use less filling.

¾ cup dried borlotti beans (or pinto beans), soaked (or 12 ounces canned)
¾ cup dried black beans, soaked (or 12 ounces canned)
2 inch strip kombu (see page 303)
1 medium carrot, peeled and finely diced
kernels from 1 corn cob (or 1 cup canned corn)
½ cup sweet potato, peeled and finely chopped
1 red pepper, finely diced
14 ounces canned tomatoes (or fresh to equal)
olive oil, for frying
1 onion, finely chopped
2 garlic cloves, finely chopped
1 heaped teaspoon dried thyme
½ teaspoon ground cumin
1 to 2 tablespoons fresh cilantro (preferably stem and root)
approximately ¼ teaspoon chilli powder (or more to taste) or ¼ dried chipotle chile (see page 32), roughly chopped
8 pieces flat bread (or 6½ ounces corn chips)
large handful grated cheddar cheese (optional)
⅓ cup chopped black olives

GUACAMOLE
1 large (or 2 smaller) ripe avocados
juice of 1 lime (2 to 3 tablespoons)
1 large garlic clove, finely crushed (sometimes you might need more)
sea salt, to taste
freshly ground black pepper, to taste
1 tablespoon finely chopped fresh cilantro leaves
1 tomato, peeled, seeded and diced (optional)
1 finely chopped fresh chile (optional), to taste

1 quantity fresh salsa (see page 37) or salsa ranchera (see page 39)
2 tablespoons chopped fresh flat-leaf (Italian) parsley

Using dried soaked beans
Pour the soaked beans into a sieve. Shaking gently, rinse and drain.

Put the beans and kombu in a large saucepan and add enough water to cover well (approximately 8 cups). Simmer for 1 hour over a gentle heat. Add the carrot, corn kernels, sweet potato, pepper and tomatoes to the pot. At this point, you may need to add a little more water if it is running low—the mixture should now be covered with approximately ¾ inch liquid.

Meanwhile, heat 1 teaspoon of oil in a frying pan. Add the onions, garlic, thyme, cumin and cilantro and sauté over a gentle heat for 5 to 7 minutes. Add your choice of chile, then stir this mixture into the cooking beans.

Partly cover with a lid and continue to cook at a slow simmer for another 45 minutes, stirring occasionally. Remove the lid and continue to cook over a gentle heat for another 30 to 45 minutes (stirring frequently) until you have a thick mixture. If making nachos you will want a runnier mixture, so stop cooking now. If making burritos it needs to be thicker. Mashing the beans with a spoon will help thicken the mixture. The whole cooking process takes 2 to 2½ hours. As the mixture starts to thicken, stir it often, as it will stick. Taste during cooking and add extra chilli if you like.

Using canned beans
If using canned beans start by sautéing the onion and herb mix in the saucepan, then add the vegetables, then the beans (drained), tomato, chile and enough water to just cover the mix. Cook as above until required consistency.

Make the guacamole just before serving. Put the avocado flesh and lime juice in a mixing bowl and mash roughly with a fork. Add the garlic, salt, twist of black pepper and cilantro and mix through. Check for taste, adjusting where necessary. If using tomato and chile, add and gently incorporate.

To make burritos
Lay the bread on the table in front of you, squared up. Place the grated cheese (if using) in the center and top with 2 generous tablespoons of beans. Fold the top and

bottom edges so they overlap by ½ inch. Fold in the sides—they should not touch. Put each parcel seam side down in a frying pan with a little olive oil that is hot but not sizzling. Cook for 3 to 5 minutes until golden, then turn and cook for another 3 to 5 minutes until golden. Place on a paper towel to absorb any extra oil. Serve the hot burritos with the salsa and guacamole. Sprinkle with chopped olives and parsley. Serve with a green salad.

To make nachos

Spoon the beans over the corn chips in an ovenproof dish. Top with grated cheese and melt in the oven. Top with salsa, guacamole, olives and parsley or cilantro. Serve with a green salad.

Chickpea and vegetable tagine

VEGAN

This recipe will be gluten-free if wheat-free tamari is used.

This stew is a good example of using baked vegetables (winter squash, garlic and peppers) to add depth of flavor to a dish.

SERVES 4 TO 6

½ cup dried chickpeas, soaked
olive oil, for frying
1 pound, 9 ounces winter squash (jap (kent) or butternut), peeled and cut into rough 1¼ inch cubes
2 red peppers
1 garlic bulb
2 teaspoons fresh thyme (or rosemary)
2 red onions, cut in half and roughly sliced
2 to 4 carrots, cut on the diagonal into 1¼ inch pieces
2 sweet potatoes, peeled and cut into 1¼ inch cubes
½ white sweet potato, peeled and cut into 1¼ inch cubes
14 ounces fresh tomatoes (or canned tomatoes to equal)
¼ to ½ cinnamon stick
honey (optional), to taste
fresh cilantro leaves, to garnish
quinoa (see page 118) (optional), to serve

SPICE MIX

2 teaspoons tamari

¼ teaspoon ground cumin

pinch ground coriander

pinch ground fennel seeds

zest of ½ lemon (or ½ to 1 teaspoon preserved lemon)

½ to 1 teaspoon grated ginger

1 garlic clove, crushed

1 tablespoon chopped cilantro leaves

2 teaspoons pear juice concentrate

Pour the soaked chickpeas into a sieve. Shaking gently, rinse and drain.

Put the chickpeas in a large pot, covered with a generous amount of water, and cook over a gentle heat for 2½ to 4 hours, or until they are soft and yield their starchy centers. Check occasionally and add water if necessary, and remove the froth from the top. Drain well.

Preheat the oven to 350°F. Massage a small amount of olive oil over the cubed squash and place in a roasting pan. Cut the tops off the peppers and remove the seeds and membrane. Rub the outside with olive oil and stand upright, cut side down, in the same pan. Bake the squash and peppers for 1 hour, or until the pepper skin is well wrinkled and begins to blacken and the squash is lightly browned. Remove the squash and set aside. Remove the peppers and put into a bowl and top with a plate. Cool slightly, then peel off the skins and cut the flesh into wide strips, reserving any juice.

Meanwhile, take the bulb of garlic and break the cloves apart. Place them in a square of baking paper, drizzle with a little good olive oil, and sprinkle with the thyme or rosemary. Twist the paper together, to form a bag and cook in the oven for 20 minutes or until the cloves are soft. Allow to cool, then snip the tops off and squeeze out the soft purée.

To prepare the spice mix, combine the ingredients.

Heat 2 to 3 tablespoons of oil in a large pot. Add the onions and gently sauté for approximately 5 minutes. Add the spice mix, carrots and sweet potato, together with the garlic purée and roasted pepper, along with any juice. Rinse out the bowl that held the spice mix with ¼ cup of water and add this to the stew. Add the tomatoes and chickpeas, along with the cinnamon stick. Cover and cook over a very gentle heat for 20 minutes, then add the cooked squash and a little water if it looks too dry. Gently stir. Cook for a further 20 to 40 minutes, or until the vegetables are just soft and the juices have been released. Test for taste, you may need to add a little honey to sweeten.

Garnish with fresh cilantro and serve with freshly cooked quinoa.

Chickpea fritters

GLUTEN FREE / VEGAN

This dish is quick to make and extremely versatile. You can use these fritters in a burger with lots of greens, such as spinach and tabouleh, some tahini and tomato jam, or a selection of salads.

MAKES APPROXIMATELY 10 SMALL FRITTERS

½ cup dried chickpeas, soaked
1 small onion, roughly chopped
2 garlic cloves
½ teaspoon ground coriander
½ teaspoon ground cumin
freshly ground black pepper, to taste
2 tablespoons chopped fresh flat-leaf (Italian) parsley
2 tablespoons chopped fresh cilantro leaves
1 tablespoon chopped fresh mint
1½ tablespoons chickpea flour
olive oil, for frying

Pour the soaked chickpeas into a sieve. Shaking gently, rinse and drain.

Put the soaked chickpeas in a food processor and add the onion and garlic. Pulse for a few seconds. Add all the other ingredients (except the oil) and process until finely ground. Form the mixture into small patties, approximately 1½ inches in diameter and about ½ inch thick.

Heat a little olive oil in a frying pan, just enough to cover the bottom of the pan well. Place the patties in the frying pan and cook over a moderate heat (with a gentle sizzle), for 5 to 7 minutes on each side. Don't be tempted to rush them—the insides take a while to cook. Set to drain on a paper towel. The fritters can be kept warm in the oven until ready to serve.

Socca—chickpea pancakes

GLUTEN FREE / VEGAN

Socca is peasant food—pancakes made from chickpea flour, olive oil and water and cooked in brick ovens. The beauty of socca is that it provides a bread/pancake-like result that is gluten-free.

The uncooked mixture will keep for up to 3 days in the fridge.

1¼ cups chickpea flour
¼ teaspoon sea salt
pinch teaspoon ground cumin
¼ cup olive oil (plus 4 tablespoons, extra)

TOPPINGS
2 tomatoes, chopped
2 teaspoons chopped fresh rosemary (or basil)
1 quantity caramelized onions (see page 35)
roasted pepper (page 34)
1¾ ounces goat cheese (or a good melting cheese)

Socca can also be served the traditional way—bake the untopped batter for 25 to 30 minutes. Drizzle with olive oil, sprinkle with pepper and serve sliced into wedges.

Sift the flour into a bowl and mix in the salt and cumin. Add 1¼ cups of water, a little at a time, whisking to form a smooth paste. Add the olive oil and whisk the mixture together. Let the mixture sit at room temperature for 1 hour.

Brush a 10½-inch springform cake pan or deep-sided pizza pan with 1 tablespoon of olive oil. Pour in the batter and bake for 20 minutes. Top with your choice of toppings, then bake for a further 10 minutes or until the top is set. To serve, drizzle with the remaining olive oil, season with pepper and cut into wedges.

How to prepare lentils, split peas and black-eyed peas

Lentils, split peas and black-eyed peas are the easiest of the legume family to use. The fresher the lentil or pea, the quicker they will cook. Ones bought in a healthfood shop tend to be better quality and fresher than those bought in the supermarket, where they are often stale.

Rinsing or soaking

For basic use, rinse the lentils, split peas or black-eyed peas well first. While it's not essential to pre-soak these legumes, soaking does make them more digestible (see page 74 for soaking). Lentils, however, shouldn't need to be pre-soaked as this may cause them to break up when they are cooked. For these, simply pick them over to remove any discolored ones or pieces of grit, then rinse.

Cooking lentils, split peas and black-eyed peas

It is important to choose the right lentil or pea for your dish. Some lentils, such as red ones, naturally turn to mush when cooked, and are perfect for dal or a soup, while whole red lentils tend to retain more of their shape. Brown and the smaller green lentils and black-eyed peas hold their shape and are ideal for more sturdy dishes. Lentils are cooked when they are tender to the bite.

Method for cooking lentils, split peas and black-eyed peas

SERVES 4 TO 6

After any necessary soaking, discard the water, drain well and put them in a large heatproof saucepan. Cover with about 1½ inch of water and bring to the boil over a medium heat.

As soon as it reaches boiling point turn the heat down as low as possible. Begin timing from this point, based on the cooking times below, adding more water if necessary. Yields are approximated as it will depend on the age of the lentil or pea.

If you want them to hold their shape, then choose brown, green, whole red lentils or black-eyed peas. Ultimately all the others break down.

1 cup dried brown lentils, 30 to 45 minutes
makes 2½ cups

1 cup dried green lentils, 30 to 45 minutes
makes 2½ cups

1 cup dried black lentils, 30 to 45 minutes
makes 3 cups

1 cup dried red lentils, 25 to 30 minutes
makes 2 cups

1 cup dried whole red lentils, 1½ to 2 hours
makes 2¾ cups

1 cup dried split peas, 45 minutes to 2 hours
  makes 2½ cups

1 cup dried black-eyed peas, 45 minutes to 1 hour
  makes 2¾ cups

1 cup dried mung (moong) dal, 30 minutes to 1 hour (longer if whole)
  makes 2 cups

1 cup dried channa dal, split 2 to 2½ hours, whole 2½ to 3 hours
  makes 2¼ cups

1 cup dried toor (toovar) dal, 40 minutes to 1½ hours
  makes 2½ cups

1 cup dried urad dal, 40 minutes to 1½ hours
  makes 2¾ cups

Vegetarian shepherd's pie

GLUTEN FREE / VEGAN

A little lighter than traditional shepherd's pie, this makes an excellent Sunday night meal or cold winter breakfast as savory lentils served on toast (served without the mash).

This is a popular dish, here given a healthy twist. Peas and sweet potato add sweetness and depth, counterbalancing the astringency of the brown lentils, while miso helps to create depth of flavor.

SERVES 4 TO 6

1⅓ cups dried brown (or green) lentils
2 fresh bay leaves
olive oil, for frying
1 onion, finely chopped
pinch mixed dried herbs (or a few sprigs of fresh thyme)
2 garlic cloves, finely chopped
about 1 to 2 cups finely chopped vegetables (carrot, peeled sweet potato, mushrooms, leeks, parsnips, tomato and peas work well)
1 tablespoon genmai miso

SWEET POTATO MASH
2 to 3 sweet potatoes, peeled and chopped
1 teaspoon hulled tahini

sea salt, to taste
1½ tablespoons hulled sunflower seeds
1½ tablespoons sesame seeds
1½ tablespoons pepitas (pumpkin seeds)

Sort through the lentils and rinse. Put in a heavy-based saucepan along with the bay leaves and cover with ¾ to 1¼ inches of water or stock. Cook for 30 minutes over a low heat.

Meanwhile, preheat the oven to 350°F. Heat 1 tablespoon of oil in a frying pan. Add the onion and herbs and sauté over a gentle heat for 2 to 3 minutes. Add the garlic and cook for 2 to 3 minutes longer, being careful not to burn the garlic.

Add the onion mixture to the cooking lentils along with the chopped vegetables (excluding peas, if using) and miso. Check the liquid level, and add extra if it is low. Continue to cook over a gentle heat for 20 minutes, then add the peas. Continue to cook until the mixture thickens, stirring occasionally, as the lentils will stick easily as they start to reduce.

Meanwhile, make the sweet potato mash. Steam the sweet potatoes for 15 to 20 minutes until soft. Then put immediately in a bowl along with the tahini and mash well—this is much easier to do when hot. Season with salt.

Put the lentil mixture in an ovenproof dish. Cover with the mashed sweet potatoes and sprinkle with the seeds. Bake for 25 to 30 minutes. Serve with steamed broccoli or green beans.

Lentils or peas that have been husked and split are also known as dal, and they come in many varieties. They are very handy to keep in the pantry—quick to cook and much easier to digest than beans.

Dal

GLUTEN FREE

Dal is all a matter of personal preference—some people like it cooked with vegetables, others not. Some prefer it with strong cumin, chile or ginger overtones, others like a milder dal.

SERVES 2 TO 4

3 cups dried red lentils
olive oil (or ghee), for frying

½ onion, finely diced
2 to 3 garlic cloves, finely chopped
2½ inch piece ginger, finely chopped
½ teaspoon yellow mustard seeds
1 teaspoon red mustard seeds
4 cardamom pods (seeds only)
¼ teaspoon garam masala
¼ teaspoon ground turmeric
1 teaspoon ground cumin
½ teaspoon ground coriander
2 tablespoons finely chopped fresh cilantro
1 fresh red chile, finely chopped (or more to taste)
1 tablespoon apple juice concentrate
2 to 3 teaspoons tamari

This recipe will be gluten-free depending on the tamari used and vegan if olive oil is used.

Rinse the lentils. Place the lentils and 2½ cups of water in a pot and cook over a low heat that just encourages a gentle bubble (a heat diffuser is useful here). Cook for 15 to 20 minutes, stirring occasionally.

Heat 1 tablespoon of oil or ghee in a frying pan. Add the onion, garlic, ginger and mustard seeds and gently sauté for 5 minutes, then add the cardamom seeds, garam masala, turmeric, cumin and ground coriander. Cook over a gentle heat for a few seconds, until fragrant, and then pour the cooked lentils into the frying pan, so that every bit of flavor is captured. Pour the lot back into the saucepan. Add the cilantro, chile, apple juice concentrate and tamari. Add ½ cup more water at this time if it is too thick. Continue to cook on a very gentle heat for approximately 15 minutes, stirring frequently—it will start to stick as it thickens.

Taste and adjust the flavors if necessary—does it need more cumin, chile, garam masala? If it is still too astringent, it will need sweetening—a little more juice concentrate, chutney or mirin, or you may prefer to serve with chutney.

There are many different methods of flavoring and bringing balance to a dal, such as adding golden raisins, sweet chilli sauce, a small amount of chutney or even stone fruits.

VARIATIONS

Peeled, seeded and finely diced tomato flesh (approximately 1 cup), and/or a little coconut milk (1 to 2 tablespoons) are delicious added with the apple juice concentrate and tamari. Leftover salsa also works very well.

care about what you eat:
absolutely insist that it be delicious and true

soy

In the legume family the soy bean is considered to have one of the highest amino acid profiles. Because of this, products such as soy milk, miso, tofu and tempeh are widely used as alternatives to traditional protein sources such as dairy products, meat and fish. The estrogens (isoflavones) in the soy plant are said to prevent cancer, lower cholesterol, relieve menopausal symptoms and protect against osteoporosis. However, many people disagree and point to the large range of 'anti nutrients' in soy. Among their concerns are that soy can disrupt the healthy functioning of the thyroid gland; it contains an extremely high phytate level that blocks absorption of minerals; it can interfere with the digestion of proteins; and the isoflavenes it contains can disrupt hormone balance and function. It's fair to say that the jury is still very much out with regard to soy—but there are some points worth considering. Long fermentation helps to reduce the phytate level and digestive enzyme inhibitors. Tamari, shoyu, tempeh and miso are soy products that benefit from this process. Many soy products are made from soy protein isolate (SPI), which is simply a highly refined, denatured product that is very difficult to digest. When using soy, seek out products made from whole soy beans (preferably organic—as this is your only insurance they are not genetically modified).

Tofu

This is soy bean curd made from the milk extracted from cooked soy beans. The best-quality tofu is made from soy beans that are organically grown, which is then coagulated with nigari (calcium and magnesium salts derived from sea water). This binds the protein together to produce curds, which are then pressed. The amount of whey discarded will determine the type of tofu—soft or silken tofu with a high water content, or firm with less water.

How to buy tofu

Fresh

This comes in blocks of approximately 7 to 9 ounces and is sold in tubs of water at healthfood stores. Fresh tofu has a very limited life span (2 to 4 days) and needs to be kept in the fridge, soaked in water. This water will need to be changed daily. Silken tofu is rarely available fresh.

Packaged

There are some excellent brands of packaged (sealed) tofu available and, although much more expensive than fresh tofu, they are extremely convenient. Silken tofu is usually bought in this manner, and is extremely fragile. Leftover tofu is best kept covered in water in a container and sealed. With the water changed daily it will last for up to 3 days in the fridge.

As well as plain tofu, there are many marinated and cooked varieties. Some of these include barbecued tofu, tofu cutlets and smoked tofu. These products do not have to be kept in water once opened.

Tofu does not freeze well. The result is generally crumbly and rubbery in texture.

Second-generation tofu products

These include tofu and vegetarian patties, soydogs and bacon. Choose very carefully as many (not all) of these are made from SPI or textured soy protein, together with large amounts of artificial flavors and colors. There are few truly good products available in this category.

How to use tofu

Tofu on its own can be quite bland and can taste fairly 'blah' unless put to use properly. It also has a spongy mouthfeel, which many people find unpleasant. However, knowing how to handle tofu and finding compatible ways to use it changes it from something quite uninspiring to something really delicious. Here's how to do it.

It should be remembered that tofu is not a 'whole' food—that is, it is only derived from cooked whole soy beans (and in many cases, soy protein isolates (SPI)). Many vegetarians misguidedly use it as a prime source for their protein needs, rather than relying on a wide and balanced diet.

Developing flavor—marinating

Unless you specifically don't want the tofu to influence the flavors in a dish (that is, if using it for texture, whiteness and nutrients), marinating is an essential basic for tofu. It is best to use only firm tofu in this way—silken tofu is extremely fragile and best kept for cream bases. Once marinated, tofu can be crumbled and used as an addition to patties, vegetable stuffings and stir-fries or threaded onto kebabs.

Prepare enough marinade to soak halfway up the side of the tofu in a dish. It is preferable to marinate for 6 to 8 hours (turning the tofu halfway), which allows the tofu time to fully absorb the flavors. Good results, however, can still be gained with shorter marinating times. Soy sauce (preferably tamari) is often used as a base for marinades. Marinating should always be done in the fridge.

Asian marinade

VEGAN

The basic.

TO MAKE MARINADE FOR 9 TO 10½ OUNCES TOFU OR TEMPEH

This recipe will be gluten-free if wheat-free tamari is used.

1½ tablespoons tamari
1½ tablespoons mirin
3 teaspoons pear juice concentrate
1 teaspoon grated ginger
1 teaspoon finely chopped fresh cilantro leaves
1 garlic clove, finely chopped

Combine all the ingredients with ¼ cup of water in a bowl.

Hearty all-purpose marinade

VEGAN

This is a good, deeply flavored marinade without the strong soy/Asian overtones.

TO MAKE MARINADE FOR 9 TO 10½ OUNCES TOFU OR TEMPEH

This recipe will be gluten-free if wheat-free tamari is used.

5 dried shiitake mushrooms
2 tablespoons finely chopped green onions (scallions)
2 garlic cloves, crushed
¼ cup apple juice
1½ tablespoons tamari
1 teaspoon dried oregano (or fresh)
1 teaspoon dried basil (or fresh), finely chopped
pinch freshly ground black pepper

Place the mushrooms and 1/2 cup of water in a saucepan and bring to the boil. Turn off the heat, cover with a lid and let sit for 30 minutes. Strain the liquid into a bowl, squeezing the mushrooms well to extract all the juice. Combine the liquid with the remaining ingredients.

Teriyaki marinade

This is an excellent marinade, and very versatile.

This recipe will be gluten-free if wheat-free tamari is used.

TO MAKE MARINADE FOR 9 TO 10 1/2 OUNCES TOFU OR TEMPEH OR 2 MEDIUM CHICKEN BREASTS

- 3 teaspoons grated ginger
- 1 teaspoon ginger juice
- 3 tablespoons tamari
- 1 teaspoon roasted sesame oil
- 1 1/2 tablespoons honey
- 3 teaspoons mirin
- 1 1/2 tablespoons finely chopped fresh cilantro leaves (optional)

Combine all the ingredients with 1/4 cup of water in a bowl.

Developing body and texture

Baking or broiling marinated firm tofu results in a product that is deeply flavored, extremely hardy and with excellent mouthfeel. While marinated tofu can be fried, it will not be as firmly textured; and baking or broiling the tofu offers an alternative to frying it in oil. Baking, in particular, achieves a dense result, and basting with extra sauce or marinade during the cooking process will further increase the depth of flavor. Tofu cooked on a heavy cast-iron grill is especially delicious, giving the finished product a distinctly barbecued flavor.

Vegetarian burgers

VEGAN

This is a tasty and sustaining meal, which can be made with tofu or tempeh.

SERVES 4

10½ ounces firm tofu (or tempeh), cut into 4 thin slices
1 quantity hearty all-purpose marinade (see page 98)
olive oil, for frying
3 onions, thinly sliced
1 tablespoon mirin
1 avocado, sliced
4 pieces whole grain bread or burger buns (toasted if prefered)
1 large tomato, sliced
4 slices beets (canned or fresh)
handful grated carrot
green salad leaves (lettuce, arugula)
handful snow pea (mangetout) sprouts
barbecue sauce (see page 43) (or tomato sauce), to serve

Marinate the tofu (or tempeh) for between 20 minutes and 8 hours in the fridge.

Heat 1 to 2 tablespoons of olive oil in a frying pan. Add the onions and cook over a gentle heat, stirring often, for 15 minutes, or until the onions are very soft. Add the mirin and continue to cook over a gentle heat for 10 to 15 minutes, stirring often. You should end up with beautifully soft, richly flavored and lightly colored onions.

To fry

Heat 1 to 2 tablespoons of oil in a frying pan, add the tofu slices and cook for 5 minutes on each side, until golden.

If you find the tofu sticking it means that the grill was not hot enough at the start. Just scrape it off, brush it generously with olive oil, and place back on the grill.

To chargrill

Brush the tofu with olive oil and place it on a pre-heated, very hot char-grill pan. Cook for approximately 1 minute, or until nicely lined. Brush the other side and turn. Cook for another minute.

Put the avocado on the bread, then add the onions and tempeh. Top with tomato, beets, carrot, salad leaves and sprouts and anything else that takes your fancy. Serve with barbecue sauce.

Spring rolls

VEGAN

These are always well received. With sweet ginger sauce they make a delicious meal. They cannot be made too far in advance and are best eaten shortly after they are cooked. The filling, however, can be prepared an hour or so beforehand.

MAKES ABOUT 20 ROLLS

3½ ounces tofu
1 quantity teriyaki marinade (see page 99)
1 to 1¾ ounces rice (or mung bean) vermicelli
½ to 1 teaspoon roasted sesame oil
1¾ to 3½ ounces smoked tofu, finely diced
¾ cup grated carrot
½ cup finely chopped green onion (scallions)
½ cup finely chopped bean sprouts
½ cup finely chopped snow peas (mangetout)
½ cup shredded Chinese cabbage
¼ cup lightly roasted hulled sunflower seeds
1 tablespoon lightly roasted sesame seeds
2 tablespoons finely grated ginger (do not use if serving with the dipping sauce)
20 to 30 spring roll wrappers (about 8 inches square) (or Asian rice paper)
olive oil, for frying
1 quantity sweet ginger sauce (see page 44) (optional)

You may want to marinate 10½ ounces of tofu and use the remaining 7 ounces for another recipe.

Marinate the tofu (or tempeh) in the teriyaki marinade for 2 to 8 hours in the fridge.

Cook the vermicelli in boiling water for 3 minutes, then drain well. Roughly chop and place in a large bowl and toss with the sesame oil. Add the remaining ingredients (except the spring roll wrappers, olive oil and sweet ginger sauce) and mix well.

If using spring roll wrappers, lay one on the table in front of you, with one of the corners facing you. Lightly brush a little water around the edges of the wrapper. Place a tablespoon of the mixture in the middle, fold in the edges and roll tightly.

If using rice paper, have a large bowl of very warm water at your side. Soak 2 rice papers for about 30 seconds, or until soft. Be careful not to over-soak the papers—too soft and they will break when you try to roll them. Remove the papers to one side of a clean dish towel. With the other side, pat dry. Put a small portion of filling on the paper and proceed to wrap. Keep the rolls covered with a damp cloth while preparing the rest.

The spring rolls made with spring roll wrappers can be either shallow fried or baked. Those made with rice papers can be shallow fried or eaten fresh as they are.

To shallow fry

To shallow fry, put about ½ inch oil in a frying pan over low to medium heat. Once hot, add the spring rolls and fry for 5 to 10 minutes, turning regularly until golden brown all over.

To bake

To bake, preheat the oven to 400°F. Lay the spring rolls on a lightly oiled tray. If you like, lightly brush the top of the rolls with oil also to give a glossier finish. Bake for 20 to 30 minutes, or until lightly browned.

Serve with sweet ginger sauce.

VARIATIONS

Cooked shrimp or fresh cilantro leaves can be added to the mix for additional flavor.

Thai spiced tofu balls

VEGAN

Delicious on their own served with a dipping sauce or in a salad with cilantro and chile dressing (see page 154), these are lovely to serve up as a pre-dinner nibble or entrée.

MAKES ABOUT 16 BALLS

10½ ounces firm tofu
2 teaspoons grated ginger
2 tablespoons chopped fresh chives
4 tablespoons finely diced red onion
3 tablespoons fresh cilantro leaves

1 tablespoon fresh mint leaves
2 garlic cloves, crushed
2 tablespoons diced red pepper
2 teaspoons sweet chilli sauce
2 teaspoons finely chopped lemon grass (white part only)
2 cups cooked short/medium grain brown rice
½ cup sesame seeds
olive oil (or sesame oil), for frying

This recipe will be gluten-free if wheat-free tamari is used and if the sweet chilli sauce does not contain gluten.

Put all the ingredients, except the sesame seeds and oil, in food processor and blend until combined, being careful not to over-process.

Roll the mixture into about 16 balls or patties as desired. Coat each ball in sesame seeds and place in the fridge for 30 minutes. Put about ½ inch oil in a frying pan over low to medium heat. Once hot, add the tofu balls in batches and fry for 5 to 10 minutes, turning regularly, until golden brown all over. Put on paper towels to absorb any excess oil.

Pad Thai

VEGAN

This is a classic Thai noodle dish, enriched with tofu. It is a perfect summer dinner, but is best prepared just before serving to avoid the rice noodles breaking down.

SERVES 4

3½ to 5½ ounces firm tofu, cut into bite-size cubes
½ quantity Asian marinade (see page 98)
7 ounces dried rice noodles (approximately ½ inch in width)
juice of 1 lime (2 to 3 tablespoons)
1½ tablespoons tamari
1½ tablespoons soft brown sugar
1½ tablespoons sweet chilli sauce
olive oil, for frying
3 garlic cloves, crushed
2 teaspoons finely grated ginger
2 carrots, julienned

This recipe will be gluten-free if wheat-free tamari is used.

1 head broccoli, cut into small florets

1 red pepper, julienned

6 to 8 green onions (scallions), cut on the diagonal (plus 3 to 4 extra, cut finely on the diagonal)

3½ ounces bean sprouts

3½ ounces sunflower sprouts (or other sprouts)

½ to 1 cup chopped roasted cashews

8 to 10 sprigs cilantro leaves

1 fresh red or green chile, julienned

Marinate the tofu in the Asian marinade for at least 1 hour in the fridge and up to 8 hours.

Place the noodles gently in a bowl and soak according to the packet instructions. They are very fragile so avoid pressing them down.

To make the sauce, combine the lime juice, tamari, sugar, chilli sauce and ¼ cup of water. Mix gently and set aside.

Prepare all the remaining ingredients before you start to cook.

Using a wok, heat approximately ¼ cup olive oil. It is important the oil is hot, but not smoking. Remove the tofu from the marinade, pat dry and put into the wok. Fry the tofu for 6 to 10 minutes, until it is golden. You will need to turn the tofu often, ensuring that it is cooked on all sides, and the oil should be gently sizzling. When golden, remove the tofu and place in a bowl lined with paper towel. Discard the oil.

Add 1 to 2 tablespoons of fresh oil to the wok and heat over medium-high heat. Add the garlic and ginger and cook for 10 seconds. Add the carrot, broccoli and pepper and continue to cook, stirring occasionally, for 3 minutes. Drain the noodles. Add the sauce and noodles together with the tofu, green onions, bean sprouts and sunflower sprouts. Mix well and cook for 2 minutes. Turn onto a serving plate and garnish with chopped cashew nuts, cilantro, chile and extra green onions.

Tempeh

Tempeh is a soybean cake made by fermenting cooked soybeans. To make tempeh, soy beans are cooked, split and sometimes blended with other grains such as rice or millet. They are then inoculated with *rhizopus oligosporus* bacteria and spread on trays 1¼ to 1½ inch thick. Left to ferment for approximately 24 hours, the spores spread quickly, forming a thin fuzz (mycelium) over the beans, transforming them into a firm cake.

The flavor and texture of tempeh is nutty and hearty. Because tempeh uses the whole bean (unlike tofu) it contains all its nutrients and can be considered a wholefood.

How to buy tempeh

Most tempeh available is organic (but do check) and comes in vacuum-sealed packs, which you can find in the refrigerated section of your healthfood store or supermarket. Brands differ in taste: some are definitely better than others. Once opened, tempeh lasts for 3 to 6 days. Look for clean tempeh—dark grey or black spots indicate deterioration. Tempeh freezes well.

Tempeh comes in two forms, uncooked and cooked.

Uncooked

Uncooked tempeh must be steamed, fried or baked before use. It is available plain or flavored. The flavored tempeh, also called 'seasoned' or 'tasty' tempeh is well priced and an excellent staple to have on hand. Shoyu is sometimes added so, if you are gluten-intolerant, you will need to read the ingredients carefully.

Cooked

Generally labeled 'ready to eat' or 'cutlets,' these tempeh pieces are thinner than uncooked tempeh and have been marinated and cooked to develop flavor. You can heat these and use them immediately with great-tasting results. Without heating, they are a tasty addition to a salad. Shoyu is often added to these, so check the packaging if you are gluten-intolerant.

The fermentation of tempeh delivers many benefits—it greatly reduces the oligosaccharides (those nasty complex sugars in beans that can cause flatulence), it makes the protein easy to digest and, most importantly, it deactivates the phytates and enzyme inhibitors present in beans.

How to use tempeh

Because of its sturdy texture and great flavor, tempeh is an excellent replacement for red meat, although large slabs can be a little overwhelming. Rather, use it as you would ground meat: in 'sausages' and patties, or cut into smaller pieces for sauces and stews. Tempeh can also simply be fried in oil—use either the 'ready to eat' or a well-marinated tempeh.

Although tempeh—the 'ready to eat' in particular—is a great replacement for meat, it requires considerable development of flavor for the best results.

Basic marinated tempeh

This is a great way to make your own 'ready to eat' tempeh—far superior to that bought in a store. (It is also a great way to prepare tofu.)

10 ½ ounces tempeh (or tofu)
1 quantity Asian marinade (see page 98), hearty all-purpose marinade (see page 98) or teriyaki marinade (see page 99)

Preheat the oven to 350°F.

Slice the tempeh into slices ½ inch thick. Put in an ovenproof dish and pour over the marinade. Leave to sit for between 10 minutes and up to 4 hours in the fridge.

Cover with foil and bake for 35 to 40 minutes. Remove the foil, baste with any remaining marinade and cook for a further 10 minutes, until golden.

You now have a well-flavored, 'ready to eat' tempeh that can be used in the same way as the store-bought variety.

Tasty tempeh bits

Quick to make and absolutely delicious—these are a great vegetarian replacement for crispy bacon and a flavorsome addition to salads.

This recipe will be gluten-free if the marinade contains wheat-free tamari and the tempeh does not contain shoyu.

10 ½ ounces tempeh
1 quantity hearty all-purpose marinade (see page 98) (or teriyaki marinade (see page 99)
olive oil, for frying

Cut the tempeh into small cubes (about ⅝ inch). Put the tempeh in a dish and pour over the marinade. Leave to sit for between 10 minutes and 4 hours in the fridge.

Heat 1 to 2 tablespoons of olive oil in a frying pan over low heat. Add the tempeh pieces and cook gently for 10 to 15 minutes until crispy, adding a little extra oil if necessary. The tempeh should be cooked slowly, stirring frequently—otherwise you will find it will burn. Turn the tempeh bits onto a paper towel to drain. Use immediately or store in a container, in the fridge for up to 4 days.

Tempeh and millet loaf

A good way to add flavor to tempeh, this dish holds together well and tastes great.

Ground tempeh is a great basic, and a fundamental way to develop flavor in tempeh before using it, or adding it to other dishes. It can be frozen or kept in the fridge for up to 4 to 6 weeks.

MAKES 1 SAVORY LOAF

GROUND TEMPEH

10½ ounces basic marinated tempeh (see page 102)
(or seasoned or 'ready to eat' tempeh)
olive oil, for frying
1 teaspoon roasted sesame oil
1 onion, finely chopped
3 garlic cloves, finely chopped
½ teaspoon dried basil
½ teaspoon dried sage
½ teaspoon dried thyme
½ teaspoon dried oregano
1½ to 2¼ tablespoons tamari
2¼ tablespoons tomato paste (concentrated purée)

⅓ cup hulled millet, unsoaked
1 cup roughly chopped sweet potato
olive oil, for frying
shiitake mushroom gravy (see page 42), to serve

This recipe will be gluten-free if the marinade contains wheat-free tamari and the tempeh does not contain shoyu.

Begin by preparing the minced tempeh. Cut the tempeh into very small, thin pieces. Using a large frying pan gently heat 1 to 2 tablespoons of olive oil and the sesame oil. Fry the tempeh over a medium heat, stirring occasionally to avoid sticking. Cook for 10 minutes; by this time the tempeh should have begun to color.

Add the onion, garlic and herbs and continue to cook for a further 5 minutes or until the onions have begun to soften. Continue to stir occasionally. Add 2 tablespoons of tamari and the tomato paste. Cook over a gentle heat for 1 to 2 minutes. Taste and add the extra tamari if you feel it needs it. Put to the side.

Rinse the millet well, pat dry with a dish towel and put in a heavy-based saucepan with 2 cups of water (or stock). Cover with a lid and bring to the boil over a gentle heat. As soon as it reaches boiling point, turn the heat down as low as possible (a heat diffuser is useful here). Cook the grain for 15 to 20 minutes. When it is ready, small steam holes should appear on the surface. Set aside to cool.

Steam the sweet potato for 15 to 20 minutes, until just cooked—overcooked and watery sweet potato will not hold the mixture together—then roughly mash. Put in a bowl and combine with the tempeh mince and cooked millet.

Preheat the oven to 350°F. Lightly brush a small ovenproof china loaf pan with olive oil (or line and grease a metal one) and add the mixture. Pack well. Bake for 30 to 50 minutes, or until dry to the touch.

Serve with shiitake mushroom gravy.

The tempeh and millet loaf mixture can also be shaped into balls and cooked as 'meatballs.'

Sweet and sour tempeh

VEGAN

This is a delicious dish, far superior to anything you'd buy from a fast-food restaurant. It's quick to put together, especially if you marinate in advance. The vegetables used below are a suggestion only—feel free to use what works for you. Serve with rice for a hearty meal.

SERVES 4 TO 6

MARINADE

½ cup pineapple juice
¼ cup tamari
1 to 2 garlic cloves, finely chopped
1 teaspoon grated ginger
1 teaspoon roasted sesame oil

9 ounces seasoned or 'ready to eat' tempeh, cut into ¾ inch cubes

SAUCE

2 teaspoons cornstarch (or kudzu powder or arrowroot)
½ cup pear juice concentrate
¼ cup tamari
1½ tablespoons apple cider vinegar

VEGETABLES

1 carrot, cut on the diagonal into thin slices
2 celery stalks, cut into thin slices
1 red pepper, cut lengthways into thin slices

For a quicker option, use store-bought 'ready to eat' tempeh or tempeh 'cutlets,' neither of which needs marinating.

1 head broccoli, cut into florets
6 to 8 baby corn
¼ to ½ cup pineapple pieces, cut into ½ inch dice
1 to 2 green onions (scallions), sliced thinly
10 to 15 snow peas (mangetout), halved on the diagonal

This recipe will be gluten-free if the marinade contains wheat-free tamari and the tempeh does not contain shoyu.

Combine all the marinade ingredients and add the tempeh and put aside.

To make the sauce, put the cornstarch in a bowl and add ¼ cup of the water. Mix to a smooth paste, then add a further ¼ cup of water. Add all the other ingredients and mix together well.

Put the tempeh and all the marinade in a large frying pan. Cook over a very low heat for 10 to 15 minutes, until the marinade has nearly evaporated. Turn the tempeh often so both sides are evenly cooked and glazed. Remove the tempeh from the pan and set aside.

Add 1 to 2 tablespoons water to the pan to lift the sediment from the base of the pan. Add the carrot, celery, pepper, broccoli and corn, cover with a lid and cook over a low heat for 10 minutes, until they are nearly tender. Return the tempeh to the pan along with the pineapple. Add the sauce and bring to the boil, stirring constantly. Stir in the snow peas and green onions and remove from the heat. Serve over cooked grain, such as rice, quinoa, millet or barley.

goodness needs to be available
to your body every single day

grains

Throughout history, grains have held a symbolic significance for many cultures. Ancient pagan cultures prayed to the gods for successful harvests; and it is from the Roman goddess of agriculture and fertility, Ceres, that the word 'cereal' derives. In an age-old tradition, Catholics continue to use bread as part of the ritual of Mass. Grains are held in such high regard with good cause—they form the only food group that contains all of the major nutrients needed by the body—complex carbohydrates, protein, unsaturated fats, and a wide range of vitamins and minerals. To be beneficial though, grains must be whole, which means unrefined. Most commercially available grains are refined; that is, grains that have had the bran and germ removed, leaving a center of starch and carbohydrate. This is done to extend the shelf life and avoid spoilage. What you end up with, however, is a grain with much of its nutritional value removed. Good organic whole grains provide slow release fuel and fiber that enables the body to run properly. They also provide the nutrients as nature designed them—in the correct proportions for the body's optimum usage.

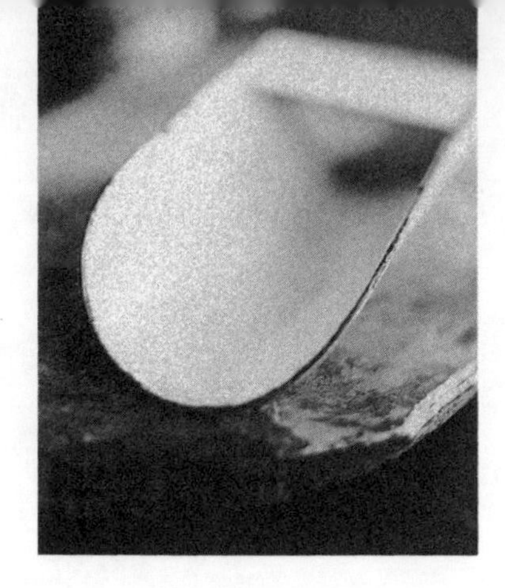

How to prepare grains

Whole grains have as much as possible of their natural, edible parts intact. Only the outer inedible husks are removed, giving access to the grain. They are available at all wholefood, healthfood and natural food stores. Because of their fat content, whole grains will need to be stored in a cool, dark place—preferably the fridge. Like beans, you need to be a bit organized as many grains need some presoaking.

Dry roasting grains

Some grains respond well to dry roasting before soaking, and develop great flavor (buckwheat and millet in particular). To roast grains, simply cook in a dry frying pan over a gentle heat for 5 to 10 minutes, or until fragrant and lightly colored, stirring often.

Soaking grains

Most people agree that whole grains benefit from soaking. This is because grains contain phytic acid and enzyme inhibitors in the outer layer, or bran, which interferes with the absorption of many minerals, notably calcium, magnesium and zinc. During soaking and fermentation, lactobaccilli bacteria begin to break down the phytic acids and enzyme inhibitors, creating lactic acid at the same time. The bacteria also break down gluten—a protein that is very difficult for the human digestive system to handle. Because of this, soaking often increases tolerance to wheat, while nutritionists have recorded an increase in vitamin content in the grain, most notably the B vitamins. The most convincing reason for pre-soaking grains, however, is that it can dramatically reduce cooking times.

It is recommended that you always soak the hardier grains—such as barley, wheat, rye and spelt—which results in a far softer, easier to digest end product. (Wheat, in particular, is a high/strong gluten grain, and is always best soaked.) Soak the grains for 6 to 12 hours to get the best results.

A useful routine is to soak them overnight in a large bowl with 2 teaspoons of whey, buttermilk or yogurt stirred gently through. Soaking should be done at room temperature, allowing a little fermentation to occur.

It is important to note that grains have only been refined in the last 60 to 70 years of human evolution, during which time big business has taken over the major production of our food. It is ironic that in recent years industry's answer to grain modification has been to 'enrich' the product with nutrients that the process of refining has removed.

Cooking grains

The following section provides some basic techniques for cooking grains. You will end up with a cooked, fluffy and generally intact grain, though some grains such as millet and buckwheat do tend to lose their form. The cooked grain can then be used to serve with a meal, incorporate into a stuffing or pattie mix with a wealth of other applications only limited by your imagination. The yields for cooked grains, given below, are approximate, it will vary depending on the age of the grain, soil growing conditions and other factors.

Method for cooking grains

If using soaked grains (see page 117), discard the water, drain well and pat dry. Pour the grains into a sieve, and rinse under running water, shaking gently. If using unsoaked grains, rinse well and pat dry with a dish towel. Put the drained grain into a heavy-based saucepan, add required amount of water (see below), cover with a lid and bring to the boil. As soon as it reaches boiling point turn the heat down as low as possible (a heat diffuser is useful here). Begin timing from this point, based on the cooking times below.

Placing a clean dish towel or paper towel over the grains while they stand will help to absorb excess moisture, resulting in a fluffier, less wet, grain.

SERVES 4

1 cup pearled barley
soaked, 2¼ cups liquid, 50 to 70 minutes
unsoaked, 2½ cups liquid, 60 to 80 minutes
makes 3 to 4 cups cooked

1 cup kasha (toasted buckwheat)
soaked, 1¾ cups liquid, 15 to 20 minutes
unsoaked, 2 cups liquid, 15 to 20 minutes
makes 2½ to 3½ cups cooked

1 cup hulled millet
soaked, 1¾ cups liquid, 15 to 20 minutes
unsoaked 2 cups liquid, 15 to 20 minutes
makes 2½ to 3 cups cooked

Wheat berries must be soaked.

1 cup quinoa
soaked, 1¾ cups liquid, 15 to 20 minutes
unsoaked, 2 cups liquid, 15 to 20 minutes
makes 2 cups cooked

1 cup wheat berries
soaked, 4 cups liquid, 2 hours
makes 2 to 3 cups cooked

For longer-cooking grains, check if there is any water left by tipping the pot on an angle 5 minutes before the end of the cooking time. If there is, continue to cook until no liquid remains. When it is ready, small steam holes should appear on the surface.

Take the pot off the heat and leave to stand, covered, for 5 minutes. This allows the internal heat and steam to finish the cooking process.

Method for cooking polenta

Ground corn cooked with water is one of the most basic of foods, and also one of the most delicious. The key to good polenta is to cook it for at least 20 minutes; this ensures a full softening of the harsh grain. It also helps to use a deep, good-quality pot with a heavy base and a large wooden spoon. The finished product should be beautifully creamy.

It takes a strong arm to stir polenta but it is well worth the effort.

SERVES 4

4 cups stock (or water) for a firm polenta
(plus 1 cup for a soft polenta)
sea salt, to taste
1 cup polenta

Using a large heavy-based saucepan, bring the stock or water and salt to the boil. Start adding the polenta to the water slowly, stirring as you go. Lower the heat to a gentle simmer and cook for 20 to 30 minutes, stirring frequently (especially as it starts to thicken).

Add your choice of flavorings and stir well.

VARIATIONS

Polenta benefits enormously when extra elements are added. Butter and grated parmesan cheese are traditionally added, but below are some other suggestions that can be added to the recipe above after the polenta is cooked.

- Add 2 teaspoons finely chopped fresh rosemary.
- Add 2 teaspoons finely chopped fresh basil.
- Add 1 to 2 tablespoons unsalted butter.
- Add 1/4 to 1/2 cup of grated parmesan cheese and 1 to 2 tablespoons of butter.

Your polenta can now be used in either of two ways:

Using soft polenta

This is served straight from the pan. Put onto the serving plate with an indentation or well in the center to contain a topping. This can be as elaborate as a sauce or stew, or as simple as a dash of good olive oil, a handful of flat-leaf (Italian) parsley, or some pesto and freshly ground black pepper. Adding some roasted or grilled vegetables as a side with a salad of fresh greens makes a superb lunch or light dinner.

Using firm polenta

Polenta has the great advantage of setting in a fairly solid state, and will take the shape of whatever form it is molded to. Simply pour the warm polenta into a lightly oiled dish of desired depth. This recipe fits a dish of 7 inches diameter and a depth of 1¾ inches filled to the top, but you can just as easily set it in a larger dish and end up with a thinner polenta. The polenta can then be cut and fried with a little olive oil or grilled.

To shallow fry, coat triangular pieces in a little cornmeal. Put about ½ inch of oil in a frying pan over low to medium heat. Once hot, add the polenta and fry for 5 to 7 minutes, or until golden, then turn and cook the other side. Remove and set on a paper towel to drain excess oil.

Grilling can be done using a cast-iron chargrill pan or a non-stick sandwich maker. Using firm polenta, lightly brush the top and bottom of each triangle with olive oil and put on a hot grill. With the stove top grill plate, cook for 5 minutes, or until a skin has developed. Turn and cook for a further 5 minutes. Using a sandwich maker, cook for 10 minutes.

Serve with your choice of the following: grilled vegetables and/or oven-baked tomatoes (see page 34), roasted peppers (see page 34) with a leafy salad, fresh tomato sauce (see page 35) or pesto (see page 45).

Method for cooking rice

APPROXIMATELY 1 CUP RICE MAKES 2½ CUPS COOKED

Free boiling method (for white basmati or jasmine rice)
Rinse the rice well to remove any excess starch.

Bring a heavy-based saucepan with 4 cups of water to the boil, add the rinsed rice, stir well to keep it from sticking together, and continue to boil for approximately 15 minutes, until cooked.

After 10 minutes check to see whether it is ready and continue cooking if necessary. When ready, drain, fluff with a fork and either return to pot to keep warm or serve.

Absorption method (for brown rice)
If using unsoaked grains, rinse well, pat dry with a dish towel, and put in a heavy-based saucepan with 2 cups of liquid for short/medium grain and 1¾ cups if using long grain (including brown basmati). If using soaked grains (see page 117), discard the water, drain well and pat dry with a dish towel; add 1¾ cups of water (or stock) for short/medium grain or 1½ cups for long grain (including brown basmati) in a heavy-based saucepan.

Try not to remove the lid during the cooking process as this also allows steam to escape.

Cover with a lid and bring to the boil over a gentle heat. As soon as it reaches boiling point turn the heat down as low as possible (a heat diffuser is useful here). Begin timing from this point, based on the cooking times below.

soaked, 30 to 40 minutes
unsoaked, 40 to 50 minutes

Placing a clean dish towel or paper towel over the grains while they stand will help to absorb excess moisture, resulting in a fluffier, less wet grain.

When it is ready, small steam holes should appear on the surface.

The finished result is a delicious grain for use in salads. It is also great for stuffing mixes, and will keep in the fridge for 2 days.

Hearty grain-based meals

Nourish body and soul with a warming bowl of healthful grains—your body will thank you for it. The recipes in this section are sure to become some of your favorite standbys.

Barley risotto with roast squash and mushrooms

The high amount of starch in barley makes for a creamy consistency—perfect for risotto. The key to a good risotto is the stock—it will need to be rich and well flavored. This is a hearty and delicious risotto, perfect for the cooler weather.

SERVES 3 TO 4

1 cup pearled barley, soaked
1 pound, 12 ounces winter squash (jap (kent) or butternut), cut into rough 2-inch cubes
olive oil, for frying
2 tablespoons finely chopped fresh rosemary
4 to 5 cups vegetable stock (see page 48)

1 red onion, finely chopped
2 garlic cloves, finely chopped
1½ tablespoons mirin (plus 1 tablespoon extra, to taste)
9 to 12 ounces well-flavored mushrooms
(such as Swiss brown, portabello), sliced
handful fresh flat-leaf (Italian) parsley, finely chopped (plus extra to serve)
tamari, to taste
freshly ground black pepper, to taste
1 quantity tamari seeds (pumpkin only) (see page 33)

This recipe will be gluten-free depending on the tamari used.

Pour the soaked grains into a sieve. Shaking gently, rinse and drain.

Preheat the oven to 350°F. Put the squash in a roasting pan and toss with 2 to 3 tablespoons of olive oil and 1 tablespoon rosemary. Cook for 1 hour, until soft and even a little browned. When ready, set aside.

Bring the stock to a gentle simmer and keep it simmering gently. Using a large heavy-based saucepan, cook the onion, garlic and remaining 1 tablespoon of rosemary in 1 tablespoon of olive oil for 5 to 6 minutes over a gentle heat. Add the mirin and allow to sizzle gently. Immediately add the drained barley and stir. Add about 2 cups of the warm stock, stir well, cover and cook at a gentle simmer. After approximately 10 minutes, check and add more stock if it is running low, stirring gently. Continue in this manner until the barley is cooked—about 1 to 1½ hours.

While the risotto is cooking, gently sauté the sliced mushrooms in a little olive oil or butter for 10 minutes, or until cooked.

When the barley is cooked, check for taste—adding the tamari, extra mirin and black pepper as necessary. Attend to the consistency of the risotto—if you find you have added too much stock and the risotto is runny, simply continue to cook over a medium to high heat, without the lid, until the mixture has reduced. It is very hard to overcook barley. If too thick, add a little extra stock. Add the cooked mushrooms, parsley and squash. Serve sprinkled with the tamari seeds and extra parsley.

VARIATIONS

- Add ½ cup freshly grated parmesan cheese when serving.
- Add strips of roasted pepper (see page 34) with the squash and mushrooms.

Barley pilaf

WHEAT FREE

This is a lovely way to add flavor to simply cooked barley.

SERVES 4 TO 6

1 cup pearled barley, soaked
olive oil (or ghee), for frying
1 onion (or leek), finely chopped
½ teaspoon dried thyme (or 2 sprigs fresh)
2 garlic cloves, finely chopped
1 teaspoon grated ginger
up to 3 cups vegetable stock (see page 48)
2 celery stalks, finely diced
2 carrots, finely diced
½ small sweet potato, finely diced
1 cup roasted chopped walnuts (or roasted seeds)
handful fresh flat-leaf (Italian) parsley, finely chopped

Pour the soaked grains into a sieve. Shaking gently, rinse and drain.

Heat 1 tablespoon of olive oil (or ghee) in a large heavy-based saucepan over gentle heat. Add the onion (or leek), thyme, garlic and ginger and sauté for 2 to 3 minutes. Add the barley and 2 cups of stock. Cover with a lid and cook over a very low heat for 20 minutes. Add the vegetables and extra stock if it begins to look dry, and stir through. Cover and cook over a very low heat for 40 minutes. Add the chopped walnuts or toasted seeds, parsley and some pepper if needed and fluff with a fork.

This can be served with sautéed kale or shiitake mushroom gravy (see page 42), or use it as a stuffing or a savory grain breakfast.

Buckwheat with leek and walnuts

GLUTEN FREE / VEGAN

SERVES 2

2 cups kasha (roasted buckwheat), unsoaked
olive oil (or ghee), for frying
1 leek, well rinsed, roughly cut
1 sprig fresh thyme
½ cup finely chopped roasted walnuts (or tamari seeds)
handful fresh flat-leaf (Italian) parsley, roughly chopped

Put the buckwheat in a heavy-based saucepan with 2 cups of water, cover with a lid and bring to the boil. As soon as it comes to the boil, turn the heat down as far as it will go and cook for 15 to 20 minutes. About 5 minutes before the end of cooking, remove the lid, tip the pan on an angle and, if there is any water left, cover once more and continue to cook until you see small steam holes on the surface. Remove from the heat, put a dish towel under the lid to absorb any steam and leave for about 5 minutes. Then set aside to cool completely.

Meanwhile, heat 1 tablespoon of oil or ghee in a saucepan. Add the leek and fresh thyme and gently sauté for 5 to 8 minutes.

Fold the leek, roasted walnuts or seeds and parsley into the buckwheat and serve.

Mushroom and kasha bake

With an almost loaf-like consistency, this is a good way to use buckwheat.

SERVES 4

¾ cup kasha (toasted buckwheat), unsoaked
olive oil, for frying
1 small onion, finely chopped
1 teaspoon mixed herbs (dry or fresh)
10½ ounces well-flavored mushrooms (such as Swiss brown or portabello)
1 to 2 garlic cloves, finely chopped
1 tablespoon fresh flat-leaf (Italian) parsley, finely chopped

1 to 2 tablespoons tamari
sea salt, to taste
freshly ground black pepper, to taste
1 egg, lightly beaten

This recipe will be gluten-free depending on the tamari used.

Put the kasha in a heavy-based saucepan with 1½ cups of water, cover with a lid and bring to the boil. As soon as it comes to the boil, turn the heat down as far as it will go and cook for 15 to 20 minutes. About 5 minutes before the end of cooking, remove the lid, tip the pan on an angle and, if there is any water left, cover once more and continue to cook until you see small steam holes on the surface. Remove from the heat, put a dish towel under the lid to absorb any steam and leave for about 5 minutes. Then set aside to cool completely.

Preheat the oven to 350°F. Heat 1 tablespoon of olive oil in a frying pan. Add the onion and mixed herbs and sauté over a low heat for approximately 5 minutes.

Brush the mushrooms with olive oil and finely slice. Add them to the onion and continue to cook for 10 minutes, until all their juices have been released. Add the garlic and parsley and cook for 5 minutes, until the juices are reduced.

Put the mushroom mixture into a mixing bowl and add the cooled kasha, tamari, salt and pepper. Mix well and leave to cool.

Add the egg, mix well and put mixture into a lightly oiled, oven-proof dish (approximately 6 inches square and 2½ inches deep). Bake for 50 minutes. When cooked it will be slightly puffed and evenly colored.

Serve with large pieces of roasted winter squash and steamed greens, tossed with a little butter and garlic.

Tempeh bolognese lasagne

VEGAN

This is a truly delicious meal, hearty and great tasting. Polenta works very well when used as lasagne sheets and is a good option if you are gluten-intolerant—it is far superior to the gluten-free sheets available commercially. The various elements do take some time to prepare, but once they are all done it is easy to put together.

To make this gluten-free, choose a gluten-free marinade with gluten-free tamari or be sure to choose a seasoned tempeh that doesn't contain shoyu.

SERVES 4 TO 6

1 pound, 5 ounces winter squash (jap (kent) or butternut), cut into rough 1¼-inch cubes
1 sprig fresh rosemary, leaves only
olive oil, to bake (plus 1 tablespoon extra, to fry)
1 bunch spinach
4 cups vegetable stock (see page 48) (or water)
1 cup polenta
2 cups well-flavored mushrooms (such as Swiss brown or portabello), sliced
1 to 2 garlic cloves, finely chopped
1 to 2 tablespoons finely chopped fresh flat-leaf (Italian) parsley (plus handful extra, to garnish)
1 quantity tofu 'ricotta' (see page 40)

TEMPEH BOLOGNAISE

10½ ounces basic marinated tempeh (see page 102) (or seasoned or 'ready to eat' tempeh)
olive oil, for frying
1 teaspoon roasted sesame oil
1 onion, finely chopped
½ teaspoon dried basil
½ teaspoon dried sage
½ teaspoon dried thyme
½ teaspoon dried oregano
1½ to 2½ tablespoons tamari (plus 3 teaspoons tamari, extra)
28 ounces canned tomatoes (or fresh to equal)
1½ tablespoons tomato paste (concentrated purée)
1 tablespoon roughly chopped fresh basil leaves
1 to 2 teaspoons apple juice concentrate

Preheat the oven to 350°F. Toss the squash pieces in the rosemary and a little olive oil. Put the squash on a baking tray and bake for 1 hour, or until soft and caramelized. Set aside.

If you are using a stainless steel pan, the tempeh may stick a little to the bottom. Using a slotted spatula makes it easier to scrape it off the bottom of the pan.

To make the tempeh bolognaise, cut the tempeh into very small, thin pieces. Using a large frying pan, gently heat 1 to 2 tablespoons of olive oil and the sesame oil. Add the tempeh and cook for 10 minutes over a medium heat, stirring occasionally, by this time the tempeh should have begun to color.

Add the onion and herbs and continue to cook, stirring occasionally, for a further 5 minutes, or until the onions have begun to soften. Add 1½ tablespoons of tamari and stir. Cook over a gentle heat for 1 to 2 minutes. Taste and add the extra tamari if you feel it needs it.

Add the tomatoes and roughly break them apart. Add all other ingredients. (If you are using fresh tomatoes, you may need to add approximately ½ cup of water.) Cook at a slow, gentle simmer for 40 to 45 minutes, stirring often.

To prepare the spinach, cut the leaves from the root and wash well. Put in a large saucepan, and cook for 3 to 4 minutes over a low heat, until wilted, stirring occasionally. Strain through a colander and squeeze out any remaining liquid. Set aside.

To make the polenta lasagne sheets, put the stock (or water) in a large saucepan, bring to the boil and add a pinch of salt. Add the polenta slowly, stirring as you go. Reduce the heat to a gentle simmer and cook for 20 to 30 minutes, stirring frequently (especially as it starts to thicken). The polenta is ready when it has developed a creamy appearance.

Using an offset spatula makes spreading out the polenta very easy.

Line one or two large baking trays with non-stick baking paper. While the polenta is still hot, spread a thin layer on the tray (approximately ¼ inch thick). Cover and set aside to cool. To use, simply cut the polenta into manageable pieces (too large and they are difficult to lift out whole without cracking). Trim any dry edge pieces if needed.

Heat 1 tablespoon of olive oil in a frying pan and gently sauté the mushrooms for 15 minutes, until all their juices have been released. Add the tamari, garlic and parsley and cook for a further 5 to 10 minutes, until the juice is reduced.

To assemble the lasagne, put half the bolognaise mixture on the base of a lasagne dish. Gently lift the polenta pieces (it can be easier to move the sheets inverted attached to the baking paper) and put them over the sauce to make a layer (it may need further trimming to fit).

Cover the polenta with squash, mushrooms and spinach. Gently cover with another layer of polenta. Spread the tofu ricotta over this. Cover this with the remaining polenta and top with the remaining bolognaise mixture. Bake for 1 hour to 1 hour 10 minutes, or until you can see the mixture bubbling on the sides and the polenta edges are beginning to crisp. Sprinkle with the parsley and let it sit for 10 minutes before cutting, this allows it to 'set' and makes cutting considerably easier. Serve with a green salad with basil dressing (see page 150).

Polenta sheets can be made up to 2 days before use and kept, covered in plastic, in an airtight container.

VARIATIONS

You can add a variety of ingredients to this lasagne. Roasted peppers (see page 34) added with the squash, pesto (see page 45) dotted on the vegetables, fresh tomato sauce (see page 35), pitted kalamata olives and grilled vegetables are great additions in place of the squash.

Adding 1/2 cup of red wine with the tomatoes will make a richer, more flavorsome sauce.

Gratin of polenta, with goat cheese and salsa ranchera

GLUTEN FREE / VEGETARIAN

With subtle chili warmth, this is a dish packed full of flavor. A bowl of this is true comfort food.

SERVES 4 TO 6

- 4 cups vegetable stock (see page 48) (or water)
- 1 cup polenta
- 1 quantity salsa ranchera (see page 39)
- 7 ounces mild goat cheese (such as blanc or chevre)
- small handful roughly chopped fresh flat-leaf (Italian) parsley

Using a large, deep saucepan, bring the stock to the boil and add a pinch of salt. Add the polenta slowly, stirring as you go. Lower the heat to a gentle simmer and cook for 20 to 30 minutes, stirring frequently (especially as it starts to thicken). It takes a strong arm to stir polenta but is well worth the result. The polenta is ready when it has developed a creamy appearance. Transfer to a lightly oiled dish (approximately 11¼ x 7½ inches). The polenta should be about ⅝ inch thick. Allow to cool completely.

Preheat the oven to 400°F. To assemble the gratin, cut the cooled polenta, while still in the dish, into 12 squares. Cut these squares diagonally to create triangles.

Use a large, shallow ovenproof dish for the gratin. Spread about ¾ cup of the salsa over the bottom, then arrange the polenta triangles upright, across the width of the dish. Add the goat cheese in large chunks between the polenta, and pour over the rest of the salsa. Try to leave the tips of the polenta uncovered, these will become crisp in the oven.

Bake for 30 to 45 minutes, or until the sauce is bubbling and the polenta tips look lightly browned. Sprinkle with parsley before serving.

VARIATIONS

Many things work with polenta cooked in this way.

- Sprinkle with a good grated melting cheese over the top before baking, or add the polenta once cooked.
- Serve with ratatouille (see page 168).
- Add pieces of baked eggplant between the polenta.
- Use fresh tomato sauce (see page 35) instead of the salsa ranchera.
- Serve with cooked mushrooms with garlic and parsley

Corn fritters

GLUTEN FREE / VEGETARIAN

Corn fritters are a great meal any time of the day. The mixture keeps well in the fridge for up to 3 days. It is actually preferable to use canned corn kernels for this, which are more tender, but if you use fresh corn, simply steam them and then cut the kernels off.

MAKES 8

olive oil, for frying
1 onion, finely chopped
2 garlic cloves, finely chopped
28 ounces canned corn kernels (or fresh to equal)
3 tablespoons fresh flat-leaf (Italian) parsley, finely chopped
3 tablespoons cornstarch (or kudzu powder)
3 tablespoons cornmeal (golden)
2 eggs, lightly beaten

TO SERVE
1 quantity fresh salsa (see page 37)
1 avocado, finely diced
small handful fresh flat-leaf (Italian) parsley, finely chopped

This is a great dish to serve for breakfast.

Preheat the oven to 235 to 275°F. Heat 1 tablespoon of oil in a frying pan. Add the onion and garlic, and sauté for 3 to 4 minutes, until just soft. Combine remaining ingredients in a bowl, add the onion and garlic and stir well.

Heat 2 tablespoons of olive oil in a frying pan over medium heat. To make each fritter, put approximately 3 tablespoons of the mixture into the pan (don't be tempted to flatten them out too much), and cook for 4 to 5 minutes on one side. It is important that the heat is high enough to create a good sizzle, without being too high that it cooks the outside before the inside is ready. Turn over and cook for a further 4 to 5 minutes. Remove and drain on a paper towel and then move to the oven to keep warm. Repeat with the remaining mixture.

Serve with fresh salsa, avocado and sprinkled with parsley.

Millet patties

GLUTEN FREE / VEGAN

These are best made into patties while the mixture is still warm; once the millet cools (especially after being in the fridge) it loses its stickiness.

MAKES 6 TO 8

1 cup hulled millet, unsoaked
4 1/4 ounces sweet potato, peeled
4 1/4 ounces carrots (plus 1 extra, finely diced)
olive oil, for frying
1/2 onion, finely chopped
1 garlic clove, crushed
1 teaspoon dried basil
3 teaspoons tamari
1 to 2 tablespoons finely chopped fresh flat-leaf (Italian) parsley
1 tablespoon chopped, fresh basil
freshly ground black pepper, to taste
cornmeal (or flour), for dredging
carrot and ginger sauce (see page 45) or shiitake mushroom gravy (see page 42), to serve (optional)

Rinse the millet well, pat dry with a dish towel, and put in a heavy-based saucepan with 1 cup of water. Cover with a lid and bring to the boil over a gentle heat. As soon as it reaches boiling point, turn the heat down as low as possible (a heat diffuser is useful here). Cook the grain for 15 to 20 minutes. When it is ready, small steam holes should appear on the surface. Scoop into a large bowl and allow to cool slightly.

Meanwhile, steam the sweet potato and carrot for 15 to 20 minutes, or until soft. Drain, then mash well. The mash mustn't be too wet, otherwise the mixture won't hold together.

Heat 1 teaspoon of olive oil in a frying pan over medium heat. Add the onion, garlic, diced carrot and dried basil and gently sauté for 5 minutes, until soft. Add to the millet along with all the other ingredients. Mix together well and mold into patties.

Heat about 3 tablespoons of oil in a large frying pan over medium heat. Roll the patties gently in cornmeal and fry for 2 to 3 minutes on each side, until lightly browned. Drain on a paper towel before serving.

Scented quinoa pilaf

GLUTEN FREE / VEGAN

This is a simple but delicious way to use quinoa. It can be served warm or cold.

SERVES 3 TO 4 AS AN ACCOMPANIMENT

olive oil, for frying
2 to 3 green onions (scallions), finely chopped
½ teaspoon ground cumin
¼ teaspoon ground ginger
¼ teaspoon ground cinnamon
¼ teaspoon ground coriander
1 cup quinoa
2 cups vegetable stock (see page 48) (or water)
¼ cup currants
½ cup roasted pine nuts
handful cilantro leaves, finely chopped

Heat the olive oil in a saucepan over a moderate heat. Add the onion and spices and cook for 5 minutes. Rinse the quinoa and drain well. Pat dry with a dish towel then add to the saucepan and stir through. Add the stock. Cover with a lid and bring to the boil. As soon as it comes to the boil, turn the heat down low and cook for 15 to 20 minute. Check if there is any water left by tipping the pot on an angle about 5 minutes before the end of the cooking time. If so, continue to cook until no liquid remains. When it is ready small steam holes should appear on the surface. Remove from the heat, place a dish towel under the lid to absorb any steam and leave for about 5 minutes.

Put the quinoa in a bowl and add the currants, pine nuts and cilantro and gently mix through.

Rice balls

VEGAN

These are often found at macrobiotic food shops and are very popular. Now you can make your own. The secret to getting them to stick together is to knead the mixture well. This allows the starch inside the grain to help bind the mixture together. Another secret is to use well-cooked brown rice (if it is a little undercooked, the starchy center will remain trapped).

These can be gluten-free if there is no shoyu in the tempeh and if wheat-free tamari is used.

MAKES 8 TO 10

¼ cup arame (see page 303)
olive oil, for frying
½ onion, finely diced
1 garlic clove, crushed
1½ to 2 cups grated carrot
3 cups cooked medium/short grain brown rice (equivalent to about 1 cup raw rice)
4½ ounces basic marinated tempeh (see page 102) (or 'ready to eat' tempeh), finely diced
½ cup hulled sunflower seeds, finely ground
1½ tablespoons tamari
1 teaspoon roasted sesame oil
1 cup cooked, well-drained sweet potato
¼ cup roasted sesame seeds (plus extra for rolling)

Soak the arame in a small bowl of water for about 15 minutes, then rinse and drain.

Heat a teaspoon of oil in a frying pan. Add the onion and garlic and gently sauté for 5 minutes. Add the carrot and continue to cook for 4 to 5 minutes, until soft.

Place all the remaining ingredients into a large bowl, and add the cooked carrot mixture. Knead together well until it holds together. Form into balls about the size of a tennis ball and roll in sesame seeds—you should get 8 to 10 balls.

Put about ½ inch oil in a frying pan over low to medium heat. Once hot, add the rice balls in batches and fry for 8 to 10 minutes, turning gently until the sesame seeds are golden. Drain on paper towel. Alternatively, you can bake them in the oven at 350°F for approximately 30 minutes, until golden.

Serve cold with a salad for a wonderful lunch, or warm with steamed vegetables for dinner. You may like to serve them with tomato sauce or tamari served on top. They freeze well.

Sushi nori

VEGAN

Nori rolls are basically rice and filling wrapped inside a flat sheet of seaweed. Most nori rolls you see commercially use white rice, with sugar syrup. Brown rice will work just as well and it actually tastes much nicer. The most difficult part is the rolling, but this does come with practice. The rolls can be made up to 1 hour before serving, but are best cut just before for maximum freshness.

MAKES 4 NORI ROLLS

RICE

3 cups cold cooked medium/short grain brown rice
1½ tablespoons mirin
3 to 5 drops roasted sesame oil
3 teaspoons sesame seeds, roasted

Roasted sesame oil is very strong and its flavor can easily overpower everything else. A drop here is measured as just that—a tiny drop.

TAHINI SPREAD

½ cup hulled tahini
3 teaspoons mirin (or to taste)
1 teaspoon tamari
1 teaspoon sweet chilli sauce (or to taste)
1 teaspoon finely chopped fresh cilantro leaves

FILLING

2¾ ounces basic marinated tempeh (see page 102) (or 'ready to eat' tempeh), cut into strips approximately ½ inch wide
1 cup finely grated carrot
1 avocado, cut into thin slices
3 green onions (scallions), thinly sliced
a few slices of pickled ginger

For a gluten-free roll, use wheat-free tamari and avoid tempeh that contains shoyu.

4 nori sheets

TO SERVE
dipping sauce
pickled ginger
wasabi

Place the rice and remaining rice ingredients in a bowl. Mix the ingredients together gently.

Combine all the tahini spread ingredients in a bowl and mix well. Adjust the sweet chilli sauce and mirin to taste. The tahini can thicken as you mix and make a very stiff paste, too thick for spreading. If this happens, simply add a little water and continue to mix until it becomes smooth—it will take a minute or so for the tahini and water to combine.

The secret to putting nori together easily and with a minimum of fuss is to have everything ready, lined up for assembly. You will also need a bowl of water for sealing the roll, a clean, wet cloth and a dry dish towel. Have a plate ready for the finished nori.

It is important that you prepare the nori on a clean, dry surface (using a nori mat to roll if preferred). Lay the nori sheet down, with the smooth side facing the work surface (nori sheets have indented lines on them to allow for easy rolling.) With clean, dry hands, scoop up approximately ¾ cup of rice, and roughly form into a ball the size of a tennis ball. Using your fingertips, press the rice thinly (and gently) over the nori sheet, leaving ¾ inch at the edges closest and furthest from you. It is important that the rice is evenly spread and covers the entire width of the nori sheet, especially the edge. If you find it a little too sticky using your fingers, try using a fork to pat down the rice.

At this stage, wipe your hands with the damp cloth, removing any rice that has stuck to them. Spread a little tahini spread over the rice, a few inches in from the edge closest to you. Put one-quarter of the filling ingredients along the edge closest to you. Don't be tempted to use too much filling, as it will become difficult to roll.

With clean fingers, wet the edge of the nori furthest from you. Wipe your hands on the dry towel, removing any excess water. Begin to roll the nori, starting from the edge closest to you. The aim is to keep the filling well tucked in and to keep the roll tight. If the roll is too loose, the filling will fall out when cut, if it is too tight, the nori will split as you roll. Toward the end of the roll you may sometimes get a build-up of rice. If this happens, use a sharp knife to remove it, leaving a clear width of wet nori sheet (approximately ¾ inch) for sealing. Continue rolling over the wet edge of the nori; you should now have a light seal. Run your fingers over this, giving it a little pressure to complete the seal. Repeat to make 4 rolls.

Serve with dipping sauce (this can be simply tamari and mirin mixed together), pickled ginger and wasabi.

You need a really sharp knife to cut nori rolls, as you depend on sharpness, not pressure to do the job. If you use too much pressure on the rolls during cutting, the filling starts to come out. The best technique is to use a light, sawing motion. If not using them immediately, cover and make airtight, and put in the fridge.

VARIATIONS

- Add finely sliced strips of deseeded cucumber to the roll.
- Add finely sliced strips of red pepper to the roll.
- Add spears of blanched, cooked asparagus to the roll.
- Add shrimp or salmon to the roll.
- Add wasabi to the roll. This is a wildly hot Japanese horseradish—put just a tiny amount on the rice, before using the tahini.

'Fried' rice

GLUTEN FREE / VEGAN

This is a hearty meal that looks and tastes great, yet is really just brown rice and steamed vegetables. At first glance this looks like a complicated recipe; it really isn't, but it does have quite a few parts, many of which can be done ahead of time.

SERVES 4 TO 6

5½ to 7 ounces firm tofu, cut into ¾ to 1¼ inch cubes
1 quantity Asian marinade (see page 98)
1 cup long grain brown rice (or 2 cups cold cooked long grain brown rice)
1 to 2 carrots, cut in half lengthways and then cut on the diagonal into thin slices
2 celery stalks, sliced finely on the diagonal
1 red pepper, cut lengthways into thin slices

5 to 8 baby corn, halved
1 head broccoli, cut into small florets
4 to 5 asparagus spears, sliced on the diagonal into 1½ to 2 inch lengths
10 to 15 snow peas (mangetout), halved lengthways
olive oil, for frying
fresh cilantro leaves, to garnish
1 quantity carrot and ginger sauce (see page 45)
1 quantity tamari seeds (see page 33)

First, marinate the tofu in the Asian marinade for 1 to 12 hours in the fridge.

If cooking the rice, rinse well. Pat dry and put in a heavy-based saucepan with 2 cups of water. Bring to the boil over a gentle heat, then turn the heat down as low as possible and cook for 30 to 40 minutes. When it is ready, small steam holes should appear on the surface.

Meanwhile, toast the seeds, make the carrot sauce and prepare all the vegetables. Heat ¼ cup of olive oil in a wok. It is important that the oil is hot, but not smoking. Remove the tofu from the marinade and put it into the wok (reserv-ing the marinade). Fry the tofu for 6 to 10 minutes, until it is golden. You will need to move the tofu constantly, ensuring it cooks on all sides. The oil should be making a gentle sizzle, indicating a good temperature. When golden, remove the tofu and put in a bowl lined with paper towel. Discard the oil.

Add a little of the reserved marinade to the wok (approximately ¼ cup). This will provide steam to help cook the vegetables. Add all the vegetables except the snow peas and cover with a lid. Cook on a low heat for 5 to 8 minutes. Lift the lid and check the vegetables; they should be ever so slightly undercooked. Add the snow peas, rice and tofu and stir to mix. Replace the lid. Continue to cook until the vegetables are just cooked (3 to 5 minutes). Turn out into a bowl. Pour over sufficient carrot and ginger sauce to moisten and sprinkle with the toasted seeds. Finish by garnishing with cilantro leaves. Serve any leftover sauce in a jug or bowl.

VARIATIONS

Any seasonal vegetables that can be lightly cooked will work well —zucchini, baby (pattypan) squash, asparagus, cauliflower florets, kale, green beans and green peas would all be good.

Jambalaya

GLUTEN FREE

Jambalaya is a pilaf, a well-flavored and easy meal to prepare, perfect for Sunday night dinner. Because this is one of those dishes you put together when you are looking for great taste with minimal effort, canned beans are used here.

This will be vegan if vegetable stock is used.

SERVES 4

olive oil, for frying
1 cup long grain brown rice
1 onion, finely diced
½ cup finely chopped celery
1 cup red and green pepper, finely diced
kernels from 1 corn cob (or 1 cup canned corn)
1 carrot, finely diced
2 garlic cloves, finely chopped
¼ to ½ teaspoon cayenne pepper (or to taste)
½ to 1 teaspoon freshly ground black pepper
1 teaspoon dried oregano
1¾ to 2¼ cups stock
14 ounces canned kidney beans, drained (or freshly cooked to equal)
handful fresh flat-leaf (Italian) parsley, roughly chopped

Start with ¼ teaspoon cayenne, and adjust the heat level at a later time during the cooking process.

Heat 1 tablespoon of olive oil in a frying pan over low to medium heat. Add the rice and gently sauté for 5 minutes, then add the onion and cook for a further 2 minutes. Add all the vegetables, garlic, cayenne, black pepper and oregano and cook for 2 minutes, stirring frequently.

Add 1¾ cups of stock. Cover with a lid and bring to the boil. Turn down the heat immediately and simmer over a very low heat for about 40 minutes. Check after 20 minutes and add the extra liquid if it is low. Once cooked, check for taste, then add the kidney beans and toss until heated through. Add a good handful of chopped parsley and serve.

VARIATIONS

- Add some chopped, fried bacon while the onion is sautéing.
- Add more varieties of vegetables, such as peas, broccoli and sweet potato.

- Add spicy sausage, a traditional ingredient in a jambalaya. Cut it into bite-size pieces and add with the vegetables.
- Add raw shrimp toward the final 10 minutes of cooking.

Risotto

Most risotto sold commercially uses large quantities of butter, mascarpone cheese and/or other saturated fats to give it a fullness of flavor, which can be extremely rich. It is very easy, however, to make a delicious risotto with little or no fat by focusing on good-quality stock and building flavor in elsewhere.

A strong, well-flavored stock is the beginning and end of a good risotto. The stock should reflect the overall flavor of your risotto: the earthy autumn and winter risottos of mushrooms, roasted root vegetables and winter squash will benefit from deeply flavored, earthy stocks (beef or mushroom-based vegetable stocks); the lighter spring and summer risottos of fava beans, asparagus and green peas are best with a lighter stock (chicken or a simple vegetable stock).

Basic risotto

DAIRY FREE

Use this basic recipe as a base to create your own risotto, with the addition of seasonal ingredients, for example roasted peppers (see page 34) or winter squash.

SERVES 3 TO 4

5 cups vegetable stock (see page 48)
oil (or butter or ghee), for frying
½ onion (or 2 shallots or 1 leek), finely sliced
4 to 5 fresh sage leaves (or 1 to 2 tablespoons fresh rosemary or 4 to 5 fresh sprigs thyme)
1½ cups arborio rice
1½ tablespoons mirin (or more to taste)
1 to 2 teapsoons tamari (to taste)
pecorino (or parmesan) cheese, to serve
3 tablespoons chopped fresh flat-leaf (Italian) parsley

This recipe will be gluten-free depending on the tamari used.

Begin by gently heating the stock (it should be simmering, not boiling).

Heat 2 tablespoons of oil in a heavy-based saucepan. Add the onion and sauté for 2 to 5 minutes over a gentle heat, stirring occasionally, and then add the sage (or rosemary or thyme) and stir through.

Add the rice and stir it gently, coating it in the oil and onion for approximately 1 minute, then add the mirin. Stir the onion and rice gently and allow the mirin to steam and sizzle, for 1 to 2 minutes, until it evaporates and reduces a little.

Ladle approximately 1 cup of stock into the rice and stir gently. The heat should be slow and low, enough to encourage a very gentle simmer. Continue to stir the risotto, adding more stock as it is absorbed into the rice. Once you have used nearly all of the stock, taste the rice. It is ready when it still has a slight crunch. The risotto will continue to cook once it has been removed from the heat.

If you are using cheese, add the finely grated pecorino or parmesan (approximately 2 tablespoons or to taste). Season with salt and pepper, and sprinkle generously with chopped flat-leaf (Italian) parsley. Test for taste—you may need to add a little tamari or extra mirin, but generally, if you have used a good stock this should not be needed.

Spring risotto

DAIRY FREE

This is an absolute favorite. Stock for this risotto should be sturdy but light, such as chicken or vegetable, and it is important that a good amount of butter is used. If you can find green garlic, this is a good risotto to use it in. Fresh, young green peas also work well here.

SERVES 3 TO 4

5 cups vegetable stock (see page 48) (or chicken stock)
butter (or oil or ghee), for frying
1 to 2 small leeks, well rinsed, roughly cut
1 garlic clove, crushed (or 2 to 3 stems green garlic, finely sliced)
5 to 6 sprigs fresh thyme

This recipe will be gluten-free depending on the tamari used, and will also be vegan if vegetable stock is used.

- 1½ cups arborio rice
- 1½ tablespoons mirin (or more to taste)
- 1 to 2 teaspoons tamari (to taste)
- 1 cup young fava beans
- 10 to 12 asparagus spears
- Herbamare, to taste

Begin by gently heating the stock (it should be simmering, not boiling).

Heat 2 tablespoons of oil in a heavy-based saucepan. Add the leeks, garlic and thyme and sauté for 2 to 5 minutes over a gentle heat, stirring occasionally.

Add the rice and stir it gently, coating it in the oil and leek for approximately 1 minute, then add the mirin. Stir the leek and rice gently and allow the mirin to steam and sizzle for 1 to 2 minutes, until it evaporates and reduces a little.

Ladle approximately 1 cup of stock into the rice and stir gently. The heat should be slow and low, enough to encourage a very gentle simmer. Continue to stir the risotto, adding more stock as it is absorbed into the rice. Once you have used nearly all of the stock, taste the rice. It is ready when it still has a slight crunch. The risotto will continue to cook once it has been moved from the heat.

While the risotto is cooking, shell the beans and slip them out of their skins, then set aside in a bowl. Break or cut off the woody ends of the asparagus and discard. Cut the tips to lengths of approximately 1½ inch and set aside. Cut the remaining asparagus into slices ½ inch long.

Melt a little butter in a frying pan and add the fava beans and sliced asparagus (not the tips). Cook over a gentle heat for approximately 10 minutes, stirring occasionally, then set aside.

Bring a small saucepan of water to the boil. Add the asparagus tips and cook for about 20 seconds. Pour into a colander and run under cold water for a few seconds.

Add all the ingredients to the prepared risotto rice. Test for taste; you may need to add a little tamari or mirin but, generally, if you have used a good stock this should not be needed. Another way to add extra flavor at this point is to use heavily reduced stock, hitting it with concentrated flavor.

Summer risotto

This is really quite a flexible risotto—and a lovely way to celebrate summer.

SERVES 3 TO 4

about 15 cherry tomatoes (or 6 roma (plum) tomatoes)
sea salt, to taste
freshly ground black pepper, to taste
5 cups vegetable stock (see page 48)
olive oil (or butter), for frying
½ onion, diced
6 to 8 fresh basil leaves, roughly chopped
1½ cups arborio rice
1½ tablespoons mirin
1 roasted pepper (see page 34), cut into strips
about 12 kalamata olives, pipped and cut in half
grilled fennel (or grilled zucchini) (see pages 193-4) (optional)
pesto (see page 45), to serve
flat-leaf (Italian) parsley, to serve

If using cherry tomatoes, preheat the oven to 350°F, toss the tomatoes with a little oil, salt and pepper and roast for approximately 20 minutes. For roma tomatoes, roast for about 50 minutes, until soft.

Heat the stock (it should be simmering, not boiling). Heat 2 tablespoons of oil (or butter) in a heavy-based saucepan. Add the onion and basil and sauté for 2 to 5 minutes over a gentle heat, stirring occasionally. Stir in the rice, coating it in the oil and onion for about 1 minute, then add the mirin. Stir the onion and rice gently and allow the mirin to steam and sizzle, for 1 to 2 minutes, until it evaporates and reduces a little.

Ladle approximately 1 cup of stock into the rice and stir gently. The heat should be slow and low, enough to encourage a very gentle simmer. Continue to stir the risotto, adding more stock as it is absorbed into the rice. Once you have used nearly all of the stock, taste the rice. It is ready when it still has a slight crunch. The risotto will continue to cook once it has been moved from the heat. When ready, add the tomatoes, pepper, olives and sliced fennel or zucchini and serve with a small dollop of pesto and parsley.

salads

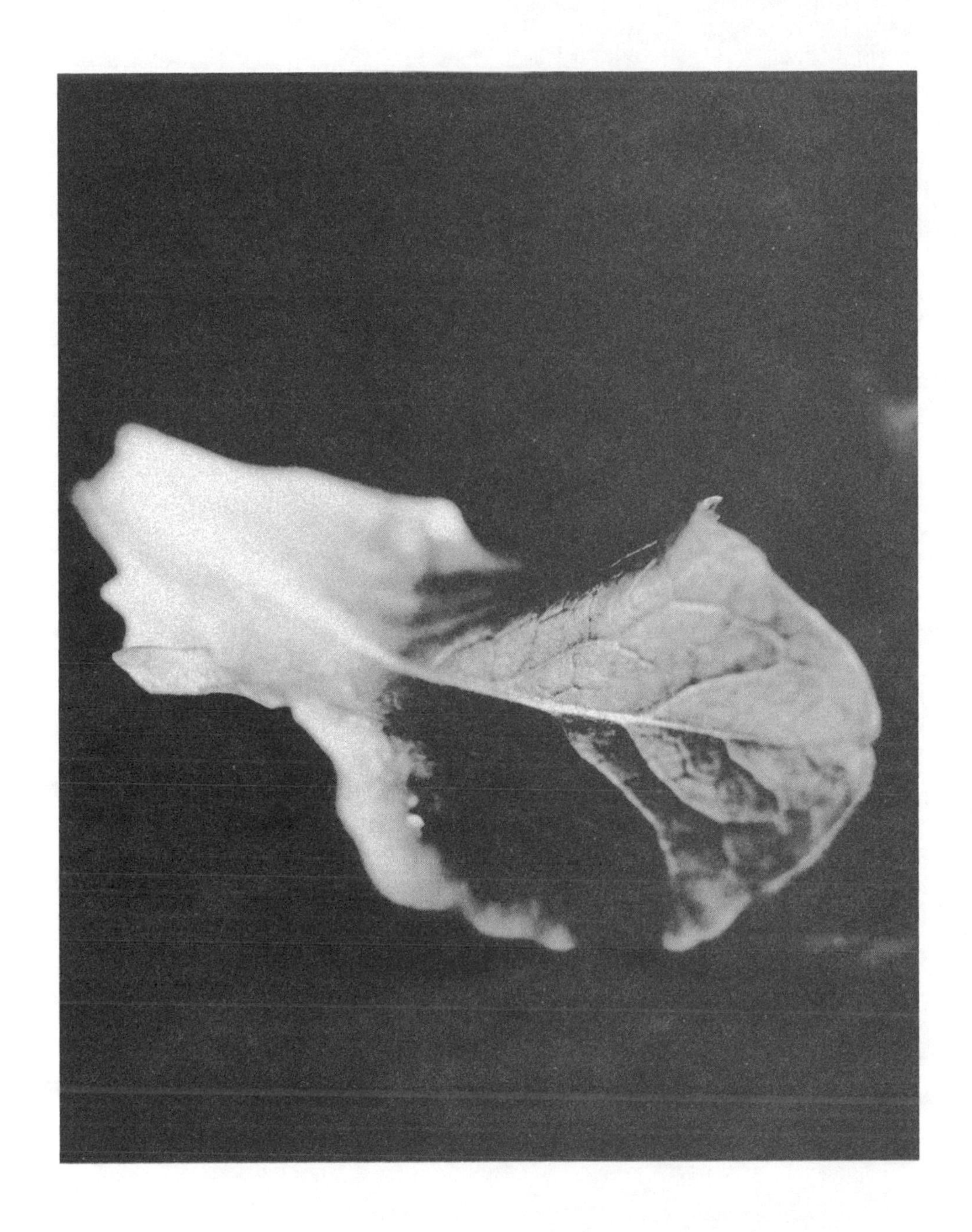

A salad can range from a bowl of beautiful, just-picked green leaves to a complex mixture of beans and vegetables. It can be chilled and raw or cooked and warm, tossed together or presented as separate offerings—in short, a salad can be whatever you want it to be. Salads offer the best opportunity to get maximum goodness from your food: those freshly picked, bursting-with-life green leaves are full of nourishment; that drizzle of good-quality oil, packed with essential nutrients, is the absolute best way to ingest oil (raw and unheated). The only essential rule to follow when making a salad is to use the freshest of ingredients for, in a salad, no disguise is possible. The success of the end product will depend entirely on the quality of its components—old and tired ingredients will only ever make a dull and boring salad.

Beyond a bowl of leaves

Sometimes a diverse mixture of leaves, each with their own distinctive flavor, alive and bursting with nutrients, is just what the doctor ordered. To this can be added a range of other foods that not only add to the overall nutritional benefit of a salad, but also add flavor and interest. The following recipes are full of goodness and they celebrate simple wholesome ingredients.

Green salad with basil dressing

VEGAN

SERVES 4

1 large (or 2 small) romaine lettuce (or other fresh green lettuce)
approximately 15 arugula leaves, stems removed
3 sprigs fresh flat-leaf (Italian) parsley, leaves only, roughly torn
1 avocado, peeled and sliced
1 cucumber, peeled if the skin is very tough, seeds removed if desired, sliced thinly
3½ ounces sunflower sprouts (or other sprouts)

BASIL DRESSING
handful fresh basil
½ cup extra virgin olive oil
1 to 2 garlic cloves, crushed
½ teaspoon whole grain mustard
1½ tablespoons apple cider vinegar
1 to 2 teaspoons apple juice concentrate

Wash the salad leaves well, making sure to remove any traces of sand. Drain and dry well. Depending on the size of the lettuce leaves, tear into smaller pieces and set aside.

To make the dressing, put the dressing ingrendients into a blender in the order listed, and blend until smooth.

Put all the salad ingredients into a bowl, toss gently and drizzle with approximately 3½ ounces of the dressing and serve.

A dressing adds another dimension of taste to a salad, and in its simplest form consists of an oil and an acid, usually vinegar or lemon. The basic formula is three parts oil to one part acid. For the best results, however, always taste your dressing and adjust accordingly.

Sea caesar salad

VEGAN

This is a perennial favorite with a vegan twist. Here nori strips and tempeh replace the traditional anchovy and crispy bacon.

SERVES 2

CROUTONS
1 to 2 thick bread slices, cut into cubes
extra virgin olive oil (optional), for tossing
pinch dried basil
pinch dried sage
pinch dried thyme

1 baby romaine lettuce
handful tasty tempeh bits (see page 107)
1 avocado, sliced lengthways
10 nori strips ¾ x 2 inches wide
finely chopped fresh flat-leaf (Italian) parsley, to serve

This salad will be gluten-free if the tempeh used does not contain shoyu.

CREAMY TOFU MAYONNAISE

2½ ounces silken tofu

1 to 2 garlic cloves

1 teaspoons wholegrain mustard

1½ tablespoons balsamic vinegar

1 tablespoons shiro miso paste

¼ cup extra virgin olive oil

Any leftover mayonnaise will keep in the fridge for up to 2 weeks.

Preheat the oven to 350°F. To make the croutons, toss the bread cubes with a little olive oil (optional), some dried basil, sage and thyme and mix together. Put on a baking tray and bake for 15 minutes, until the cubes are a little crisp (shaking the tray occasionally). Be careful not to dry the bread out too much—you will find the denser the bread the more you want just the outside to be crisp.

Some bread responds better to crouton making than others. For example, a heavy and dense sourdough will make rock-hard croutons. It is possible to make excellent gluten- or wheat-free croutons but you need decent bread to start with.

To make the tofu mayonnaise, put the tofu, garlic, mustard, vinegar and miso in a blender. Put the lid on and, while the blender is running, slowly drizzle in the oil. Start very, very slowly and be patient—if you do it too fast it will fail to combine. Once the mayonnaise starts to combine you can add the oil in a faster stream.

To assemble the salad, tear the leaves from the lettuce and arrange in two large serving bowls. Start with larger leaves first and layer with smaller leaves. Add the tempeh bits, then drizzle as much mayonnaise as desired over and around the salad. Arrange the avocado slices attractively on top, then add the croutons. Sprinkle on top, first the nori strips and then the parsley and serve.

Jeanie's tabouleh

VEGAN

This is my best-friend's recipe—a grain-free version of the classic salad, bountiful with greens and 'earthed' with sprouted lentils.

SERVES 4

DRESSING

3 teaspoons apple juice concentrate

3 teaspoons apple cider vinegar

3 teaspoons lemon juice

- 9 ounces ripe tomatoes
- ½ bunch (4 to 5 stems) Swiss chard (young, fresh leaves)
- ¼ cup roughly chopped roasted walnuts
- 1¼ cups sprouted lentils
- 9 ounces cucumber, finely diced
- 4 sprigs fresh flat-leaf (Italian) parsley, finely chopped
- 5 mint leaves, finely chopped

To make the dressing, mix all the dressing ingredients together and set aside.

Cut an X at the bottom of each tomato, to pierce the skin. Bring a large saucepan of water to the boil, then plunge 2 to 3 tomatoes at a time for 20 to 30 seconds. Remove from the pan and allow to cool just a little, then peel the skin away from the cross. Set aside to cool completely, then dice.

Wash the Swiss chard well, discarding the stem unless very young and tender. Dry and slice as finely as possible.

Combine all the salad ingredients and toss through the dressing.

Honey and sesame squash salad

DAIRY FREE

This is a great salad to serve as a main meal on a hot summer's day. Roast squash and tempeh make it richly satisfying.

SERVES 2

- 7 ounces winter squash (jap (kent) or butternut), cut into 1¼-inch cubes
- extra virgin olive oil, to drizzle
- 2 teaspoons honey
- 3 teaspoons sesame seeds
- 1 red pepper
- good handful of salad leaves
- 12 arugula leaves (minus stems)
- handful tasty tempeh bits (see page 107)
- 6 marinated artichoke quarters

1 avocado, sliced lengthways
cilantro leaves, to garnish

CILANTRO-CHILE DRESSING
¼ cup sesame oil
3 teaspoons brown rice vinegar
3 teaspoons lime juice
1 teaspoon grated ginger
10 sprigs fresh cilantro
1 garlic clove
1 teaspoon roasted sesame oil
1½ tablespoons apple juice concentrate
8 small mint leaves
3 kaffir lime leaves (vein removed)
1 small red chile (or to taste)

Cilantro-chile dressing is a fabulous summer dressing. Its flavor improves when left to sit in the fridge, with the lime leaves infusing into the wildly fragrant sesame oil.

Preheat the oven to 350°F. Put the squash on a baking tray, drizzle with olive oil and honey and sprinkle with sesame seeds. Bake for 1 hour, until the squash is soft and caramelized. Remove from the oven and allow to cool.

Meanwhile, wash the pepper well and cut the top off close to the stem. Remove the inside core and seeds. Stand upside down in a baking dish and rub well with olive oil. Bake for 30 to 50 minutes, or until the skin is well wrinkled and beginning to blacken. Remove and put into a bowl and top with a plate to cool. Remove the skins, slice into 12 strips and set aside.

Mix the dressing ingredients together until well combined. Pour into a glass jar and shake well.

Arrange the salad leaves on a serving plate, giving it a little height. Add the arugula leaves. Scatter over the squash and tasty tempeh bits and add the artichokes and avocado. Position the roast pepper strips attractively, and top with cilantro leaves. Drizzle over the dressing and serve immediately.

Bean, noodle and grain-based salads

With their protein and fiber, these hearty ingredients can turn a salad into a satisfying meal in itself. Rice and buckwheat noodles both make excellent bases for Asian salads, while chickpeas match wonderfully with Indian or Moroccan spices. Cannellini and borlotti (cranberry) beans, or young tender fava beans shine when mixed with garlic, basil and Mediterranean flavors, while black-eyed peas and black beans make wonderful bases for salads with a Mexican touch.

If you are avoiding gluten or wheat, salads are a wonderfully versatile way to include grains such as barley, quinoa, buckwheat or rice in your diet.

Brown rice salad

DAIRY FREE

This salad is a popular favorite. A small amount will anchor a plate of lighter salads and deliver substance to a lunch.

This salad will be gluten-free if the tempeh used does not contain shoyu and the tamari is wheat-free.

SERVES 8

1½ cups brown rice
4½ ounces basic marinated tempeh (see page 102)
(or 'ready to eat' tempeh), cut into very small pieces
1 carrot, very finely diced
1 red pepper, very finely diced
½ red onion, very finely diced
1¼ cups sprouted legume mix
kernels from 1 corn cob
handful fresh flat-leaf (Italian) parsley, finely chopped

RICE SALAD DRESSING

1 tablespoon extra virgin olive oil
2 teaspoons apple juice concentrate
1½ tablespoons tamari
1 garlic clove, crushed
1 teaspoon wholegrain mustard
1 tablespoon cilantro leaves, finely chopped

Rinse the rice well, pat dry with a dish towel; put 3 cups of water for short/medium grain and 2½ cups if using long grain to a heavy-based saucepan along with the rice.

Cover with a lid and bring to the boil over a gentle heat. As soon as it reaches boiling point, turn the heat down as low as possible (a heat diffuser is useful here). Cook the grain for 40 to 50 minutes. When it is ready, small steam holes should appear on the surface. Set aside to cool completely.

You can make the dressing either by hand or in a blender. If making by hand, whisk the olive oil, apple juice concentrate and tamari together. Then whisk in the garlic, mustard and cilantro. If making in a blender, put all the ingredients in together and blend until well combined. Set aside.

Mix the cooked rice with the remaining salad ingredients in a large bowl, then turn into a salad bowl. Drizzle with the salad dressing, toss well and serve.

Curried chickpea salad

DAIRY FREE / GLUTEN FREE / VEGAN

This salad can be kept in the fridge for up to 6 days, and just keeps getting better. As with the brown rice salad, a small amount will anchor a range of lighter salads, adding substance to create a complete meal.

SERVES 6 TO 8

2 cups dried chickpeas
olive oil, for frying
½ small onion, cut into fine crescents
1 to 2 tablespoons curry powder
¼ cup currants (or golden raisins)
1 tablespoon pear juice concentrate

Soak the chickpeas overnight in 1½ to 2 cups of water with 2 teaspoons of whey, buttermilk or yogurt stirred gently through. Discard the soaking water and rinse well.

Put the chickpeas in a large heavy-based saucepan covered by approximately 4 inches of water. Cook over a gentle heat for 2½ to 4 hours, or until they are soft and yield their starchy centers. Check occasionally and add water if necessary, and remove the froth from the top. Drain.

Heat a teaspoon of oil in a frying pan. Add the onion and gently sauté for 3 minutes or until soft. Add the curry powder and currants, and continue to sauté for another minute. Add the chickpeas and pear juice concentrate, as well as a small amount of water if the mixture is too dry. Continue to sauté over a gentle heat for 5 to 10 minutes to allow flavors to infuse. Turn onto a plate and serve either hot, warm or cold.

Harvest salad

GLUTEN FREE / VEGAN

This is a salad that demands you set the table outside under the trees and complement it with good bread, some dips, great cheeses and good wine.

SERVES 2 TO 4

⅓ cup cannellini beans
2 inch piece kombu (see page 303)
1 red pepper
olive oil, to coat
2 handfuls arugula, well washed
10½ ounces green beans, blanched, cut into 2 to 2½ inch lengths
1 cup pitted kalamata olives
handful fresh flat-leaf (Italian) parsley, roughly chopped

FLAXSEED AND BALSAMIC DRESSING
¼ cup flaxseed oil
1 tablespoon balsamic vinegar
¼ teaspoon wholegrain mustard
2 garlic cloves, crushed
1 teaspoon apple juice concentrate.

A dressing is a great way to include flaxseed oil in your diet—other flavors mask its assertive taste while it provides a bountiful source of the precious omega 3 essential fatty acids. Only make a small quantity at a time and use immediately as the oil is rapidly affected by light and heat.

Soak the beans overnight in 1½ to 2 cups water with 2 teaspoons of whey, buttermilk or yogurt stirred gently through. Discard the soaking water and rinse well.

Put the beans to a heavy-based saucepan with enough water to cover them by about 4 inches. Add the kombu and simmer for approximately 1 to 1½ hours (a heat diffuser is useful here) or until the beans are soft and yield their starchy center to light pressure. Be careful not to overcook the beans. Discard the cooking water and set aside.

Preheat the oven to 350°F. Cut the top off the pepper and remove the insides. Rub the outside with olive oil and stand upright, cut side down, in a baking dish. Cook for 1 hour, or until the skin is well wrinkled and begins to blacken. Remove and put into a bowl and top with a plate to cool. Peel off the skins and cut the flesh into wide strips and set aside.

To make the dressing, whisk the dressing ingredients together.

Form the bed of the salad with the rocket and then top with green beans. Spoon on the cannellini beans, then add the roasted red pepper strips, olives and flat-leaf parsley. Drizzle with the dressing.

VARIATIONS

A beautiful marinated feta makes a delicious addition to this salad, as do grilled artichokes and eggplant (see page 193) or oven-baked tomatoes (see page 34).

Roast vegetable salad with goat cheese

GLUTEN FREE

This is the most popular salad I make and it is a fabulous way to use roasted vegetables—virtually any combination will work. For a great meal, serve with a green salad (see green salad with basil dressing, page 150) and good bread. The recipe is fundamentally a formula, tossing the vegetables with salt, pepper and finely chopped herbs (rosemary, basil, oregano and sage) or with a little ground cumin.

SERVES 4 TO 6

1 pound, 12 ounces winter squash (jap (kent) or butternut), cut into slices
4 to 5 potatoes (fingerlings are an excellent choice), unpeeled and cut into rough 1¼ to 2½ inch pieces
1 orange sweet potato, cut into rough 1¼ to 2 inch pieces
2 carrots (baby carrots left whole or larger cut into 2 to 3 pieces)
2 to 3 parsnips, peeled and cut into smaller pieces, removing the woody core
3 to 4 baby beets, well washed
2 red peppers
sea salt, to season
freshly ground black pepper, to season
½ teaspoon ground cumin

extra virgin olive oil, to drizzle
4½ to 7 ounces marinated goat cheese
good handful fresh flat-leaf (Italian) parsley, finely chopped

When roasting ingredients, especially for salads, try not to overcrowd the pan. This will make some of them steam, rather than roast.

Preheat the oven to 400°F. The vegetables need to be baked separately to cook well. Put the squash on one tray, the potatoes on another, carrots, sweet potato and parsnip on another and the beets in a dish covered with foil. This way no steaming (apart from the beets) can take place. Stand the peppers upside down in one tray, with your choice of seasonings. Drizzle a little oil over all the vegetables, season with salt, pepper and cumin and massage, so the oil covers the entire surface area of the vegetables.

Bake for 40 minutes to 1½ hours, or until the peppers are well wrinkled and begin to blacken. Remove the peppers, put into a bowl and top with a plate to cool. Remove the skins and cut into strips. Continue to cook the other vegetables if necessary, until they are golden and well cooked (this may be at different times).

Turn the vegetables into a serving bowl or large platter (rubbing the skin off the baby beets before using). Add the red pepper strips, dot with the goat cheese and drizzle with a little of the marinating oil. Top with freshly chopped parsley and serve, warm or cold.

VARIATIONS

Baked or grilled mushrooms, grilled artichokes (see page 193), pitted kalamata olives and oven-baked tomatoes (see page 34) all make delicious and hearty additions to this salad.

food … must be authentic and real

vegetable soups and stews

It's been a hard day, things have not all gone according to plan and you are ready for a little comfort food. To hold the gentle curves of a bowl in your hands, the warmth seeping through to your bones, the smells winding their way to your nose, is in itself essentially nourishing. Meals in bowls are usually soupy, stewy affairs, fairly easy to put together, easily digested and very nurturing. Generally, a stew is thicker than a soup. Both can be as quick as a brief simmer on the stove top, or as long as an extended, slow bake in the oven. They are infinitely flexible, extremely undemanding and freeze well. Then, when you do find yourself at the end of a tough day, exhausted and in need of comfort, there it is! Ready to reheat, to pour into that waiting bowl: ready to warm you, nourish you and befriend you. But perhaps the real healing power of the bowl is the gentle encouragement to snuggle up in your favorite chair. For even if you have the healthiest meal on the planet in that bowl, it is the relaxing, the letting go that is the real healing.

The healing bowl

Making delicious vegetable soups and stews is easy. Traditionally, butter and cream are used to add depth and flavor and a beautiful richness of mouthfeel. Although it is just as easy to make a healing low-fat vegetable or vegan version, there are certain rules that can't be broken.

The vegetables themselves must be of the best quality

Old or wilted vegetables will result in a poorly flavored soup. The more singular the soup (that is, the less variety of vegetables used) the more important this is.

Stock is the foundation of the soup

A well-balanced stock will provide much-needed depth and roundness. The stock must also match the soup you are making—a delicatc soup like asparagus will need a full, but light stock made from vegetables as opposed to a hearty, mushroom-based vegetable stock.

Develop flavor

Do this by slowly sautéing the onions and herbs in fat (1 tablespoon of olive oil or 1 to 2 teaspoons butter or ghee). As each vegetable is prepared, add them to the pot and stir them in. This should take approximately 10 to 15 minutes.

Consider how to develop the thickness of the soup

Control the thickness of the soup through the amount of liquid added and evaporation. Reduction in itself, is one of the most potent tools you have to concentrate and develop flavor.

Use lentils and beans

This greatly increases the heartiness of soups. Truly, they make for meals in a bowl. Legume and vegetable soups actually improve with age; served the day after they are first cooked, the flavors become even more developed.

Giambotta

GLUTEN FREE

This classic Italian vegetable stew differs from minestrone in that the vegetables retain their individuality, both in shape and flavor. It is a light-bodied stew (typical of those cooked briefly on the stove top) that displays the freshness and quality of the vegetables. The attractiveness of the stew is heightened if you use baby vegetables left whole, with a little of their green tops left on. As the vegetables require little cooking time, a well-flavored stock is essential. The vegetables included can vary, although fennel plays an important role in adding subtle sweetness. Artichoke and fava beans are both fabulous additions in spring, with fresh green beans in summer. Served with pesto this is a great summer meal.

SERVES 2

olive oil, for frying

1 onion, sliced lengthways into ½ inch slices

4 to 5 basil leaves, roughly chopped

4 to 5 baby potatoes

5 to 8 baby carrots

1½ cups vegetable stock (or chicken stock) (see page 48)

3 roma (plum) tomatoes, peeled, seeded and sliced lengthways

3 to 4 baby zucchini, halved

¼ to ½ fennel, sliced lengthways into ½ inch pieces

10 baby (pattypan) squash

10 green beans, sliced on the diagonal into 2 inch pieces (smaller ones can be left whole)

3 stems green garlic, roughly chopped (or 1 garlic clove, finely chopped)

freshly ground black pepper, to taste

handful fresh flat-leaf (Italian) parsley, roughly chopped

pesto (see page 45), to serve

Heat 1 tablespoon olive oil in a frying pan. Add the onion and basil and sauté for 3 minutes. Add the potatoes and carrots, along with the stock. Cover with a lid and continue to cook over a gentle heat for 6 to 8 minutes, or until the vegetables are just barely cooked. Add the tomatoes, zucchini, fennel, yellow squash, green beans, garlic and pepper to taste. Cover with a lid and continue to cook for 5 to 6 minutes, or until the vegetables are just cooked. Put into bowls, sprinkle with parsley, top with pesto and serve.

VARIATIONS

Add oven-baked tomatoes (see page 34) and grilled zucchini (see page 194) for greater depth of flavor.

Ratatouille

GLUTEN FREE / VEGAN

This is a classic French stew made with late summer vegetables. It can be cooked on top of the stove, or baked in the oven. It is useful to precook some of the vegetables, thus increasing the depth of flavor dramatically. Ratatouille is infinitely variable and forgiving, and is delicious served hot with soft or grilled polenta and a sprinkle of parmesan cheese, or at room temperature or cold with some good bread. Leftovers of ratatouille can also make a fabulous addition to frittatas or lasagne.

SERVES 3 TO 4

3 to 5 eggplants
olive oil, to drizzle
2 red peppers
6 roma (plum) tomatoes, halved
pinch dried basil
5 to 6 garlic cloves
fresh herbs (such as basil, or sage, or thyme, or marjoram), to season
1 red onion, sliced lengthways into ½ inch pieces
handful fresh basil, roughly chopped
6 to 8 baby zucchini (or l large), sliced diagonally into 1¼ inch pieces
freshly ground black pepper, to taste
handful fresh flat-leaf (Italian) parsley, roughly chopped

Preheat the oven to 350°F. Roughly chop the eggplant into large cubes and put in a roasting pan. Drizzle the eggplant with a little olive oil and rub well. Cut the tops off the peppers and remove the insides. Rub the outside with olive oil and stand upright, cut side down, in the same baking dish. Lay the tomatoes in a separate tray. Drizzle with olive oil and sprinkle with a little dried basil.

Bake for 30 to 40 minutes or until the eggplant is just cooked and the pepper skin is well wrinkled and begins to blacken at the top. The peppers may take a little longer than the eggplant. Remove the tomatoes and leave to stand on the tray. Remove the peppers, put into a bowl and top with a plate to cool. Peel off the skins, cut the flesh into wide strips and set aside. Leave the eggplant to stand also.

Meanwhile, put the garlic in a square of baking paper, drizzle with a little good olive oil, and sprinkle with fresh herbs. Twist the paper together, to form a bag, and bake in the oven for 20 minutes, or until the cloves are soft.

Using a large heavy-based saucepan, gently heat 1 tablespoon of olive oil. Add the onion and basil and cook for 3 to 5 minutes over a gentle heat.

Add all the other ingredients—the roasted eggplant, roasted pepper flesh, roasted tomatoes, roasted garlic (with skins on), whole baby zucchinis and a pinch of black pepper. Cover with a lid or with a piece of foil, and bake in the oven for 40 to 60 minutes, or until the stew is soft and juicy. Remove the garlic, press out the soft inner flesh and discard the skins. Sprinkle with parsley and serve.

Creamy asparagus soup

GLUTEN FREE / VEGAN

This is a lovely light yet sustaining soup. Flavor comes from an abundant use of asparagus and young leek. A small amount of rice is added instead of the more traditional flour and milk to thicken the soup and create a creamy texture.

SERVES 4

2 pounds, 4 ounces asparagus
olive oil (or ghee), for frying
2 small leeks, well rinsed and finely sliced
4 to 5 sprigs fresh thyme
1½ to 2 tablespoons short grain white rice
6 cups vegetable stock (see page 48), to cover
freshly ground black pepper, to taste
sea salt, to taste
fresh flat-leaf (Italian) parsley, to serve

Break off the woody ends of the asparagus spears and discard. Cut off the tips to a 2 to 2½ inch length and set aside. Cut the remaining stems into slices ½ to ¾ inch long.

Heat 1 tablespoon of olive oil in a large saucepan. Add the leeks and thyme and sauté over a low heat for 5 minutes. Add the rice, cut asparagus stems and the stock. Cook over a gentle heat for 20 minutes, or until the rice is very soft.

While the mixture is cooking, blanch the asparagus tips in boiling water for approximately 2 minutes, and drain immediately. Set aside.

Cool the soup slightly, transfer it to a blender and purée until smooth. Check for taste, adding salt and pepper if necessary. Return to a clean pan and gently reheat. Add the asparagus tips and gently stir through. Serve sprinkled with chopped parsley.

Squash, sweet potato and ginger soup

VEGAN

This is a classic soup. A mixture of butternut squash and jap (or kent) squash, with a small portion of sweet potato, helps develop body in the finished flavor, while the ginger provides freshness.

SERVES 4 TO 6

olive oil, for frying
2 to 3 small leeks, well rinsed and finely sliced (or 1 large onion, diced)
1½ inch piece ginger, finely chopped
1 garlic clove, finely chopped
1 bunch cilantro, stems only roughly chopped, leaves left whole
2 pounds, 12 ounces winter squash (jap (kent) or butternut), peeled and roughly chopped
1 medium sweet potato, roughly chopped
5 cups vegetable stock (see page 48) (enough to just cover the vegetables)
tamari, to taste
finely ground black pepper, to taste
pear juice concentrate, to taste
coconut milk, to finish (optional)

This recipe will be gluten-free if wheat-free tamari is used.

Heat 1 tablespoon of olive oil in a large heavy-based saucepan. Add the leeks, ginger, garlic and cilantro stems and sauté gently over a low heat for 10 minutes. Add the squash, sweet potato and stock. Cover with a lid and cook over a gentle heat for 30 minutes.

Cool the soup slightly, then transfer it to a blender and purée until smooth. Check for taste, adding tamari and pepper if necessary or a small amount of pear juice concentrate to deepen and balance the flavor. Return to a clean pan and gently reheat the soup and serve sprinkled with cilantro leaves, or drizzled with a little coconut milk and cilantro leaves.

Jeanie's roast vegetable soup

VEGAN

This is my friend Jeanie's brainwave, and a good example of using means other than fat to develop flavor. Here the vegetables are roasted, concentrating and developing their flavor before being added to the soup.

Don't use potatoes—they make the soup too gummy.

This recipe will be gluten-free if wheat-free tamari is used.

When roasting ingredients, try not to overcrowd the pan. This will make some of them steam, rather than bake.

SERVES 4 TO 6

4 to 5 garlic cloves
1 pound, 10 ounces winter squash (jap (kent) or butternut), peeled and cut into large chunks
10½ ounces sweet potato, cut into fairly large slices
7 ounces purple sweet potato, cut into fairly large slices
4 medium carrots, cut lengthways
2 small rutabaga, peeled and cut into quarters
1 to 2 parsnips, peeled, and cut into quarters lengthways with the woody core removed
3 large brown onions, unpeeled, whole
½ teaspoon ground cumin
sea salt, to taste
freshly ground black pepper, to taste
olive oil, to drizzle
8 cups vegetable stock (see page 48)
3 teaspoons tamari
1 teaspoon pear juice concentrate

Preheat the oven to 400°F. Wrap the garlic in a small piece of baking paper, twisting it to seal into a package, to prevent it drying out.

Put the vegetables in one or two roasting trays with cumin, salt and pepper. Drizzle with a little olive oil and massage, so the oil covers the entire surface area of the vegetables. Put the wrapped garlic in with them.

Bake for 60 to 80 minutes, removing the vegetables as they turn soft and caramelized. Remove the garlic after 15 to 20 minutes or when it's soft to the touch. When cool, peel off the skin and set aside.

Squeeze the inside cooked flesh from the onions, discarding the skins and put into a heavy-based saucepan along with the other roasted vegetables. Cover with the stock. Add the cooked garlic. Cover and cook over a gentle heat for 30 to 40 minutes.

Remove the lid and allow the mixture to cool a little. Transfer to a blender and purée until smooth. Check for consistency. If it is too thick add a little more liquid; if it is too thin, return it to a clean pan and simmer until reduced to the desired thickness. Check the seasoning, adding tamari and pear juice concentrate if required.

Spicy black bean soup

VEGAN

Here, the beans are cooked in the soup, adding great depth of earthy flavor to the finished soup. This is a soup with a delicious smoky heat coming from the addition of chipotle chile.

SERVES 4 TO 6

1 cup black beans
olive oil, for frying
1 onion, finely diced
½ teaspoon dried thyme
½ to 1 teaspoon ground cumin
1 tablespoon finely chopped cilantro stem
1 garlic clove, crushed
2 carrots, finely diced
1 medium sweet potato, peeled and diced
kernels from 1 corn cob (or 1 cup canned corn)
½ red pepper, finely diced
12 cups vegetable stock (or water) (see page 48)
2 inch strip kombu (see page 303)
3 teaspoons tomato paste (concentrated purée)
chipotle chile, to taste (see page 32)
3 teaspoons apple juice concentrate
½ to 1 tablespoon tamari
1½ tablespoons fresh cilantro leaves, finely chopped, to serve

This recipe will be gluten-free if wheat-free tamari is used.

Soak the beans overnight in 1½ to 2 cups water with 2 teaspoons of whey, buttermilk or yogurt stirred gently through. Discard the soaking water and rinse well.

Heat 1 tablespoon of oil in a large heavy-based saucepan. Add the onion and sauté gently over a low heat for 3 minutes. Add the thyme, cumin, cilantro and garlic and continue to cook for 3 more minutes.

Rinse the black beans well and add to the pot along with the carrots, sweet potato, corn, pepper, stock or water, kombu, tomato paste and chile. Partially cover with a lid and continue to cook at a slow simmer for about 1½ hours. Add extra liquid if it is low. After this time, add the apple juice concentrate and tamari. Continue to cook for 30 minutes, until thickened. Check for taste, sprinkle with the cilantro and serve.

Late summer minestrone

GLUTEN FREE / VEGAN

Minestrone is an infinitely variable Italian soup with a tomato base. There are many ways to make minestrone, depending greatly on what vegetables are seasonally available. This version is thick with beans and vegetables, with the flavor of garlic and basil in the pesto exploding in your mouth. For a richer minestrone, add some pasta (any kind) to the soup and let it cook in the broth. This is a vegetarian version, but feel free to add some good, organic bacon or pancetta to the sautéing onions and garlic. When fennel is in season, it makes a welcome addition (finely chopped) to this hearty soup.

SERVES 4 TO 6

olive oil (or ghee), for frying
1 onion, finely chopped
3 garlic cloves, finely chopped
½ to 1 teaspoon dried basil
¼ teaspoon ground fennel
a few fresh oregano leaves, roughly chopped (or ½ teaspoon dried)
6 to 8 fresh basil leaves, roughly chopped
2 to 3 carrots, finely diced
½ red pepper, finely diced
2 celery stalks, finely diced
12 ounces sweet potato, finely diced

10 ounces green beans, cut into 2 inch lengths
14 ounces precooked kidney or cannellini beans (see pages 74–76) (or canned)
14 ounces precooked borlotti (cranberry) beans (see pages 74–76) (or canned)
14 ounces canned tomatoes (or fresh to equal)
about 2½ cups vegetable stock (see page 48)
1 to 2 teaspoons apple juice concentrate
freshly ground black pepper, to taste
1 zucchini, diced
4 to 5 small baby (pattypan) squash, diced
1 teaspoon tamari
3 tablespoons fresh flat-leaf (Italian) parsley, roughly chopped

Heat 1 tablespoon of oil in a large saucepan. Add the onion, garlic and herbs and gently sauté over a medium heat for 3 minutes, allowing them to develop color.

As you prepare each of the vegetables add them to the pot, except the zucchini and squash (as they require less time to cook). Add all the beans and tomatoes along with the stock, using just enough liquid to cover. (If using fresh tomatoes use less liquid as they will release juices as they cook.) Add 1 teaspoon of the apple juice concentrate and a little black pepper, then cover with a lid and cook over a low heat for 40 to 50 minutes. After this time, add the zucchini and squash. Remove the lid and continue to cook for 10 to 20 minutes. Check for taste and add a little tamari, tomato paste or apple juice concentrate if necessary. Continue to reduce until the soup reaches the desired consistency. Check again for taste, add the parsley and serve.

VARIATION

If you want to include pasta in the minestrone, add it about 15 minutes before the end of cooking. This will thicken the soup.

Moroccan minestrone

GLUTEN FREE / VEGAN

This is a highly fragrant soup, made with brown lentils and chickpeas.

SERVES 4 TO 6

3 cups cooked chickpeas (1 cup uncooked)
olive oil, for frying
1 onion, finely diced
3 celery stalks, finely sliced
2 inch piece ginger, finely chopped
½ teaspoon ground cinnamon
1 teaspoon turmeric
1 tablespoon chopped fresh cilantro leaves
1 cup dried brown lentils, sorted and well washed
14 ounces canned tomatoes (or fresh to equal), roughly chopped
3 teaspoons tomato paste (concentrated purée)
8 cups vegetable stock (see page 48)
1½ tablespoons tamari (or to taste)
2 tablespoons pear juice concentrate (or to taste)
1 tablespoon finely chopped fresh flat-leaf (Italian) parsley, to serve
1 tablespoon finely chopped fresh cilantro leaves (extra), to serve

If using raw chickpeas, soak them overnight in 1½ to 2 cups of water with 2 teaspoons of whey, buttermilk or yogurt stirred gently through. Discard the soaking water and rinse well.

This soup is best served fairly thick; if it is too thin, continue to cook until reduced to desired consistency.

Put the chickpeas in a large heavy-based saucepan, cover with a generous amount of water, and cook over a gentle heat for 2½ to 4 hours, or until they are soft and yield their starchy centers. Check occasionally, adding water if necessary, and skimming off the froth from the top.

For cooked chickpeas, start from here. Heat 1 tablespoon of oil in a large heavy-based saucepan. Add the onion and celery and sauté gently over a low heat for 6 to 8 minutes. Add the ginger, cinnamon, turmeric and cilantro, and continue to cook for another 1 minute. Add the lentils, chickpeas, tomatoes, tomato paste and stock. Cook over moderate heat for 45 to 60 minutes. Taste the soup and add tamari and pear juice concentrate as needed. Stir through the parsley and cilantro, and serve.

Soothing red lentil and vegetable soup

GLUTEN FREE / VEGAN

This is a spicy soup with wonderful aromas. For something extra special, drizzle a little coconut cream through the soup when in the bowl and sprinkle with cilantro.

SERVES 4 TO 6

olive oil (or ghee), for frying
1 onion, finely diced
2 celery stalks, finely diced
2 tablespoons chopped cilantro stems
2¾ to 3¼ inch piece of ginger, grated
1½ teaspoons ground cumin
1 teaspoon ground coriander
1 teaspoon curry powder
1¼ cups dried red lentils, well rinsed and sorted
12 ounces sweet potato, peeled and finely diced
2 to 3 carrots, finely diced
8 cups vegetable stock (see page 48)
2 teaspoons tamari (or to taste)
2 to 3 teaspoons mirin (or to taste)
1 to 2 tablespoons finely chopped fresh cilantro leaves

Heat 1 teaspoon of oil (or ghee) in a large heavy-based saucepan over a gentle heat, add the onion, celery, cilantro stem and ginger and cook for 5 minutes. Add the cumin, ground coriander and curry powder and cook for another 1 minute, stirring. Add the lentils, vegetables and stock.

Continue to cook over a gentle heat for approximately 1 hour, stirring occasionally, until it reaches the desired consistency. Check for taste, adding tamari and mirin as needed, then stir through the cilantro before serving.

This dish is commonly known as 'dashi' and it can be bought in granule form from healthfood shops.

Shiitake and kombu broth

GLUTEN FREE / VEGAN

This is a flexible broth that forms the base for a savory noodle bowl as well as miso soup. Rich in nutrients from both the kombu sea vegetable and shiitake mushrooms, this is a deeply nourishing broth.

MAKES APPROXIMATELY 6 CUPS

2 strips kombu (see page 303)
7 to 8 dried shiitake mushrooms
5 to 6 slices ginger
1 carrot (unpeeled), roughly chopped
1 large sweet potato (unpeeled), roughly chopped
1 small onion, halved

Put all the ingredients in a saucepan with 7 cups of water, partially cover with a lid and cook over a gentle heat for 30 to 40 minutes. Make sure the broth simmers slowly to avoid evaporation. Cool and strain into a bowl, keeping only the shiitake mushrooms and the liquid. Thinly slice the mushroom caps, discarding the tough stem and return them to the liquid. If you find it too hard to slice the mushroom caps they can be discarded also. The kombu can also be thinly sliced, if desired. Serve immediately

Many blessings noodle bowl

GLUTEN FREE / VEGAN

This recipe uses shiitake and kombu broth as its foundation, but is enriched in flavor with tamari and mirin, and made heartier with tofu, vegetables and buckwheat noodles. The amounts of tamari and mirin used will depend heavily on the strength of the stock—trust your taste when adding. Ginger (in the form of ginger juice) is another flavor that can add dimension to the soup.

SERVES 4

1 quantity shiitake and kombu broth (see recipe above)
7 to 8 fresh shiitake mushrooms, finely sliced

1 teaspoon kudzu powder (or cornstarch), to thicken
1 to 3 tablespoons tamari
1 to 2 tablespoons mirin
3½ to 7 ounces firm tofu, cut into small cubes
2 carrots, julienned, blanched and drained
5½ to 7 ounces buckwheat (soba) noodles, cooked
4 to 5 green onions (scallions), finely cut on the diagonal

The addition of kudzu slightly thickens the broth and helps it to coat the noodles.

Have ready the hot shiitake and kombu broth (with the dried shiitake mushrooms discarded after cooking). Add the fresh shiitake mushrooms to the broth and simmer, covered for 5 minutes, or until the mushrooms are tender.

Put the kudzu or cornstarch in a small bowl and add a small amount of broth to create a thin paste, then return to the main broth. Add the tamari, mirin (checking and adjusting taste), tofu and the carrots and gently heat, stirring constantly until boiling. Remove from the heat and set aside while you put serving portions of the buckwheat noodles in individual bowls. Immediately cover with desired amount of broth, top with green onions and serve.

Miso soup

GLUTEN FREE / VEGAN

A particularly nourishing and cleansing soup, here the shiitake and kombu broth is enriched with unpasteurized miso and seasonal vegetables. The broth can also be served more simply—with wakame, shiitake mushrooms and firm tofu that has been cubed.

Miso is highly alkalinizing and excellent for reducing the effects of environmental toxins.

SERVES 4

1 quantity shiitake and kombu broth (see previous page)
1 wakame leaf (see page 303)
1 carrot, julienned
kernels from 1 corn cob (or 1 cup canned corn)
4 to 6 snow peas (mangetout), julienned lengthways
handful cabbage, finely sliced
1 to 2 kale leaves, finely sliced
grated ginger (or ginger juice) (optional)

3 to 4 tablespoons genmai miso, unpasteurized
2 to 3 green onions (scallions), finely cut on the diagonal
cilantro leaves, to garnish

Have ready the shiitake and kombu broth. Add the wakame to the broth and allow to sit for 15 minutes. Remove from the broth and cut into slices, discarding the rib. Set aside.

Add the vegetables to the broth and gently cook for 5 to 10 minutes, being careful not to overcook. Add ginger to taste if desired (there is already some in the broth). Return the wakame to the pot.

You will find that the miso will separate as it sits. This is entirely normal.

Begin to add the miso gradually, and stir. Adjust the taste—you may not need to use all the miso. To benefit from all the goodness of the unpasteurized miso, be careful not to boil the soup. Spoon into serving bowls, top with green onion and cilantro and serve.

when you cook … you are providing more nourishment than packaged food ever could

vegetable dishes

Vegetables are the heart and soul of what we eat. They are nature's pharmacy, providing the nutrients we need to nourish and protect us. Just as there is a profound difference in taste and goodness between organic and non-organic produce, so there is between freshly harvested and older produce. Unlike grain, which can actually hold the life force intact for centuries (coded within the DNA), most vegetables begin to spoil from the minute they are picked. Some of the hardier root vegetables, such as winter squash and onions, are an exception. Disconnected from the life force, all organic beings deteriorate: flowers, fruit, animals, vegetables and humans. In foods, this power manifests in the body-compatible form of vitamins, minerals, trace elements, carbohydrates, amino acids, fats, essential fatty acids and enzymes. When fruit and vegetables are as fresh and the best quality that they can possibly be, it is reflected in the taste and provides us with health, vigor and joy.

Simple vegetable dishes

Roasting, grilling and blackening are invaluable basic tools for developing flavor and contributing depth of taste to many vegetarian meals. This is particularly important in a meal or dish with little fat or dairy, where you must build flavor in other ways.

Roasting vegetables

The slow and indirect heat of the oven makes roasting one of the best mediums for developing and intensifying flavor in vegetables. During cooking, the moisture becomes more concentrated, resulting in a deep and intensely flavored vegetable. A good ovenproof dish (tray), preferably enamel-coated cast-iron, is essential for baking vegetables to create crispness (glass or ceramic doesn't allow enough heat to reach the vegetables directly). Some fat is necessary for the process: it is the fat that insulates the vegetables from the drying effect of the oven. Root vegetables, in particular, have little moisture of their own and benefit from the use of fat.

Some vegetables will cook more quickly than others and the way they are cut will have a direct relation to the time it takes to cook them. Large, thick pieces of potato will take far longer than the thin ends of parsnip. Remember, also, that freshly harvested vegetables will cook faster. To coordinate the baking process of a group of different vegetables, either cut them appropriately so everything ends up cooking at approximately the same time, or steam some of the hardier vegetables (such as the squash and potatoes) first.

When roasting ingredients, especially for salads, try not to overcrowd the dish. This will make some of them steam, rather than bake. The same applies when cooking large amounts of roast vegetables—do so in batches (for example, all the squash in one dish, the potatoes on another and then a mix of others).

The more fat used in roasting (to coat the vegetables), the moister the vegetables will be on the inside and the crispier on the outside. If you would prefer to use less fat, it is a good idea to steam root vegetables partly first to make the inside tender.

Root vegetables cooked on the hearth

A simple way to cook root vegetables is to roast them in the coals of a fire, wrapped in foil. They need only be washed and scrubbed before wrapping. They will come out with lightly crisped skins and beautifully soft flesh. Garlic and herbs can be added to contribute deeper complexities of flavor. If you are adding garlic, it will need to be stuck inside individual pieces of vegetable to stop it burning. Winter squash responds extremely well to this method of cooking. Cut in chunks with the skin left on, even the hardiest of squash cooks quickly with a delicious, slightly smoky result.

This is how it works. Make a parcel of vegetables. Don't be tempted to make the parcels too big: 1 potato, 2 chunks of sweet potato, 4 to 5 baby carrots, 2 chunks of squash per parcel is plenty. The wrapped vegetables are placed on hot embers, away from the direct flame. If the coals are red hot, cover them with a little ash—otherwise the bottoms of the vegetables will end up black. Turn the parcels every 15 minutes—this will avoid one side being exposed to the heat source for too long.

The time will depend on the size of the parcel, the vegetables being cooked and the heat of the fire. Generally, they will cook more quickly than in an oven—potatoes for example, will take only 30 to 40 minutes. It is easy to tell when they are cooked, just pick them up with tongs and squeeze. They should be soft. If in doubt, unwrap them and check (being mindful of the steam).

Roasted winter vegetables with rosemary and sage

GLUTEN FREE / VEGAN

Root vegetables, such as beets, carrots, celeriac, onions, parsnip, potatoes, sweet potatoes (orange and white), rutabaga and turnips, are particularly suited to this method of cooking.

SERVES 4 TO 6

1 garlic bulb
3 medium potatoes, cut into rough 1½ inch cubes
6 pieces of winter squash (jap (kent) or butternut), cut into rough 1½ inch cubes
6 slices of sweet potato, cut into rough 1½ inch cubes
6 slices of white sweet potato, cut into rough 1½ inch cubes
4 carrots, cut into smaller pieces (or baby carrots left whole)
2 parsnips, peeled and cut into smaller pieces, removing the woody core
sea salt, to taste
freshly ground black pepper, to taste
2 to 3 sprigs fresh rosemary, finely chopped (plus extra, to serve (optional))
1 tablespoon fresh sage, finely chopped
1 to 2 tablespoons olive oil, for brushing

Preheat the oven to 350 to 400°F.

You will first need to wrap the garlic in a small piece of baking paper, twisting it to seal. Garlic dries out and burns extremely quickly. The paper will help to protect it. Put the vegetables in a couple of ovenproof dishes (or roasting pans) with the salt, pepper, rosemary and sage. Drizzle the oil over them and massage, so the oil covers the entire surface area of the vegetables. Pop the wrapped garlic in with them.

Bake for 1 to 1½ hours, or until the vegetables are golden, well-cooked and slightly caramelized. (The cooking time will depend entirely on the vegetable and the size they have been cut, and will vary each time you cook them.) The garlic should be removed after the first 20 to 30 minutes, or when it is soft and squishy to the touch. When cool, peel off the outside paper and roughly break up into cloves. Add the cooked garlic to the finished vegetables. Sprinkle with a little extra rosemary if desired.

Roasted summer vegetables with fresh basil

GLUTEN FREE / VEGAN

The summer vegetables, pepper, eggplant, mushrooms, tomatoes and zucchini, respond brilliantly to the slow, indirect heat of baking. With a higher moisture content than root vegetables, they don't require as much oil.

SERVES 4 TO 8 (DEPENDING ON USE)

1 (or 2 small) eggplant, cut into slices ¾ to 1¼ inch thick
olive oil, for brushing
handful fresh basil, roughly torn
1 to 2 red peppers, cut into strips
1 to 2 medium zucchinis, cut into slices approximately 2 inches thick
2 to 4 tomatoes (preferably roma (plum)), cut in half lengthways
6 to 8 mushrooms, with stems
2 to 5 garlic cloves, with skins left on
freshly ground black pepper, to taste
sea salt, to taste
pesto (see page 45), to serve (optional)

Preheat the oven to 350 to 400°F. If using older, larger eggplants, you will need to salt the eggplant slices to extract the bitter juices. Lay the eggplant slices on the draining section of the kitchen sink and sprinkle liberally with salt. Allow to sit for 30 minutes. Wash well in water and pat dry with a dish towel.

Brush the bottom of an ovenproof dish or roasting pan with olive oil and add the roughly torn basil. Arrange all the vegetables on the basil and brush them lightly with the olive oil. Wrap the garlic (sprinkled with a few dried herbs) in baking paper to make a parcel and put in the dish. Sprinkle with a little sea salt and pepper.

Don't be tempted to pile layers of vegetables into the dish—they really need some room for the air to circulate and help dry them out a little. Too many layers and the end result will be a stew.

Bake for 20 minutes, then check the garlic—it should be soft. Remove the garlic from the oven, then return the vegetables for another 40 minutes, or until cooked and lightly colored. Allow the garlic to cool, then peel off the skin and serve the flesh with the vegetables.

Served with good bread, pesto, good cheese and organic wine, this dish is the harvest celebrated. Leftovers can be used in salads, sandwiches or omelets, or reheated.

Three glazed vegetables

GLUTEN FREE / VEGAN

Glazed and roasted is a tasty way to serve rutabaga and turnips, and guaranteed to delight anyone who is used to turning their noses up at these humble roots. With an assertive flavor, this dish is best served as a side dish.

SERVES 3 TO 4

1½ tablespoons mirin
1½ tablespoons apple juice concentrate
2 garlic cloves, crushed
3 carrots (if large, cut into 2 to 3 pieces on the diagonal)
3 small turnips, peeled and cut in half
2 small/medium rutabaga, peeled and cut into quarters
pinch dried mixed herbs

Preheat the oven to 350 to 400°F. Mix the mirin, apple juice concentrate and garlic together. Brush a large baking dish generously with some of this mixture. Put the prepared vegetables in the dish and brush them with a little more of the mixture, leaving some in reserve. Sprinkle over the mixed herbs. Cover with foil and bake for 30 minutes.

After this time, remove the foil and pour the balance of the liquid over the vegetables. Make sure you brush the vegetables liberally with the liquid. Continue to cook for a further 20 to 30 minutes, basting the vegetables a few times with the liquid. By the end of the cooking time it will have become a thickish glaze, and the vegetables should have a little color and shine to them.

VARIATION

This is a great way to use kohlrabi. Cut the kohlrabi into thick slices and bake it with the other vegetables.

Stuffed butternut squash

VEGAN

This delicious meal typifies late summer and the sweet tastes of autumn and makes a great dinner served with steamed greens.

SERVES 4 TO 6

1 butternut squash
olive oil, for brushing (plus extra, for frying)
2 teaspoons finely chopped fresh thyme (or rosemary)
1/4 cup hulled millet
1 onion, finely chopped
1 garlic clove, finely chopped
2 celery stalks, finely chopped
2 carrots, finely chopped
1/4 to 1/2 teaspoon ground cumin (or curry powder)
kernels freshly cut from 1 to 2 corn cobs
1/4 cup currants
1/4 cup roasted pine nuts
1 tablespoon finely chopped fresh cilantro leaves
2 teaspoons tamari
small handful pepitas (pumpkin seeds) (or hulled sunflowers or grated cheese) (optional)

This recipe will be gluten-free if wheat-free tamari is used.

Preheat the oven to 350°F. Cut the squash in half lengthways and scoop out the seeds. Brush with a little olive oil and sprinkle with some fresh thyme or fresh rosemary. Bake for 1 hour and 10 minutes, until the flesh is just soft. Leave the oven turned on.

Meanwhile, prepare the millet. Rinse the millet and drain well. Quickly pat dry with a dish towel. Put in a small saucepan with 1/2 cup of water, cover with a lid and gently bring to the boil. As soon as it comes to the boil, turn the heat down as far as it will go. Cook for 10 to 15 minutes. About 5 minutes before the end of cooking, remove the lid, tip the pan on an angle and, if there is any water left, cover once more and continue to cook until you see small steam holes on the surface. Remove from the heat, put a dish towel under the lid to absorb any steam and leave for about 5 minutes.

Heat a tablespoon of olive oil in a frying pan. Add the onion, garlic, celery and carrots and cook gently, covered, for 10 minutes, until soft (you are not frying the vegetables, just cooking them through). Add the cumin or curry powder and corn kernels and cook for a further 2 minutes.

Mix the cooked millet, all the vegetables (except the squash), currants, roasted pine nuts, cilantro and tamari together in a bowl.

When the squash is ready and cooled a little, gently scoop out the bulk of the flesh from the skin and add this to the bowl of millet and vegetables. Try to leave a little flesh on the squash (it will help it to keep its shape). Check the mixture for taste; you may need to add a little more tamari. Stuff this mixture into the squash halves (there should be plenty of it, so be generous). Either sprinkle with a few pepitas and sunflower seeds, or a little cheese and bake for 15 to 20 minutes, or until warm.

Grilling vegetables

While it is a popular method for cooking meat, grilling (broiling) is often overlooked when it comes to vegetables. Grilled vegetables, however, are well worth the effort, as they gain a distinctly barbecued flavor. In summer the barbecue is the obvious tool for the job.

The ribs on a grill pan give beautiful score marks to the food and impart a superb, smoky flavor. Grill pans do work best on gas, but can also be used on electricity. Buy the best quality, heaviest duty grill pan you can afford. While the flavor of foods cooked on a grill pan will never equal that of food grilled over a wood fire, it is none the less excellent.

If you do not have a barbecue or a house with a big open fire, the Japanese hibachi cooker is a great tool for grilling, and an excellent investment. They are great for traveling, too.

Why grill vegetables?

Grilling vegetables is probably the easiest way to create intense flavor. In some instances, the natural sugars (of fennel and onion particularly) caramelize and deliver flavor that is far superior to any other cooking method. Grilled vegetables make excellent additions to salads, stews, pies or tarts, and are invaluable when you require maximum flavor with minimal use of fat.

TIPS FOR GRILLING

- Use wood rather than briquettes or commercial charcoal. Briquettes in particular are generally petroleum-based products and will flavor the food. Don't overlook aromatic woods (such as grape vine and rosemary).
- Most vegetables can be simply sliced and grilled. If making a kebab, hardier vegetables such as potato need to be par-cooked.
- Brush the surface of the vegetable to be grilled with a little olive oil—you only need a very small amount. Too much, and you will create a lot of smoke. Some vegetables, eggplant in particular, can soak up a lot of oil, but they really only require a brush on each side. In most instances, if the vegetables stick it is because the grill is not hot enough.
- Use long-handled tongs—it gets very hot close to the grill! Below is a list of good grilling vegetables and how to grill them:

Artichoke: These need to be pre-cooked, then seared on the grill. Cook for approximately 1 minute on each side.

Asparagus: Trim the woody ends first and then grill for 3 to 5 minutes, turning occasionally.

Baby (pattypan) squash: Depending on their size, either slice the squash thickly (3/4 to 1 1/4 inches) or in half. Be careful not to overcook; grill for 2 to 3 minutes, turning occasionally.

Bell pepper: Remove the stem and seeds. Cut into quarters and grill for 5 to 8 minutes.

Corn: This needs to be grilled for 10 to 15 minutes, turning occasionally. Alternatively, you can steam the corn cob first, and briefly blacken it on the hot grill.

Eggplant: Grilled eggplant is simply wonderful and requires 3 to 5 minutes to cook, turning once.

Fennel: Slice fairly thinly. The grilling almost caramelizes the natural sugars in fennel. Grill until just lined, approximately 2 to 3 minutes, turning once.

Leek: Young, small leeks are the best to use. Wash well and grill for 5 minutes, turning occasionally.

Try brushing artichokes with a mixture of extra virgin olive oil, crushed garlic and finely chopped flat-leaf (Italian) parsley before putting them on the grill.

As an alternative to making garlic bread with butter, try it the Italian way. Firstly, make sure you have some great bread (a hardy sourdough is especially good), then toast it over the hot coals (best) or on the grill pan (still good). When cooked, rub it with a clove of garlic and drizzle with extra virgin olive oil—a sublime treat awaits you.

Mushroom: Use the well-flavored portabello or Swiss brown when grilling. Cook for 1 to 2 minutes on the skin side only.

Potato: Grilled potato chips are the best you will ever make. Finely sliced, grill for 2 to 3 minutes on each side or until lightly scored.

Winter squash: Slice finely (approximately 1/4 inch), brush with a simple marinade of olive oil, honey and garlic, and cook on a low heat for 2 to 3 minutes on each side, or until lightly scored.

Red onion: Cut into thick slices and grill for 5 to 6 minutes, turning occasionally.

Sweet potato: This needs to be sliced thinly (1/4 inch). Be careful not to burn the flesh before it has had a chance to cook through. Cook for 2 to 3 minutes each side, or until lightly scored.

Tomato: Cut in half and grill for approximately 3 minutes, turning once.

Zucchini: This vegetable is very fragile and needs to be cut into thick slices (3/4 to 1 1/4 inch). Cook for 2 to 3 minutes, turn once when just scored.

Blackening

A step further than grilling, blackening requires blistering the skin over a flame. This is traditionally done over a wood fire, but gas will also give a good result. It provides a deeper, smokier flavor than grilling. When blackening over the stove top gas flame, use a wire rack over the flame to keep the vegetable from being too close to the flame. (If you don't have a gas stove, blacken under the broiler.

Bell pepper: Put the pepper on a rack and allow the skin to blacken for 10 to 15 minutes, turning to expose all the skin evenly. Alternatively, put directly onto the gas flame, using tongs to turn occasionally.

Chile: When blackened, chiles become sweeter, subtler and hotter. As they are small and have only a thin layer of flesh, blackening happens quickly. As soon as blackening occurs, turn quickly so as not to burn the flesh. Cook for 1 to 2 minutes.

Eggplant: Blackening eggplant provides a much more subtle flavor than grilling. Put on a rack and turn every 5 to 8 minutes, until the whole is blackened.

Tomato: Well-blackened tomatoes, cooked over hot coals, are a foundation of Tex-Mex cooking. The tomatoes are simply put on a rack over the hot coals until the skin blackens and blisters, 5 to 8 minutes. Turn until all the skin is blackened.

Hearty vegetable meals

In this section, vegetables are mixed together with sauces and accompanied by grains and pasta. Together, the flavors mingle and become more complex. The finished result becomes the sum of the whole, rather than the singular note of one or even two vegetables.

Gratins and tians

A gratin refers to vegetables that are traditionally baked under a covering of cream and cheese, in a shallow dish with a large surface area. The richness of cream lends itself particularly well to softening and adding the most beautiful flavor to even the hardiest of vegetables. It is hard to replace cream with milk as the inherent stability of cream makes it perfect for use in high heat. Milk (and this includes soy milk) ultimately breaks down, separating into protein curds and whey (although this can be avoided to a degree by sprinkling a bit of flour between the vegetable layers). An organic non-homogenized whole milk will separate less than generic whole milk and certainly much less than a low-fat milk.

There are non-dairy ways to achieve good results, but they will never match the same dish cooked in cream or organic whole milk. Excellent results are still possible with soy milk and, most importantly, a strongly flavored and well-reduced stock. You can entirely eliminate dairy in this manner, or cut it with either of these two ingredients. Another way is to make a béchamel sauce, a simple mix of flour and grain or root starch to thicken.

Tians are a simpler version of these gratins—most often they are vegetables cooked with herbs, seasonings and olive oil, the juices mingling to form a delicious sauce. They are cooked in similar dishes to gratins, shallow with a large surface area, and are excellent served at room temperature with a bowl of salad and some good bread.

Gratins are a superb way to treat the less popular root vegetables such as turnips, rutabaga, celeriac and kohlrabi. Sliced very thinly, the assertive flavor of these vegetables is tempered by the milk and cheese.

Potato gratin

VEGETARIAN / WHEAT FREE

Traditionally this dish is made with large quantities of cream (or milk and cream) poured over thinly sliced raw potatoes and baked in the oven until golden. It can, however, be made with soy milk and a little cheese and still taste very good.

SERVES 2 TO 4

- 3 to 4 large potatoes
- 2 cups milk (soy or dairy)
- 1 fresh bay leaf
- 1 sprig fresh thyme
- 1 garlic clove
- 1 teaspoon unbleached spelt flour (or cornstarch or arrowroot)
- freshly ground black pepper, to taste
- sea salt, to taste
- handful grated cheese (a good melting cheese, such as a cheddar)

Preheat the oven to 300 to 325°F. Lightly grease a shallow gratin dish. Cut the potatoes into fine slices and put in a saucepan. Add just enough milk to barely cover the potatoes, then add the bay leaf, thyme and garlic. Cook over a low heat (do not boil the milk) for 10 minutes, until the potatoes are just soft.

When using milk rather than cream, it is essential to cook on a low to moderate heat, so as not to break down the milk. It is also useful to pre-cook the potatoes to hasten the overall cooking time.

Using a slotted spoon, remove the potatoes and arrange in the gratin dish, sprinkling the flour in between the layers. Sprinkle with freshly ground black pepper and salt to taste. Remove the garlic, lightly mash it with a fork and mix it with approximately ½ cup of the milk. Pour this over the potatoes. The milk should cover two-thirds of the potatoes.

This dish is dairy-free if using soy milk and if no cheese is used.

Sprinkle with desired amount of cheese and bake for 1 to 1½ hours, or until the milk is fairly well absorbed and the cheese is golden.

VARIATIONS

- Add finely sliced green garlic to infuse through the milk. If you use this you will not need to use the whole garlic clove.
- Layer cooked and well-drained kale or Swiss chard in between the potato.
- Add a layer of delicious caramelized onions (see page 35) with the potato.

Leek and butternut squash gratin

DAIRY FREE / VEGETARIAN

New season leeks often appear at the same time as butternut squash, and together they make a beautiful combination. Young leeks generally have a sweet flavor that older leeks lack.

SERVES 4 TO 6

¼ cup olive oil
2 to 3 new season leeks, well rinsed and sliced
1 teaspoon finely chopped fresh sage
2 teaspoons finely chopped fresh rosemary
1 pound 3 ounces butternut squash, peeled and sliced into ¼ inch pieces
½ cup reduced mushroom vegetable stock (see page 49)
2 slices crusty bread, such as sourdough

To reduce the stock, take 1 cup of stock and boil until it has reduced by half—the quicker the boil, the quicker the reduction... about 10 minutes.

1 to 2 garlic cloves
3 teaspoons pepitas (pumpkin seeds)
1½ tablespoons hulled sunflower seeds

Preheat the oven to 350°F. Lightly grease a large shallow gratin dish.

Heat 1 tablespoon of the oil in a frying pan. Add the leeks and gently sauté for 8 minutes, until wilted. Add the herbs, season well and mix together. Set aside.

Arrange the squash slices in the gratin dish, layering the sautéed leeks between the slices. Sprinkle with a little black pepper. Pour over the stock and cover with foil. Bake for 30 minutes, or until the squash is soft.

Put the bread, garlic and pepitas in a small food processor or blender and process until just fine. Add 2 tablespoons of olive oil and blend to combine. Sprinkle this over the squash and pat down gently. Sprinkle with the sunflower seeds.

Bake for a further 10 to 15 minutes, or until the breadcrumbs are golden and the mixture is bubbling slightly. Leave to stand for 5 minutes before serving.

Tomato gratin

VEGETARIAN

This is an excellent example of a simple gratin—vegetables baked together under a torn bread topping. Allow about one medium tomato per person.

My mom has made this gratin for as long as I can remember, always with a roast dinner. It is best when tomatoes (any variety) are at their peak, ripe and juicy from the sun.

SERVES 3 TO 4

3 to 4 ripe tomatoes, finely sliced
1 small onion, finely sliced whole into rings
1 to 2 garlic cloves, finely chopped
3 to 4 fresh basil leaves, chopped (or a sprinkle of dried basil)
freshly ground black pepper, to taste
sea salt, to taste
2 to 3 slices bread, torn into small pieces
1 to 2 teaspoons unsalted butter (or 1 to 2 tablespoons olive oil)

Preheat the oven to 350°F. Lightly grease a medium-sized gratin dish.

Layer the sliced tomatoes in the gratin dish with the onion, garlic, basil, salt and pepper. Top this with the torn bread and dot with small pieces of the butter, or drizzle with the olive oil. Bake for 30 minutes to 1 hour. The bread should appear golden, and the tomatoes a deep, cooked red when ready.

Swiss chard and pasta gratin

VEGETARIAN

This is a very loose adaptation of macaroni and cheese and an excellent way to present Swiss chard or even kale to children. The finished result will only be as good as the Swiss chard you use—that is, use the freshest possible.

Some vegetables are best done with dairy bechamel, in particular Swiss chard, where the excess calcium from the dairy milk buffers the oxalic acid in the leaves.

SERVES 2 TO 3

1 cup raw pasta shells (any variety)
1 large bunch Swiss chard (or kale to equal)
olive oil (or ghee), for frying
1 small onion, finely chopped
¼ teaspoon dried basil
handful good melting cheese (such as cheddar)
1 quantity of béchamel—dairy version (see page 40)

Cook the pasta shells in a large saucepan of salted boiling water, until *al dente*.

Meanwhile, wash the chard well, making sure you remove all the sand that tends to collect on the leaves. Remove, shake well and cut off the stems from below the leaf line and discard. Slice the leaves finely.

Heat 1 tablespoon of oil or ghee in a frying pan. Add the onion and basil and sauté for 5 minutes. Add some of the chard, but don't overfill the pan. Continue to cook for 10 minutes over a gentle heat, until wilted and reduced in volume. Remove from the pan and put in a bowl. Continue to cook the remaining chard in batches for 10 minutes a time, adding extra oil as required.

Preheat the oven to 350°F. Lightly grease a medium-sized shallow gratin dish.

Add the pasta and béchamel sauce to the bowl of chard and mix together well.

Season well, transfer to the dish and sprinkle with as much cheese as desired. Cook until warmed through and the cheese has melted.

VARIATIONS

Any mixture of vegetables will work with pasta and béchamel sauce. Sauté finely diced carrot and onion in a little ghee or olive oil for 5 minutes, until soft. Add some broccoli florets and cook for a further 3 minutes, or add some corn kernels, a handful of fresh parsley and some red pepper. (Covering with a lid will help the vegetables cook through more quickly.) Mix it all together with the cooked pasta and béchamel, put in the gratin dish and sprinkle with breadcrumbs and a little cheese if desired. Bake in a moderate oven until warmed or the cheese has melted.

Eggplant parmigiana

GLUTEN FREE / VEGETARIAN

This is a favorite dish for a late summer picnic, and lends itself to many variations. It is traditionally paired with cheese but, for a dairy-free option, you could include tofu ricotta. Use young, fresh eggplant for best results.

This dish can also be made using pre-baked or grilled eggplant slices, thus reducing the amount of fat used.

SERVES 2 TO 4

1 to 2 eggplants
½ cup corn flour
½ cup rice crumbs (or any very finely ground breadcrumbs)
1 teaspoon dried basil
olive oil, for frying
2 cups fresh tomato sauce (see page 35) (or passata)
handful of good melting cheese (such as cheddar)
grated parmesan cheese (or pecorino cheese)

Begin by preparing the eggplants. With young eggplants, wash well and cut into ½ inch slices. If using older eggplants (which will be larger), after they have been cut, lay on the draining section of the kitchen sink and sprinkle liberally with salt. Allow to sit for about 30 minutes. Then, wash well in water and pat dry with a dish towel. They are now ready for use.

Mix the corn flour, crumbs and dried basil together in a dish, then coat both sides of the eggplant in the mixture (you can be quite generous).

Heat a small amount of olive oil in a frying pan over a moderate heat. Use only enough oil to cover the bottom of the pan. (Eggplant will soak up as much oil as you give it but you don't need any more oil than this.)

Check the temperature of the oil before you start cooking by dropping a little of the flour in it—if it sizzles, it is ready. Put as many pieces of eggplant as you can fit in one layer in the pan. Cook over a moderate heat for 5 to 10 minutes, until golden, then turn and continue on the other side. When the slices are ready, leave them to drain on paper towel while you do the others. You may need to wipe the pan out between every second batch or so, discarding any old oil and flour.

Preheat the oven to 350°F.

Using a medium-sized shallow gratin dish, cover the bottom with one-third of the tomato sauce. Put a layer of eggplant slices over this, using about one-third of the eggplant, overlapping them a little. Sprinkle a little freshly ground black pepper and cover with half the remaining sauce, then another layer of eggplant slices, then the rest of the sauce and top with the cheese. Bake for 50 to 60 minutes, or until the top is golden and the sauce is bubbling.

Serve with a large Greek salad, loaded with greens, olives and garlic.

VARIATIONS

- Roasted pepper strips (see page 34), mixed with the eggplant make a great addition to this dish.
- For a richer gratin, beat together ricotta cheese and egg (1 egg to each 4¾ ounces ricotta) and layer between the eggplant.
- Tofu 'ricotta' (see page 40) can also be layered between the eggplant.

Tian of summer vegetables

GLUTEN FREE / VEGAN

This is a wonderful and quick way to make a delicious meal, using whatever vegetables are seasonally available.

SERVES 3 TO 4

3 tomatoes, sliced
3 eggplants, sliced and either grilled or baked
12 ounces zucchini, sliced on the diagonal, 1¼ inch thick
6 ounces baby (pattypan) squash, cut in half or in slices
5 mushrooms (such as Swiss brown or portabello), stems removed
1 roasted pepper (see page 34), cut into strips
2 garlic cloves, finely cut
small handful fresh herbs (such as basil, thyme or oregano)
freshly ground black pepper, to season
5½ ounces goat cheese (optional)
freshly grated parmesan or pecorino cheese (optional), to sprinkle
olive oil, to drizzle
handful fresh flat-leaf (Italian) parsley, to serve

Preheat the oven to 350°F. Lightly grease a medium sized shallow gratin dish.

Arrange the vegetables attractively in layers in the dish. It is best to start with a layer of tomato on the bottom, as it contributes a nice moistness to some of the other drier vegetables. Season with a little sea salt, freshly ground black pepper and herbs between the layers. You may also like to add a little goat cheese between the layers as an option. If you like, sprinkle with parmesan or pecorino on top.

A good way to develop a more intense flavor is to drain the juices from the tian, reduce them, then add them back.

Drizzle with olive oil and bake for 1 hour, or until the vegetables are soft. Frequent basting with the juices will help prevent the vegetables from drying out.

This can be serve with fresh parsley sprinkled on top.

Cashew curried vegetables

DAIRY FREE / GLUTEN FREE

This meal is quick and simple to put together and offers a delicious and nourishing result. Making your own curry mix really only takes a couple of minutes with a spice mill or mortar and pestle, and the result is a bright curry flavor with a fragrance that is often missing in commercial mixes. The type of liquid you use will greatly influence the taste and texture of this curry—water and stock give good results with a lighter flavor, while coconut milk makes for a richer curry.

SERVES 4 TO 6

CURRY POWDER (Makes approximately 2 tablespoons)

1 teaspoon toasted cumin seeds
2 teaspoons toasted coriander seeds
1 teaspoon toasted fennel seeds
½ teaspoon toasted fenugreek seeds
2 cardamom pods (seeds removed and husks discarded)
½ teaspoon ground cinnamon
⅛ to ¼ teaspoon ground clove
¼ teaspoon turmeric
1 dried red chile (or more)

THE STEW

1 teaspoon ghee (or 1 tablespoon olive oil)
1 brown onion, finely chopped
2 garlic cloves, crushed
2 to 3 teaspoons finely chopped fresh ginger
3 teaspoons curry powder (from above)
1 teaspoon garam masala
2 tablespoons fresh cilantro leaves, finely chopped
1 cup peeled, seeded and finely diced tomato
16 ounces vegetable stock (see page 48) (or a mixture of water and coconut milk to equal)

BASE VEGETABLES

14 ounces winter squash (jap (kent) or butternut), cut into rough 1½ inch cubes
7 ounces sweet potato, peeled and cut into rough 1½ inch cubes
3 carrots, peeled and cut on the diagonal in ¾ to 1¼ inch slices

LIGHTER VEGETABLES, CHOOSE 2 OR 3:

1 small head broccoli, cut into florets

10 beans, cut into 2 inch lengths

1 cup fresh (or frozen) peas

1 bunch of spinach, well washed with stems removed

1 zucchini, cut into small chunks

½ cauliflower, cut into florets

1 red pepper, cut into thin strips

1 to 2 teaspoons tamari (optional)

1 to 2 teaspoons pear juice concentrate (optional)

handful fresh cilantro leaves, roughly chopped

1 cup roasted cashew nuts

Begin by making the curry powder. Put the seeds in a frying pan over a low heat, being very careful to not let the pan get too hot. Shake the pan occasionally, distributing and turning the seeds. Continue until the seeds begin to change color, being careful not to let them burn. Immediately turn the seeds into a bowl to stop the cooking process. Add the remaining spices to the bowl before grinding in a spice mill or mortar and pestle.

Melt the ghee in a large saucepan and add onion, garlic and ginger. Cook over a gentle heat for 10 minutes, until lightly colored. Add the curry powder, garam masala, cilantro and tomatoes, stir through and add the liquid.

Add the squash, sweet potato and carrots. Cover and cook over a gentle heat for approximately 30 minutes, or until the vegetables are just tender. Add choice of lighter vegetables, stir through, cover and cook for a further 5 to 10 minutes. Check for taste and add a little tamari and pear juice concentrate if required. Gently stir through the cilantro and cashew nuts.

VARIATIONS

- Add 1 chicken thigh, diced into 1½ to 2 inch pieces.
- Add fresh chile, seeded and finely chopped, with the lighter vegetables.
- Add cooked chickpeas for added richness.
- Add firm tofu, cut into small cubes to the stew with the lighter vegetables.

Pies and tarts

A combination of grain and fat, pastry is a deeply satisfying soul food. In the current food climate, the fashion has been to use an unsaturated fat (oil or hydrogenated) in the place of a saturated fat (butter or (traditionally) lard) for pies and tarts. The end product is usually a mediocre pastry made with highly refined oil, and the result is not necessarily better for you than one made with saturated fat.

If you want to reduce the amount of saturated fat you eat, it would be better to eat good-quality pastry, in smaller portions every now and then; or reduce the amount of saturated fat by using less pastry (for example, having a pastry top only on a pie); or by using good quality oil instead of butter.

Shortcrust pastry

If you are only using the pastry on the bottom (for a quiche or tart) a small amount of butter (9 tablespoons) is fine. Increase the quantity up to 6 ounces when a rich, glossy lid is desired.

When making butter shortcrust pastry it needs to be understood that the type of flour, or mixture of flour, and the percentage of fat used, all affect the end result.

Whole wheat flour makes a superb, nutty tasting pastry. You can lighten this by using a mix of whole and unbleached flours, or even by replacing the whole wheat flour with atta flour (see page 319). As a general rule, the more whole wheat flour you use, the wetter the dough should be. This is to counterbalance the tendency for whole wheat flours to absorb liquid. This makes enough pastry to line a 9½ x 1¼ inch tart pan. If you are making a pie (with a bottom and a top), double the quantity.

MAKES 1 POUND

- 9 to 12 tablespoons unsalted butter
- 2 cups all-purpose flour (wheat or spelt)
- 3 to 5½ ounces ice-cold water

Using a pastry cutter or your fingertips, cut the butter into the flour in a bowl until it is incorporated into the flour, but still chunky. The chunks need to be small. If using a food processor, pulse one or two times, or until ready and turn out into a bowl.

Begin to mix the water gradually into the flour and butter (using a butter knife to cut the wet into the dry). Use only as much water as you need—the higher the percentage of whole wheat flour, the more water needed. Once the mixture looks evenly moist, bring it together into a ball (but don't knead or work it too much). Flatten, and chill for approximately 20 minutes, long enough to take the softness off the butter. The dough is now ready to use.

TIPS FOR MAKING SHORTCRUST PASTRY

- The more fat used, the more flaky the pastry. Think about how you will be using the pastry. If using butter, the amount can be increased for a richer, glossier pastry.
- Conditions must be kept cool to keep butter from melting. This is the reason a marble board is recommended when making pastry. Using ice cold water, chilled butter and as little contact with your hands as possible helps to keep the butter cold.
- Never overwork the pastry. Good pastry depends upon a gluten flour, and the more you work (handle) the pastry, the more you develop the gluten, and the tougher the pastry becomes.
- To roll the pastry, use as little flour as possible, but enough to make sure the surface is covered. Roll once or twice using a heavy decent size rolling pin, then run a knife underneath, move the pastry firmly and quickly, lightly redust the rolling area with flour and turn the dough over. Continue to repeat this process, folding the dough if necessary. Fold the pastry and move to the pan and line.
- If the pastry sticks, it usually means that the butter is beginning to melt. Simply pick it up, place it on a tray (lined with baking paper) and put it in the freezer for a couple of minutes to reset the butter. Alternatively, it might mean that the pastry is too wet—sprinkle it with a little flour and continue to roll, but remember to take note of how much flour you add for the next time you make pastry.
- If the pastry is too warm and soft, pop it on a tray (to keep it flat) and put the whole thing in the fridge or freezer for a few minutes, until it has firmed up a little.
- If the pastry cracks, this generally means that the pastry is too cold. Simply warm the pastry with your fingers for a few seconds, and press it back together.

Oil-based pastry is easy to roll—it 'greases' the rolling pin and is unlikely to stick. You may also need a small amount of flour to dust the rolling area and pin. It is, however, difficult to move and cannot be folded. To move, use one hand and a large knife to gently lift it into position. This pastry cannot be folded or it will break.

Oil-based shortcrust pastry

DAIRY FREE

This is an excellent pastry for savory tarts and pies. It makes enough pastry for a tart. If you are making a pie (with a bottom and a top), double the quantity. Because it is made with oil rather than butter, there is no need to chill it.

MAKES 12¾ OUNCES

¾ cup unbleached all-purpose spelt or wheat flour
¾ cup whole wheat spelt or wheat flour
¼ cup sesame seeds
2¼ ounces olive oil
2 ounces ice-cold water

Put the flour and sesame seeds into a bowl, add the olive oil and mix with a butter knife until the mixture resembles fine breadcrumbs. Gradually add the water to the flour mixture, until it begins to come together. Carefully press the dough together to form a ball, flatten and roll out to approximately ¼ inch thick. The dough is now ready to use.

Lining the pan

To line the pan, first you need to roll the pastry. Roll out the pastry, then carefully fold the pastry back over and around the rolling pin and lift it gently from the surface. Unroll the pastry over the pan and ease it into the pan, pressing to fit the side. Roll the pin across the top to cut off the excess dough.

Baking blind

Partly cooking pastry helps to seal it, and thus avoid seepage. It also helps to ensure a crisp and well-cooked bottom pastry. This process is called 'baking blind.' To do it, carefully place a sheet of baking paper over the pastry-lined tart pan. Fill with raw beans or pastry weights. Chill well.

Preheat the oven to 400°F.

Bake the tart shell for 10 minutes, then lower the heat to 350°F. When the pastry begins to color around the edge, remove the weights and the paper. It is now partly blind baked. For a fully cooked shell, return to the oven (minus the paper and weights) and continue to cook until lightly golden.

TIPS FOR BAKING

- The best results for tarts and pies will always come from very cold pastry going into a hot oven. This sets the fat and provides a better flake, and lighter pastry.
- Tarts should preferably be baked blind (see above), while pies with drier fillings can be placed in the fridge to firm before going in the oven.
- The dish is also important for successful pastry cooking. Metal and enamel will distribute the heat rapidly to the raw pastry, enabling the gluten to set, before the butter has fully melted, while ceramic will diffuse the heat, which can result in tart pastry being a little soggy.
- To achieve a glazed pastry, use either egg white, or egg mixed with a little water. With fruit pies, pastry can be sprinkled with sugar and cinnamon.
- Pies and tarts are cooked when the pastry is glistening and lightly browned, with flakes evident. Leave in the oven for a little longer (approximately 5 minutes) beyond this point to allow the pastry on the side and on the bottom to finished. They should then be allowed to sit for approximately 10 minutes, allowing them to settle before cutting.

Basic savory custard

This quantity of custard is enough for a simple tart with few ingredients. The more ingredients you add, the less custard you will need.

FOR A 9½ X 1¼ INCH TART PAN

2 cups milk (dairy or soy)
small sprig fresh thyme (or fresh oregano or green garlic) (to infuse soy milk)
1 fresh bay leaf
1 garlic clove, quartered
sea salt, to taste
freshly ground black pepper, to taste
2 eggs
1 egg yolk

Put the milk in a saucepan (along with your choice of seasonings if using soy milk), the bay leaf and garlic and place over a very low heat. Don't allow it to boil, but heat until it just begins to steam. Remove from the heat, cover, then put in the fridge.

When cool, remove the skin (if there is one) and herb sprig (but not the leaves) and mash the garlic clove into the custard. Season to taste with salt and pepper, then whisk in the eggs.

Tarts (open pies)

Tarts are traditionally shallow and have a milk- and egg-based custard that sets and holds the flavorings in place. They can be made with a lot of custard and a small amount of bulk (quiche lorraine is probably the most well known example) or vice versa. They are rich, with 50 to 70% cream or milk. The higher percentage of cream in a tart, the silkier the custard. Truly, there is nothing to equal the taste or texture of a tart made from an organic non-homogenized whole dairy, but compromise is possible, for instance by the use of soy milk or by using more filling and less custard.

It is very easy to depend upon high-fat custard to provide flavor in a tart, when it really should be the fillings that are relied upon to do this job. When using soy milk, quality is of utmost importance as that is what will be reflected in the finished custard. Soy milk does tend to develop a skin if not covered (generally by cheese). Cover this with a sprinkle of flat-leaf (Italian) parsley when serving.

Sweet potato, caramelized onion and artichoke tart

This is a beautiful tart, where flavor is developed not through the use of fat, but by combining delicious ingredients.

SERVES 4 TO 6

1 quantity (1 pound) shortcrust pastry (see page 208) (or oil-based shortcrust pastry) (see page 210)
2 sweet potatoes (about 1 pound, 12 ounces), peeled and cut into 1 to 2 inch cubes
1 sprig fresh thyme
olive oil, for drizzling (plus extra, for frying)
sea salt, to season
freshly ground black pepper, to season
2 onions, finely sliced
1 tablespoon mirin
10 marinated artichoke quarters, halved
1 quantity basic savory custard (see previous page)
handful grated melting cheese (such as cheddar (optional))

Preheat the oven to 350°F. Line a 9½ x 1¼ inch loose-based round tart pan with the pastry and trim the edges. Put in the fridge for at least 20 minutes, or until well chilled.

Meanwhile, put the sweet potato and thyme in a baking dish, drizzle with olive oil, add a pinch of salt and pepper and massage well. Bake for 40 minutes, or until soft.

Put a second baking tray in the oven to heat up.

Heat 1 tablespoon of olive oil in a frying pan. Add the onions and cook over a gentle heat, stirring often for 15 minutes, or until the onions are very soft. Add the mirin and continue to cook over a gentle heat for 10 to 15 minutes, stirring often until soft and lightly golden. Set aside.

Line the well-chilled pastry shell with baking paper and fill with baking beans or raw rice. Put into the hot oven on the hot baking tray and bake blind for 15 minutes. Remove the baking paper and bake for a further 5 minutes or until the base of the pastry is dry.

Spread the onions evenly over the partly-baked pastry shell. Fill the rest of the shell with the baked sweet potato and artichoke pieces. Pour over the custard, using only enough to bring the level to just below the top of the pastry. (You will probably have too much custard but this is useful if the tart leaks.) Your filling will sit higher than the level of the custard.

Carefully carry the tart to the oven and bake for about 15 minutes, then lower the temperature to 350°F and check after a further 50 minutes. By this stage the tart should be set and becoming golden on top. If you would like to top it with cheese, sprinkle over a good melting cheese approximately 20 minutes before it is ready.

Summer tart

VEGETARIAN

This is a favorite—a tart filled with the best that summer has to offer. It is particularly delicious when made with grilled corn, which gives smokiness and depth to the tart. Bacon can also be used to add smokiness. Cooked with the onion, the bacon fat replaces oil.

SERVES 4 TO 6

1 quantity (1 pound) shortcrust pastry (see page 208)
olive oil, for frying
1 red onion, finely diced
5½ ounces/4 rashers bacon, chopped (optional)
¼ teaspoon dried thyme
2 garlic cloves, peeled and finely chopped
1 small red pepper, seeded and finely diced
1 small green pepper, seeded and finely diced
kernels from 2 corn cobs (or 2 cups canned corn)

- 1 fresh chile, seeded and finely chopped (or to taste)
- sea salt, to taste
- freshly ground black pepper, to taste
- 1 quantity basic savory custard (see page 212)
- handful grated melting cheese (such as cheddar)

Line a 9½ x 1¼ inch loose-based round tart pan with pastry and trim the edges. Put in the fridge for at least 20 minutes, or until well chilled.

Preheat the oven 400°F and put a baking tray in the oven to heat up.

Heat 1 teaspoon of olive oil in a frying pan. Add the onion and bacon and sauté over a medium heat for 2 minutes, then add the thyme, garlic, peppers, corn and chile. Continue to cook over a low heat for 10 to 15 minutes, stirring occasionally, until the vegetables are fairly soft. Season with salt and pepper.

Line the well-chilled pastry shell with baking paper and fill with baking beans or raw rice. Put in the hot oven on the hot baking sheet and bake blind for 15 minutes. Remove the baking paper and bake for a further 5 minutes or until the base of the pastry is dry.

Put the vegetables in the tart shell and pour over the custard, using only enough to bring it a little below the top of the pastry. That is, your filling will sit higher than the level of the custard. Gently carry the tart to the oven and bake for 15 minutes, then lower the temperature to 350°F and bake for a further 15 minutes. Sprinkle with the cheese and bake for a further 25 to 35 minutes, or until the tart is set and firm to touch.

Spinach tart with pine nuts

VEGETARIAN

This is a bright, colorful and delicious tart to serve at picnics with a leafy salad.

SERVES 4 TO 6

- 2 red peppers
- olive oil, for drizzling (plus extra, for frying)
- 1 quantity (1 pound) shortcrust pastry (see page 208)

- 3 medium red onions, finely sliced
- 1 tablespoon mirin
- 2 bunches spinach
- 5 to 6 fresh basil leaves, roughly chopped
- 9 ounces mild goat cheese
- 1 quantity basic savory custard (see page 212)

Preheat the oven to 350°F. Cut the tops off the peppers and remove the insides. Rub the outsides with olive oil and stand upright, cut side down, in a baking dish. Cook for 1 hour, or until the skin is well wrinkled and begins to blacken. Remove, put into a bowl and top with a plate to cool. Peel off the skins, cut the flesh into wide strips and set aside.

Line a 9½ x 1¼ inch loose-based round tart pan with pastry and trim the edges. Put in the fridge for at least 20 minutes, or until well chilled.

Heat 1 tablespoon of olive oil in a frying pan. Add the onions and cook over a gentle heat, stirring often, for 15 minutes, or until the onions are very soft, Add the mirin and continue to cook over a gentle heat for 10 to 15 minutes, stirring often, until soft and lightly golden. Set aside.

Increase the oven to 400°F and put a baking sheet in the oven to heat up.

Remove the stems from the spinach and wash extremely well to remove all sand. Lift the leaves directly into a saucepan and sweat over a gentle heat for 10 minutes. Put the leaves into a colander to drain and cool, squeeze really well (otherwise your filling will be watery), then roughly chop.

Line the well-chilled pastry shell with baking paper and fill with baking beans or raw rice. Put into the oven on the hot baking sheet and bake blind for 15 minutes. Remove the baking paper and bake for a further 5 minutes or until the base of the pastry is dry.

Spread the onions evenly over the base, followed by the roughly chopped spinach and the roughly chopped basil. Top with strips of roasted pepper and chunks of goat cheese. Pour over the custard, using only enough to bring to just below the top of the pastry. (You will probably have too much custard but this is useful if the tart leaks.) Your filling will sit higher than the level of the custard.

Gently carry the tart to the oven and bake for about 15 minutes, then reduce the temperature to 350°F and bake for a further 50 minutes, or until the tart is set and golden.

Covered pies

Traditionally, covered pies have both a top and a bottom. If you want to use less pastry, however, a farmhouse or pot pie (with only the top) offers the best of both worlds. They are a fabulous way to enjoy pastry, especially on a cold winter night.

Hunza pie

VEGETARIAN

This is a loose interpretation of the classic dish. Swiss chard is a difficult vegetable to use in a dairy-free manner; the presence of oxalic acid almost always works best with the buffering effects of dairy.

Don't be alarmed by the amount of Swiss chard required—it shrinks considerably when cooked. Choose the freshest, youngest leaves possible for the best flavor.

SERVES 4 TO 6

melted butter (or olive oil), for greasing
2 quantities (2 pounds) shortcrust pastry (see page 208)
20 to 30 Swiss chard leaves
olive oil, for frying
1 onion, finely diced
1 garlic clove, finely chopped
6 to 10 fresh basil leaves (or ½ teaspoon dried)
¾ cup cooked brown rice, well drained
(equivalent to about ⅓ cup raw rice)
7 to 9 ounces feta cheese
1 to 2 tablespoons pine nuts, roughly chopped
freshly ground black pepper, to taste

Preheat the oven to 400°F.

Brush a 9½ x 1½ inch round tart pan with a little melted butter or olive oil. Roll out half the pastry, until it is large enough to generously line the pan. Then line the pan, trimming the pastry to approximately 1¼ inch above the edge of the pan. Put in the fridge for at least 20 minutes, or until well chilled. Cover the remaining pastry and put in the fridge.

Wash the chard well. Remove the stem and ribs right up into the leaf. Cut approximately 20 of the finer, inner ribs into very fine slices (discard the tougher ribs and stems). Shake the leaves dry and cut into small slices.

Using a little olive oil, cook the onion, garlic, basil and chard ribs over a low heat, for about 7 minutes, or until the ribs are beginning to soften. Turn into a mixing bowl.

Heat a further teaspoon of olive oil in the frying pan. Add the chopped leaves and cook over a gentle heat until they are wilted and soft. Be careful not to overcook them. You may need to do this in batches. As they are ready, drain off the liquid and add the leaves to the bowl. Add the rice, feta, pine nuts and black pepper to the mixture. Mix together well.

Roll out the remaining pastry to a size large enough to cover the pie.

Spoon the chard filling into the chilled pastry case, then top with the other piece of pastry. Trim both edges to approximately ½ inch wider than the pan and crimp together. Using a knife, make 2 slits in the top for the steam to escape. Bake for 15 minutes, then reduce the heat to 350°F and bake for a further 30 to 40 minutes, or until the pastry is golden.

VARIATIONS

- Mushrooms (such as Swiss browns or portabellos) make a hearty and delicious addition to this pie. Slice and cook separately in a little olive oil and crushed garlic over a gentle heat until all the mushroom liquid has reduced, then add with the rice and feta.
- For a more subtle and creamy filling, replace the feta with ricotta cheese.

Vegetable pot pie

DAIRY FREE

This is a lovely winter dish—root vegetables and marinated tofu in a herb-scented creamy sauce, covered with pastry. It is possible to omit the tofu, but the flavor contributed by the marinade is indispensable.

SERVES 4 TO 6

MARINADE

4 dried shiitake mushrooms

1 teaspoon apple juice concentrate

1 small garlic clove, crushed

3 teaspoons Kelpamare (see page 301)

1 sprig fresh thyme, leaves only

pinch dried basil

FILLING

3¾ to 5½ ounces firm tofu, cut into small dice

olive oil, for frying

1 leek, well washed and finely sliced

2 carrots, peeled and cut into ½ inch dice

2 to 3 potatoes, peeled and cut into ½ inch dice

1 small sweet potato, peeled and cut into ½ inch dice

1 cup mushroom vegetable stock (see page 49)

½ cup fresh (or frozen) peas

kernels from ½ corn cob (or 2¾ ounces canned corn)

SAUCE

3 teaspoons rice flour

3 teaspoons cornstarch (or kudzu powder or arrowroot)

¼ cup mushroom vegetable stock (see page 49)

1 cup soy milk

¼ teaspoon dried thyme

¼ teaspoon dried sage

freshly ground black pepper, to taste

1 quantity oil-based shortcrust pastry (see page 210)

To make the marinade, put the shiitake mushrooms and 1 cup of water in a small saucepan, and bring to the boil. Cover with a lid, turn off the heat and let sit for approximately 15 minutes.

Remove the mushrooms and squeeze as much liquid as possible into the saucepan, then discard. You should have 3/4 to 1 cup of mushroom liquid. Stir in the apple juice concentrate, garlic, Kelpamare, thyme leaves and basil. Add the diced tofu and marinate for approximately 1 hour in the fridge.

Heat 2 teaspoons of olive oil in a frying pan. Add the leek and sauté gently for 3 minutes. Add the carrot, potato and sweet potato and mushroom vegetable stock. Cover with a lid and continue to cook over a gentle heat for 15 to 20 minutes, or until the vegetables are just soft. Be careful not to overcook the vegetables. Remove the lid and add the peas, corn and tofu, reserving the marinade. Turn the heat down very low while you prepare the sauce.

Preheat the oven to 350°F.

To make the sauce, put the rice flour and cornstarch in a small bowl with the mushroom vegetable stock and mix until a smooth paste forms. Add 1/2 cup of the reserved marinade and mix together. Add to the pan of vegetables along with the soy milk, thyme and sage and season with black pepper. Cook over a gentle heat, stirring continuously but gently, until the mixture just comes to the boil. The sauce should look a little thin.

Transfer the mixture to a 9-inch square by 2-inch deep ovenproof dish. Roll out the pastry to a 10-inch square and carefully cover the pie. Bake for about 50 minutes, or until the pastry is golden all over—it's okay if some of the filling starts to bubble out. Sit for 5 minutes before serving.

Layering—lasagne and moussaka

These are traditional baked dishes from Italy and Greece. They should be light, but filling, with hearty flavor coming from quality ingredients. They freeze well and, served with a huge salad, are the most satisfying of meals, any time of the year.

Lasagne is traditionally topped with a creamy béchamel made from cow's milk, sprinkled with a little cheese (parmesan or pecorino or a good melting cheese). When made with organic whole dairy milk, it is delicious but, alternatively, you could use a non-dairy béchamel, see page 41. Another good technique is to mix 2 cups soy milk with 7 ounces ricotta and layer it with the other ingredients in the dish. It works well, setting to a ricotta-like consistency with a delicious flavor that is lighter than a full-cream dairy sauce. There is no rule, though, that says you have to have a white sauce—you can just as easily top the lasagne with tomato sauce. Then the tomato sauce top can be sprinkled with cheese only if desired.

Vegetarian lasagne

VEGETARIAN

Served with a delicious green salad and garlic bread, this makes a wonderful meal.

SERVES 4 TO 6

1 pound, 5 ounces winter squash (jap (kent) or butternut), roughly cut into 1¼ inch pieces
olive oil, for brushing
2 red peppers
9 ounces mushrooms (Swiss brown or portabello), sliced
2 bunches spinach
3 cups fresh tomato sauce (see page 35)
12 to 15 lasagne sheets (fresh or dried)
10½ ounces ricotta (or 1 quantity tofu 'ricotta' (see page 40), to equal)
handful grated pecorino cheese
handful good melting cheese (such as cheddar), to top
handful fresh flat-leaf (Italian) parsley, roughly chopped

Preheat the oven to 350°F. Put the squash in a baking dish. Drizzle with 1 tablespoon of oil and massage in, so the oil covers the entire surface area. Bake for 1 hour, or until the squash is soft and just beginning to brown. Remove from the oven and allow to cool. Do not turn the oven off.

Meanwhile, wash the peppers well and cut the tops off close to the stem. Remove the inside core and seeds. Stand upside down in a baking dish and rub well with

1 tablespoon olive oil. Bake for 30 to 50 minutes, or until the skin is well wrinkled and begins to blacken. Remove and put into a bowl, top with a plate and leave to cool. Remove the skins and set aside.

Heat 1 tablespoon of olive oil in a frying pan and sauté the mushrooms for 4 to 5 minutes, until tender.

Wash the spinach well, making sure all traces of sand are removed. Remove any large stalks. Put the leaves in a large saucepan with only the water that is clinging to the leaves and cook over a low heat until wilted, stirring occasionally. Drain well, squeezing out any excess water and then chop.

Spread approximately 1 cup of tomato sauce over the bottom of a 9-inch square by 2½-inch deep ovenproof dish. Lay lasagne sheets over this, to cover the area of the dish. Top with the roast squash and mushrooms, and spoon 1 cup of tomato sauce on top. Cover with another layer of lasagne sheets. Top this with the spinach, roasted peppers and ricotta and season well. Add another layer of lasagne sheets over this. Top with the remaining tomato sauce, allowing it to drizzle down the inside edges of the dish, and sprinkle with the cheeses.

Bake for 1 hour, or until the cheese is golden. Sprinkle with the parsley before serving.

Vegetarian moussaka

DAIRY FREE / GLUTEN FREE

In this dish, with a total absence of dairy, it is essential to layer varieties of flavor—grilled and roasted vegetables, and a beautifully rich tomato sauce enriched with cannellini beans. Sweet potato adds a subtle sweetness, and works with tofu ricotta to counterbalance the acidity of the tomatoes.

SERVES 4 TO 6

2 to 3 red peppers
olive oil, for brushing

2 bunches spinach
3 cups fresh tomato sauce (see page 35)
14 ounces canned cannellini beans, drained
20 slices grilled eggplant
8 slices grilled sweet potato
1 quantity tofu 'ricotta', seasoned well (see page 40)
handful fresh flat-leaf (Italian) parsley, finely chopped

Wash the peppers well and cut the tops off close to the stem, Remove the inside core and seeds. Stand upside down in a baking dish and rub well with olive oil. Bake for 30 to 50 minutes, or until the skin is well wrinkled and begins to blacken. Remove and put into a bowl, top with a plate and leave to cool. Remove the skins, cut into wide strips and set aside.

Wash the spinach well, making sure all traces of sand are removed. Put in a large saucepan with only the water clinging to the leaves, and cook over a low heat until wilted, stirring occasionally. Drain well, squeezing out excess liquid.

Preheat the oven to 350°F. Mix the beans into the tomato sauce and spread approximately 1 cup over the bottom of a 9-inch square by 2½-inch deep ovenproof dish. Layer approximately 6 eggplant slices over this. Top this with all the grilled sweet potato, and the roasted red peppers, then a further 1 cup of tomato and cannellini bean sauce. Layer about 6 eggplant slices over this and top with the spinach and tofu ricotta. Add a final layer of eggplant and top this with a generous amount of the sauce.

Bake for 1 hour or until the sauce is bubbling gently. Sprinkle with parsley to serve.

VARIATIONS TO MAKE LASAGNE AND MOUSSAKA

A good tomato sauce is the foundation of a good lasagne or moussaka. However, each product you use in the lasagne must be the very best available; in this way, dimensions of flavor are developed. Ingredient options include:

- Baked eggplant slices (these will require a thicker sauce as they do not absorb extra liquid).
- Swiss chard (best with a dairy béchamel and/or dairy ricotta to offset the oxalic acid in the leaves).

- Small amounts of arugula.
- Roasted winter squash, cut into rough chunks.
- Broiled artichokes or fennel (see page 193).
- Sautéed mushrooms (Swiss brown or portebello).
- For a richer lasagne with a meatier feel, use a tempeh bolognaise (see page 129).
- Use dairy or goat cheese ricotta in place of the tofu for a richer moussaka.
- Omit the last layer of tomato sauce and replace with a dairy or non-dairy béchamel (see pages 40-1) for a creamier moussaka. Top with a little cheese and bake until golden.

when you sit down to a real meal
... the soul is nourished

chicken and meat dishes

Good meat comes from the farmyard and fields, organically produced, not simply from a plastic wrapped tray in a supermarket or butcher. I believe that, ethically, if we choose to eat meat we owe that animal some respect and gratitude for its life. Meat should not come from animals living substandard, cramped lives and being given appalling feed, hormones and antibiotics. If you want meat to work with your body, rather than against it, then it needs to be the real thing. What you will notice when using organic meat is how much more flavor there is. Often, in the case of chicken, the flesh is noticeably darker in color and often slightly tougher, and it responds particularly well to slow cooking. There is, however, no getting around the fact that organic meat is much more expensive (this reflects the true cost of producing the animal), although there are ways to reduce the costs. Expensive cuts are not always the best, most nourishing cuts. Most of the recipes here call for traditionally cheaper cuts of meat, and include a bulk of vegetables in the meal. Meat should be a part of the meal, not the whole thing. Especially good are meats still on the bone. When cooked, bones contribute large amounts of minerals, nutrients and gelatine to the finished dish; the gelatine in particular helps the body absorb the meat's goodness and protein.

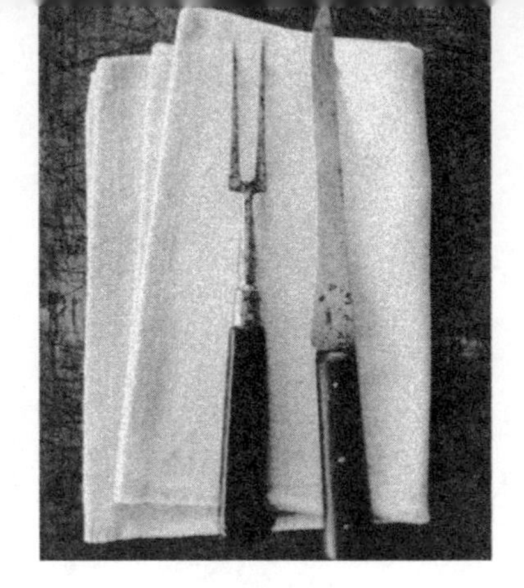

Meaty soups and stews

It is not surprising that chicken soup and Irish stew have developed the reputation for healing and restoring. Cooked on the bone, the following dishes provide a wealth of nutrients to heal and nourish. As an option for those that are young, sick, recovering, delicate or old, hold back from serving the meat, but rather mash some of the vegetables into the broth and serve.

Healing chicken soup

DAIRY FREE / GLUTEN FREE

Where else could we begin, but with this wonderful, comforting and immensely nourishing dish. This soup is infinitely variable. Seaweed, ginger, garlic and other potent foodstuffs can be added to help boost the immune system in times of need. Dried shiitake mushrooms can be another valuable addition, and could be used in place of the chicken for a vegetarian soup.

SERVES 4 TO 6

1 whole chicken, skin removed as desired (preferably with neck intact)
olive oil, for frying (optional)
1 leek (or onion), well rinsed and thinly sliced
2 to 3 carrots, finely diced
2 to 3 celery stalks, finely sliced
2 sprigs fresh thyme
6 to 8 fresh sage leaves
2 sprigs fresh marjoram
kernels from 1 corn cob (or more if desired), added with the cob
8 ounces sweet potato, peeled and finely diced
3 to 4 garlic cloves, roughly chopped (or 1 stem green garlic)
freshly grated (or sliced) ginger, to taste
1 to 1½ tablespoons white wine (or 1 teaspoon apple cider vinegar)
2 fresh bay leaves
sea salt (or dash of tamari), to taste
freshly ground black pepper, to taste
large handful fresh flat-leaf (Italian) parsley, finely chopped
1 tablespoon arame (see page 303)
3 teaspoons Kelpamare (see page 301)
8 to 10 cups vegetable stock (see page 48) (or water)
8 dried shiitake mushrooms (optional)
handful fresh flat-leaf (Italian) parsley (extra), finely chopped, to serve

Begin by placing a large heavy-based saucepan over a low heat, then add the chicken. If there is some skin left on the chicken (especially an organic one) the fat should start to render and provide a base to sauté the vegetables. If not, add a little olive oil. Add the leek, carrots and celery to the pot. Keep the heat low enough for a gentle sizzle. Add the thyme, sage and marjoram and continue to cook over a gentle heat and add the corn, sweet potato, garlic and ginger.

Add all the other ingredients (except the chopped parsley) and cover with stock. The liquid should only just cover the chicken. Cook for 1 hour.

If your chicken is an old one, leave it in the liquid to simmer for an extra 30 minutes on the bone. If the chicken is young and tender, lift it out of the liquid, then remove the flesh, shred and set aside. Return the chicken bones to the pot to simmer for 30 minutes.

After this time, remove the bones from the soup and discard (if the chicken is still intact, remove the meat from the bones, shred and set aside, discarding the bones). Taste and add more flavorings if desired (such as fresh herbs, salt (or tamari), pepper or Kelpamare). Remove as much fat as desired at this stage, from the top of the pan. Check the consistency. If the soup is too thin, you may choose to add pasta (see below) or bring to a good boil to reduce. Just before serving, remove the corn cob, return the meat to the pan and simmer for 2 minutes to warm through. Stir in the chopped parsley. The whole process should take 2 to 2½ hours. If you find it gels as it cools, you know you have a good and powerful soup.

VARIATION

There are a few ways to add texture and make this a more satisfying meal. Try including 1 to 2 tablespoons rice (white or brown) for added texture. Brown rice takes longer to cook and can be added to the soup along with the liquid, while white can be added after the initial 1½ hours of cooking and should require 10 to 15 minutes to cook. Noodles or pasta can also be added to the soup at this time, they will help to thicken it as they cook. Serve as soon as the noodles are ready.

Simple chicken stew

DAIRY FREE / GLUTEN FREE

This dish is very loosely based on the French classic *pot au feu*—where a humble meal is assembled using readily available produce. This dish is best in spring when potatoes and carrots are still young, with fresh peas making a welcome and delicious addition instead of beans. I like to serve this in a large bowl, with garlic bread.

SERVES 4 TO 6

3 pounds, 8 ounces chicken
sea salt, to taste
freshly ground black pepper, to taste
olive oil, for frying
8 to 10 small sprigs fresh thyme, roughly torn
8 shallots, peeled and left whole
3 fresh bay leaves

1 large carrot, unpeeled, washed and roughly chopped
2 celery sticks celery, roughly chopped
3 to 5 sprigs fresh flat-leaf (Italian) parsley, roughly torn (plus extra, to serve)
1 garlic clove, roughly chopped
1 teaspoon Kelpamare (see page 301)
8 to 10 baby potatoes, well washed
1 small sweet potato, peeled and diced
20 baby carrots, well washed and topped
20 small fresh green beans (or fresh peas, to equal), trimmed

Begin by cutting the chicken into portions (legs, thighs, wings, breast), removing the skin from the breast and carcass. Put the chicken pieces on a plate and the carcass in a bowl. Season the pieces with salt, pepper and thyme pressed onto the chicken. Allow to sit for 15 minutes, covered, in the fridge.

Heat 1 tablespoon of olive oil in a large heavy-based saucepan and, when hot (but not smoking), add the chicken legs, wings and thighs (return the breast to the fridge), skin side to the oil. Leave the chicken to brown for 10 minutes (resisting the urge to check it and thus release moisture), turning once and ensuring that as much skin as possible has the opportunity to brown. As the process continues, fat from the skin should render to the dish and mingle with the olive oil.

While the chicken is gently browning, peel the shallots and add along with the bay leaves. Remove the chicken pieces and set aside. Put the chicken carcass on the bottom of the pan and add the roughly chopped carrot, celery, parsley, garlic and Kelpamare with 3 cups of water. Return the browned chicken pieces to the pot. Cover and cook over a gentle heat for 35 to 45 minutes, until the chicken is cooked.

Remove the chicken pieces, put in a bowl, then cover and put in the fridge. Set a large colander over a bowl and empty the entire contents of the pot into the colander, catching the juices. Return the strained juices to the pan, along with the shallots and bay leaves, bring to the boil and immediately reduce to a gentle simmer. Add the potatoes, cover and cook for 5 minutes. Add the sweet potato and chicken breast, cover and cook on a very bare simmer for 8 minutes. Turn the breast after this time, and add the baby carrots and beans. Cover and continue to cook for another 5 minutes, or until the breast is just cooked. Lift the breast into a bowl and cover to keep warm.

Return the pot to the stove, without the lid and bring to a hard boil for 5 minutes to reduce the liquid and finish cooking the vegetables. Skim off any fat from the surface. Return the chicken pieces (except the breast) and any liquid from the bowl to the pot. Cover with the lid and cook at a very gentle simmer for 3 minutes to heat the chicken. Meanwhile, cut each chicken breast into 3 pieces.

Remove the chicken and vegetables from the pot and arrange in a serving dish. Bring the cooking liquid to a rapid boil. Add the cut breast (it should still be warm) to the serving dish and cover to keep warm. Continue to reduce the stock for another 2 to 3 minutes, until it has been reduced by up to one-third. Remove the cover from the serving dish, pour over the reduced stock and sprinkle with a handful of chopped parsley, then serve.

Irish stew

This is a classic stew, where lamb neck, rich with bone and marrow, transfers its bounty of nourishing goodness to the surrounding broth. It is simple food that when made with organic ingredients can taste deeply satisfying. Parsnip, when in season, is a must-have addition.

SERVES 4 TO 6

butter (or olive oil), for frying
1 onion, cut in half and finely sliced
2 leeks, well rinsed and finely sliced
2 sprigs fresh thyme, one roughly torn, one left whole
3 garlic cloves, roughly chopped
3 sprigs flat-leaf (Italian) parsley
1 sprig fresh marjoram
3 fresh bay leaves
6 carrots, sliced on the diagonal approximately 3/4 inch thick
4 celery stalks, roughly chopped
6 to 8 pieces best end lamb neck, on the bone, fat trimmed
10 to 12 small potatoes
sea salt, to taste
freshly ground black pepper, to taste

- 2 tablespoons pearled barley
- ¼ to ½ teaspoon Kelpamare (see page 301)
- 5 cups vegetable stock (see page 48) (or water)
- handful fresh flat-leaf (Italian) parsley, finely chopped, to serve
- handful of chives, finely chopped, to serve

HERB BUTTER

- ¼ pound (½ stick) unsalted butter, softened
- 1 tablespoon finely chopped fresh flat-leaf (Italian) parsley
- small handful fresh chives, finely chopped
- 2 teaspoons fresh thyme, finely chopped

Any leftover herb butter keeps well, covered in the fridge.

Preheat the oven to 350°F. Heat 1 tablespoon of butter in a large flameproof casserole dish. Add the onion, leek and the roughly torn thyme and sauté over a gentle heat for 2 to 3 minutes. Add the garlic and cook for another minute. Remove half this mixture to a bowl.

Tie the parsley, marjoram, whole sprig of thyme and bay leaf together. Place half the carrots and celery on top of the onion mix, topped by 3 to 4 pieces of neck, followed by half the potatoes. Sprinkle with salt and pepper, half the pearled barley and top with the tied herbs. Repeat the layering with the remaining onion mix, carrots, celery, meat, barley and potatoes. Add the Kelpamare and enough stock (or water) to barely cover the stew. Cover with a lid and put in the oven for 2½ hours.

Meanwhile, to make the herb butter, combine all the ingredients in a small bowl and put in the fridge.

Remove the stew from the oven and remove the lid. Skim off as much fat as possible from the broth. Remove the meat, place in a dish and cover. Transfer the dish to the stove over a medium-high heat for 15 to 30 minutes, to slightly reduce. The potatoes should be partly broken down, also helping to thicken the broth. Return the meat to the pot, and sprinkle liberally with chopped parsley and chives.

Serve the stew with small spoonfuls of the herb butter. This is particularly delicious mashed into the potatoes.

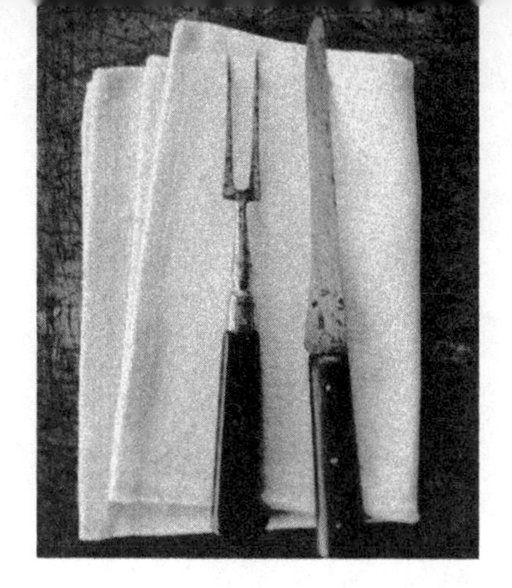

Hearty meat meals

In the following recipes, meat is used in different roles, but the result is always the same, a hearty and sustaining meal. Some, like fajitas, will be more suited to the warmer weather while others will warm body and soul on a cold winter night.

Chicken fajitas

Fabulous for summer, this is a great way to serve chicken—with lots of vegetables. These are best cooked on a grill or barbecue hot plate, but could also be done in a frying pan. Have everything ready at the table for people to put together themselves: warmed tortillas, guacamole, blackened tomato and chipotle salsa.

SERVES 4 TO 6

MARINADE

2 tablespoons finely chopped fresh cilantro leaves

3 garlic cloves, finely chopped

1 teaspoon freshly ground black pepper

¼ cup olive oil
¼ cup lime juice
1 teaspoon ground cumin
½ teaspoon dried oregano

1 pound chicken thighs, trimmed of fat, diced
1 red onion, finely sliced
1 to 2 carrots, julienned
10 to 12 snow peas (mangetout), julienned
kernels from 1 corn cob (or 1 cup canned corn)
1 red pepper, finely sliced
1 red onion, finely sliced

tortillas, to serve
blackened tomato chipotle salsa (see page 38), to serve

GUACAMOLE
1 large (or 2 smaller) ripe avocados
juice of 1 lime
1 large garlic clove, finely crushed (sometimes you might need more)
sea salt, to taste
freshly ground black pepper, to taste
1 tablespoon finely chopped cilantro leaves
1 tomato, skin and seeds removed, flesh diced (optional)
finely chopped fresh chile, to taste (optional)

Marinating is a classic technique to break down any toughness in the meat and adds wonderful flavor.

This dish will be dairy- and gluten-free depending on the tortillas.

Combine all the marinade ingredients and add the chicken. The chicken can be left in the fridge to marinate for up to 3 days.

Leaving the onions aside, mix the vegetables together in a bowl.

Toss the onion with a little olive oil and put on a hot grill. Leave for 1 minute, turning occasionally. Add all the other vegetables, followed by the chicken (discarding the marinade). Continue to cook over the hot grill, turning occasionally with tongs, for 7 to 8 minutes, until the chicken is just cooked. Warm the tortillas.

Make the guacamole just before serving. Put the avocado and lime juice in a mixing bowl, and mash roughly with a fork. Add the garlic, salt, pepper and cilantro and mix through. Check for taste, adjusting where necessary. If using tomato and chile, add and gently incorporate.

Put the chicken and vegetables onto a serving dish. Serve with the guacamole, warm tortillas and salsa.

Hunter-gatherer breast of lamb

DAIRY FREE / GLUTEN FREE

Lamb breast is a very cheap cut of meat, but when cooked becomes meltingly tender. It is a fatty cut of lamb, and you can choose to precook it, allow to cool and then remove the set fat. Otherwise, simply remove as much fat as possible before serving. When buying the breast, ask the butcher to 'square it off'—this will get rid of the thick sternum and flap. Serve with oven-baked potatoes or soft polenta. Lamb shanks could be used for this dish as an alternative to breast.

SERVES 4

2 rashers of bacon, rind removed, finely sliced
2 onions, cut in half and finely sliced
3 to 4 carrots, sliced on the diagonal ½ inch thick
3 celery stalks, sliced on the diagonal ½ inch thick
4 garlic cloves, roughly chopped
1 cup red wine
14 ounces canned tomatoes (or fresh to equal)
1 to 2 teaspoons molasses sugar
1 sprig fresh bay leaves, with 3 leaves
1 sprig rosemary, 5 inches long
1 sprig fresh thyme
2 to 4 sprigs fresh flat-leaf (Italian) parsley, with leaves (plus extra leaves, to serve)
2 pounds, 4 ounces ounces lamb breast

Preheat the oven to 275°F. Heat the bacon in a large flameproof casserole dish until it just begins to crisp and release fat. Add the onions, carrots, celery and garlic and continue to cook for 5 minutes over a gentle heat. Increase the heat and add the red wine. Add the tomatoes, 1 teaspoon of brown sugar and stir through. Turn down the heat, add the herbs and then the lamb. Sprinkle with pepper and salt and enough water to barely cover the breast. Cover with a lid and place in the oven for 3½ hours, or until the meat is tender.

Lift out the meat and put into a dish. Skim as much fat from the sauce as possible with a spoon, and then by pressing a paper towel on the surface. Return the casserole to the stove top and cook over a medium heat without the lid for 15 minutes. While the sauce is reducing, cut any fat and skin from the breast to reveal the meat, and then cut into portions (approximately 3 per breast). Return the meat to the casserole. Continue to reduce for another 15 to 30 minutes or until the sauce is very thick. Check for taste at this point, adding the extra sugar if needed. If you feel it is still fatty, press a paper towel over it to soak. If you prefer, remove any large bones before serving. Sprinkle with finely chopped parsley and serve.

Lamb and quinoa paella

DAIRY FREE / GLUTEN FREE

This is a wonderful dish to bring to the table and let everyone help themselves. While the preparation does involve a few stages, they are all quite easy to put together. You can also make this vegetarian by omitting the lamb and using tempeh instead.

SERVES 4 TO 6

10 ½ ounces lamb or mutton tenderloins (sometimes called fillet), cut into 2½ inch slices (or 9 ounces plain tempeh, cut into ¾ inch pieces)
2 teaspoons tamari
2 teaspoons pear juice concentrate
¼ teaspoon ground cumin
1 teaspoon ground fennel
zest of ½ lemon (or ½ to 1 teaspoon preserved lemon rind)
½ to 1 teaspoon grated ginger
1 tablespoon chopped fresh cilantro leaves
1 garlic clove, crushed
1 red pepper
1 pound, 2 ounces winter squash (jap (kent) or butternut), cut into rough 2 inch cubes
3 to 4 tablespoons extra virgin olive oil
pinch cumin
4 roma (plum) tomatoes, cut in half lengthways
1 garlic clove, finely chopped

1 teaspoon ginger, finely chopped
1 red onion, sliced lengthways
2 carrots, cut in half lengthways and then sliced ¼ inch thick on the diagonal
1 medium broccoli head, cut into small florets
3 to 4 kale leaves, washed and sliced 3 inches wide
kernels from 1 corn cob
3 to 4 baby (pattypan) squash, cut in half
¼ cup currants
handful fresh flat-leaf (Italian) parsley (or cilantro), finely chopped
3 tablespoons pine nuts, roasted
tamari (optional)

QUINOA
¾ teaspoon ground cumin
¼ teaspoon ground cinnamon
¼ teaspoon ground ginger
¼ teaspoon ground coriander
teaspoon turmeric
¾ cup quinoa
butter (optional), for cooking

Put the lamb (or tempeh) in a bowl with the next 8 ingredients and place in the fridge to marinate for 4 hours and up to overnight.

Preheat the oven to 350°F. Wash the pepper well and cut the top off close to the stem. Remove the core and seeds. Stand upside down in a baking dish with the winter squash. Sprinkle the squash with a little salt and pepper and a pinch of ground cumin. Drizzle with a little olive oil, including the pepper, and massage well. Cook for 1 hour, until the squash is soft and caramelized and the pepper skin is well-wrinkled and the top begins to blacken. Peel the pepper, and cut into strips.

Meanwhile, lay the tomatoes on a baking tray. Sprinkle with a little salt and pepper and drizzle with a little olive oil. Cook for 35 to 45 minutes, or until slightly darker in color.

To make the quinoa, put the spices in a small saucepan along with the quinoa and stir through. Add 1½ cups of water if unsoaked and 1½ cups if soaked. Cover with a lid, place the pan over a gentle heat and bring to the boil. As soon as it comes to the boil, turn the heat down to low and cook for 15 to 20 minutes. When ready, take the pan off the heat and cover the grains with a dish towel or paper towel to absorb any moisture. Leave to stand for 5 minutes (with the lid on).

Placing a clean dish towel or paper towel over the grains at this stage will help to absorb excess moisture, resulting in a drier, less wet grain.

Heat 1 tablespoon of olive oil in a frying pan over medium-high heat. Add the lamb (or tempeh), discarding the marinade. Cook for 2 to 3 minutes on either side, until just browned. (Tenderloin cooks very quickly and is easy to overdo.) If using tempeh, cook for a little longer until slightly crispy and lightly browned. Set aside.

Heat 1 tablespoon of olive oil in a large frying pan or wok over low heat. Add the garlic, ginger and onion and cook gently for 5 minutes. Add the carrot and cook for a further 5 minutes. Add the broccoli, with 1 tablespoon of water, and cover with a lid. Cook over a gentle heat for 5 minutes. Then add the kale and corn. Continue to cook, covered for 2 minutes, then add the baby (pattypan) squash. Cook for a further 2 minutes. The vegetables should be just cooked. If desired, add about 1 teaspoon butter. This will increase the flavor and help maximum absorption of goodness from the vegetables. Remove from the heat.

Add the quinoa, winter squash and peppers, currants, parsley or cilantro and pine nuts. Gently toss through, and put into serving dish. Check for taste, and add 1 tablespoon of tamari if necessary. Slice the lamb and arrange on top with the cooked tomato halves, and serve.

Steak and mushrooms with quince

DAIRY FREE

This is a robust and hearty dish that makes excellent use of chuck steak. Either put the mixture into a dish and top with pastry (puff or shortcrust) to make a scrumptious pie, or spoon over mashed potatoes and serve with green vegetables.

SERVES 4

2 tablespoons all-purpose flour
freshly ground black pepper, to taste

sea salt, to taste
1 pound, 5 ounces organic chuck steak, cut into 1½ to 2 inch pieces
olive oil, for frying
2 onions, finely sliced
12 ounces Swiss brown mushrooms, quartered
1½ tablespoons mirin
3 tablespoons red wine
½ teaspoon Kelpamare (see page 301)
2 garlic cloves, roughly chopped
2 fresh bay leaves
1 sprig fresh thyme
1 to 2 tablespoons quince paste

Put the flour and a little pepper and salt into a bowl. Add the meat and mix around to cover.

Heat 3 tablespoons of olive oil in a large heavy-based saucepan. When hot (but not smoking) add the meat in batches. Take care not to overcrowd the meat, which will make it stew. Keep the heat fairly high, allowing the meat to brown, turning after a minute or as soon as the meat has browned (do not overcook the meat at this stage). Brown for 1 minute on the other side.

The water can be replaced with stock or more wine. If using more wine, add more quince paste to balance.

Reduce to a medium heat and add the onion and mushrooms, stirring for 2 to 3 minutes. Add the mirin, red wine and Kelpamare, allowing it to sizzle and reduce, stirring occasionally. Turn down the heat and add the garlic, bay leaves and thyme and enough water to barely cover (no more than 1½ cups). Stir through. Add 1 tablespoon quince paste, and press this into the liquid. Cover and cook over a very gentle heat for 30 minutes.

Remove the lid and continue to cook over a very low heat, stirring occasionally, for about 25 to 30 minutes if making a stew and 35 to 40 minutes if using for a pie filling, to allow the liquid to reduce. Check for taste, and add more quince paste if necessary.

Shepherd's pie

GLUTEN FREE

Traditionally, shepherd's pie is made from leftover roast meat—mutton or lamb, however, ground lamb gives a lovely moist result. Served with green beans or broccoli (or both) this is a sustaining and warming dinner for a cold night.

SERVES 4 TO 6

olive oil, for frying
1 onion, finely diced
1 garlic clove, finely crushed
2 to 3 sprigs fresh thyme, roughly torn
1 pound, 5 ounces ground lamb
1 to 2 tablespoons Kelpamare (see page 301)
1 to 2 carrots, finely diced
1 pound, 5 ounces sweet potato, finely diced
about 1 pound, 7 ounces potatoes
1 teaspoon butter
sea salt, to taste
freshly ground black pepper, to taste
approximately ¼ cup whole milk
1 cup fresh (or frozen) peas
½ cup grated cheddar cheese (optional)

Heat 1 tablespoon of oil in a frying pan over a medium to low heat. Add the onion, garlic and thyme and sauté gently for 5 minutes. Add the ground lamb and lightly brown for 3 to 5 minutes. Add 1 tablespoon Kelpamare, the carrots and sweet potato. Add enough water to just cover the mixture and cook, covered with a lid, over a very gentle heat for 30 minutes, or until the vegetables are soft. Remove any excess fat with a spoon. Push the sweet potato into the mixture to help it thicken. Check for taste, adding extra Kelpamare if needed.

Preheat oven to 350°F. Meanwhile, keeping as much skin on as possible, peel or cut off any green skin or sprouting from the potatoes. Cut into small pieces and put in a large saucepan of salted water. Bring to the boil, and simmer until tender.

Drain, then return the potatoes to the pan. Add the butter, salt and pepper and approximately 1/4 cup of milk. Mash, adding extra milk if necessary. Set aside.

Add the peas to the lamb mixture and continue to cook over a gentle heat for 15 to 20 minutes without a lid, stirring occasionally, until the mixture has reduced to a thick consistency. Put in an ovenproof dish and top with the mashed potatoes. Sprinkle with the cheese (if using) and bake for 10 to 15 minutes or until lightly golden.

Chicken pot pie

This is a superb, hearty meal to have on a cold winter's night, topped with puff or shortcrust pastry.

SERVES 4 TO 6

butter (or olive oil), for frying
1 red onion, finely sliced lengthways
10 Swiss brown (or portabello) mushrooms, quartered, or sliced if large
4 to 5 sprigs fresh thyme
2 to 3 carrots, finely diced
2 to 3 teaspoons Kelpamare (see page 301)
kernels from 1 to 2 corn cobs (or canned to equal)
4 chicken thighs, trimmed of fat, diced
2 tablespoons all-purpose unbleached flour
1 cup vegetable stock (see page 48) (or chicken stock)
1 cup milk (dairy or soy)
handful flat-leaf (Italian) parsley, finely chopped
freshly ground black pepper, to taste
1 quantity (1 pound) shortcrust pastry (see page 208), or oil-based shortcrust pastry (see page 210)

Heat 1 tablespoon of butter (or oil) in a large frying pan. Add the onion, mushrooms and thyme and sauté over a low heat for 10 to 15 minutes, until the onions and mushrooms are lightly colored. Add the carrots and 2 teaspoons Kelpamare, cover with a lid and continue to cook for 10 to 15 minutes over a low heat, or until the carrots are just about cooked.

Preheat the oven to 350°F. Add the corn and chicken to the pan, cook over a higher heat for approximately 10 minutes or until the chicken is nearly cooked. Remove the pan from the heat, and gradually mix in the flour, stock and milk. Return to the heat and continue to cook for 3 to 4 minutes until the sauce thickens and boils gently. Add the parsley and pepper, and check for taste. You may need to add a little more Kelpamare.

Meanwhile, roll out the pastry to about 1/4 inch thick to cover a 5 to 6 cup capacity ovenproof baking dish. Pour the mixture into the dish and top with the pastry. Using a knife, make 2 slits in the top to allow steam to escape. Bake for 30 to 40 minutes, until the pastry is cooked and golden.

cakes and desserts

There are many ways to make healthy, wholesome and delicious cakes and desserts. Most of the cakes, cookies and desserts that are available commercially are made with large amounts of white flour, with white sugar to sweeten and flavor, highly processed fats to moisten and not much else. These ingredients are chosen because they are cheap and provide longer shelf life, and therefore better profits. I believe that there is room for using good-quality fats in cooking, but there are other times when lower levels are called for to cut the richness and lighten the load. I prefer to use large amounts of fruit to sweeten and moisten, more whole grains than white flours, more unrefined sweeteners and a more selective range of fats. The result is a cake that is far better for you and has far better flavor as well. These are the cakes and desserts I love to cook. Some include butter and eggs, but if you're on a dairy-free diet, you'll find recipes with quality dairy-free alternatives. Some use wheat, some are wheat-free and some are even gluten-free. Some you will cook as everyday options, while others are more suited to a celebration. What they all are, however, is nourishing and satisfying.

Creams, custards and anglaise

In traditonal desserts, dairy milk and cream (generally from cows) are essential ingredients, providing a rich, silky-smooth texture and delicious flavor. The terms 'custard' and/or 'anglaise' generally refer to a dairy cream- or milk-based sauce, often thickened with eggs. In many dairy-free alternatives, tofu and soy are the usual replacements, but these can often be too heavy. Much better is the use of almond milk or a blend of rice and coconut milk. Dairy-based desserts have their place, but the lighter non-dairy versions are equally delicious.

Almond cream

DAIRY FREE / GLUTEN FREE / VEGAN

This is a low-fat, low-sugar, dairy-free cream using the subtle sweetness of almonds. Almond cream has many applications: as frosting; as a pastry cream; as a cream replacement; or as a base in which to infuse other flavors. Almond cream is fragile, but will keep covered in the fridge for 2 to 3 days.

MAKES 2 CUPS

- ½ cup blanched almonds (see margin note)
- 3 tablespoons cornstarch
- 2 teaspoons natural vanilla extract (or 1 vanilla bean, split lengthways, seeds scraped out)
- 1½ teaspoons maple syrup
- ¼ cup coconut milk
- ¼ cup water (or weaker almond milk)

Blanched almonds are available commercially, but are much better homemade.

Put the blanched almonds and 1¾ cups of water in a blender and blend well until smooth. Peg 4 layers of cheesecloth onto a pitcher or bowl and pour the almond mix through. Pick up the cheesecloth and twist to squeeze out the remaining milk. This should make 1½ cups of almond milk. Set aside. For extra (weaker) almond milk, pour ½ cup more water through the remains and squeeze this out into a separate bowl or jug. This weaker almond milk can be used to thin the cream once it has set.

To blanch almonds, put the almonds and 2 cups of water in a saucepan and bring to the boil. Allow to boil for 1 minute. Take off the heat and sit for 5 minutes. Discard the water and remove the skins from the almonds. You now have blanched almonds.

To make the cream, put the cornstarch in a saucepan. Add vanilla and maple syrup. Slowly add the almond milk (1½ cups), stirring with a whisk or wooden spoon until a thin paste is formed.

Put the saucepan over a low heat, and slowly bring the mixture to a boil, stirring constantly. The mixture needs to bubble, ensuring the cornstarch is cooked out, but only just. As soon as it begins to bubble, remove from the heat. Pour into a bowl, allow to cool, cover and refrigerate until cold.

Spoon the mixture into a food processor and add the coconut milk and water, or any weaker almond milk. Blend for 5 minutes, until very smooth. If the mixture is too thick, add a little more coconut or almond milk.

The finished consistency is that of whipped cream.

Almond custard cream

DAIRY FREE / GLUTEN FREE / VEGAN

Layered desserts such as trifle or parfait require a sauce with a consistency somewhere between whipped cream and custard. What follows is a custard made thick with kudzu powder, but lightened by the addition of agar. When blended this allows the 'custard cream' a texture that holds more air, similar to a mousse.

MAKES APPROXIMATELY 3 CUPS

1 cup blanched almonds
2 tablespoons and 1 teaspoon agar flakes (or 1½ teaspoons powder) (see page 302)
2¼ ounces maple syrup
1 vanilla bean
1½ tablespoons kudzu powder (or cornstarch or arrowroot)
¼ cup coconut milk

Put the blanched almonds and 3½ cups of water in a blender. Blend well. Peg 4 layers of cheesecloth onto a pitcher or bowl and pour the almond mix through. Squeeze out the remaining milk from the cheesecloth. This should make 3 cups of almond milk.

Agar flakes take a long time to dissolve in soy or almond milk and must be done over a very low heat (a heat diffuser is useful here), stirring often. It usually takes about 20 to 25 minutes.

Put 2½ cups of almond milk, the agar and maple syrup in a saucepan. Lay the vanilla bean flat on a chopping board and, using a small sharp knife, cut down the length of the bean. Open the bean up and flatten to scrape the seeds. Add these to the milk in the pan.

Stir together and bring very gently to the boil, then simmer for 10 minutes if you are using agar powder; if you are using flakes, cook for 20 minutes, or until the flakes have dissolved. Stir frequently with a whisk or spoon to prevent the mixture from sticking to the bottom or boiling too hard and reducing.

Mix ¼ cup almond milk and the kudzu powder to a paste and add to the almond cream, stirring constantly as it comes to the boil. Remove from the heat and pour into a clean bowl. Allow to cool slightly before putting in the fridge to set.

When set, put what will be a fairly solid mix back in the blender. To this, add ½ cup of water (or any remaining almond milk) and the coconut milk. For a firmer cream reduce the total liquid added to ½ cup (either 50/50 water and coconut milk, or just water or coconut milk). Blend for 5 minutes, until it is silky smooth.

Vanilla anglaise

DAIRY FREE / GLUTEN FREE / VEGAN

This is a lovely light dairy-free topping, ideal for serving with apple and quince crumble (see page 258), apricot pie (see page 266) or any choice of dessert.

MAKES 1½ CUPS

½ cup blanched almonds
1½ tablespoons kudzu powder (or cornstarch or arrowroot)
1 vanilla bean
3 teaspoons maple syrup (or to taste)

Put the blanched almonds and 1¾ cups water in blender. Blend well. Peg 4 layers of cheesecloth onto a pitcher or bowl and pour the almond mix through. Squeeze out the remaining milk from the cheesecloth. This should make 1½ cups of almond milk.

Rather than using almond milk, you could use a combination of 1 cup of rice milk and ½ cup coconut milk.

Put the kudzu powder into a saucepan with ¾ cup almond milk, mix to a paste with a wooden spoon, then add the remaining milk. Lay the vanilla bean flat on a chopping board and, using a small sharp knife, cut down the length of the bean. Open the bean up and flatten to scrape the seeds. Add these to the milk in the pan along with the maple syrup.

Using vanilla extract does color the finished cream, so you may prefer to use seeds, straight from the vanilla bean.

Place the saucepan over a gentle heat and, stirring constantly, continue to cook until it comes to the boil. Immediately remove from the heat. Check for taste, and add more maple syrup if necessary.

Simple desserts

Simple desserts are a little delicious something to finish off a meal without being overly heavy and rich. Desserts have an important place in a meal and can add nourishment as well as joy and delight. The following are all fairly easy to put together, but lighter than their conventional counterparts.

Almond blancmange

DAIRY FREE / GLUTEN FREE / VEGAN

This is a lovely dessert for summer—light, fragrant and satisfying. It is designed to offset fruit (fresh, stewed, broiled or poached). Almond blancmange is best made the day it is to be eaten, but can be used the next day if the ramekins are wrapped carefully and kept in the fridge until use.

SERVES 6

1 cup blanched almonds
4 tablespoons cornstarch

3 tablespoons maple syrup
2 teaspoons natural vanilla extract

Rinse 6 ramekins (they should be no bigger than 1/2 cup capacity) lightly with water and gently shake dry.

Put the almonds and 3 1/2 cups of water in a blender and combine well. Peg 4 layers of cheesecloth onto a pitcher or bowl and strain through the mixture. Measure out 3 cups. You now have almond milk.

Put the cornstarch, maple syrup and vanilla extract in a saucepan. Add a small amount of almond milk to the saucepan, mixing to a smooth paste. Slowly add the remaining milk, so you end with a smooth mixture. Put over a gentle heat and bring to the boil, stirring constantly. Remove as soon as it comes to the boil.

Pour the mixture into the ramekins, not quite to the top. Put in the fridge for at least 1 hour to set before serving.

To remove the blancmange, simply sit the ramekins in a bowl of hot water very briefly, then turn each ramekin onto a plate and tap lightly.

An extremely finely ground starch, cornstarch is used as a thickening agent and is particularly useful where some structure is required (as opposed to for a sauce).

When using vanilla extract, the color of the finished blancmange will be darker than if you used vanilla seeds instead.

If you find you are short of almond milk, add a little more water to the almonds left in the cheesecloth and strain out a little more of the milk.

VARIATION

To create a coconut blancmange blend the almonds with 2 1/2 cups of water to make 2 cups of almond milk. Add 1 cup of coconut cream and then continue as above. This is a lovely dish to serve with tropical fruits such as grilled mango, pineapple and papaya.

Chocolate and hazlenut mousse

DAIRY FREE / GLUTEN FREE / VEGAN

This is a delicious dairy- and soy-free mousse.

SERVES 4 TO 5

1 cup blanched almonds
2 1/4 tablespoons agar flakes (or 1 1/2 teaspoon powder) (see page 302)
1/3 cup cocoa powder

1½ tablespoons kudzu powder (or cornstarch or arrowroot)

½ cup maple syrup

3 teaspoons natural vanilla extract

½ cup hazelnuts, toasted, skins removed

On a cold winter's night, this makes a fabulous dairy-free hot chocolate. Reduce the amount of agar to ¾ tablespoon of flakes or ½ teaspoon powder and omit the hazelnuts. Cook as described, but serve after bringing to the boil with the kudzu.

Put the almonds and 3½ cups of water in a blender. Blend well. Peg 4 layers of cheesecloth onto a pitcher or bowl and pour the almond mix through. Squeeze out the remaining milk from the cheesecloth. Measure out 3¼ cup and set this aside. If the measure if short, pour ½ cup more water through the remains and squeeze this out.

Put the agar and 3 cups of almond milk in a saucepan. Stir together and bring very gently to the boil, then simmer for 10 minutes if you are using agar powder; or if you are using flakes cook for 20 minutes, or until the flakes have dissolved. Stir frequently with a whisk or spoon to prevent the mixture from sticking to the bottom or boiling too hard and reducing.

While the agar is dissolving, put the cocoa and cornstarch in a small bowl and mix to a paste with the maple syrup, the remaining almond milk and vanilla extract.

When the agar has dissolved, add the cocoa mixture and stir until just boiling. Set aside and allow to cool slightly (stirring will help). While this is cooling, put the hazelnuts in a blender and process until very fine. Immediately add the liquid mixture to the blender and continue to blend until the mixture is very smooth.

Pour into a bowl, and put in the fridge for 40 minutes, or until set. The mousse is now ready to serve.

Fruit jellies

DAIRY FREE / GLUTEN FREE / VEGAN

These are a great summer treat for any time of the day. It is important to match the juice to the fruit; for example, in summer use strawberry and guava juice with fresh strawberries and blueberries. Buy good-quality fruit juice—it makes a huge difference to these jellies.

SERVES 3 TO 4

- 2 cups fruit juice
- 1½ tablespoons agar flakes (or 1 teaspoon powder) (see page 302)
- 2 cups fruit (bananas, stone fruit, fresh berries—all or any)

Put the juice and agar into a saucepan. Stir together and bring very gently to the boil, then simmer for 10 to 15 minutes for flakes, or until they have dissolved, or 8 to 10 minutes for powder. Stir frequently with a whisk or spoon to prevent the mixture from sticking to the bottom or boiling too hard and reducing. Remove from the heat and allow to cool slightly.

Place your choice of fruit in a jelly mold or bowl, and pour over the lightly cooled jelly. Cool slightly and refrigerate for 30 minutes, or until set.

Adding kudzu powder or arrowroot to the jelly will make a smoother-textured jelly. Mix 1½ teaspoons kudzu with a little juice (about 1 tablespoon). Once the agar has dissolved, add this to the pot and bring to the boil.

Millet, date and pumpkin pudding

DAIRY FREE / GLUTEN FREE / VEGAN

This is an excellent dessert to serve in the cold winter months. Leftovers can also be heated up and used as a hearty breakfast the next day. (Make sure the soy milk is free of barley malt for this to be gluten-free.)

SERVES 6

- ½ cup hulled millet
- 2¼ tablespoons kudzu powder (or cornstarch or arrowroot)
- 1½ tablespoons pear juice concentrate
- 1½ tablespoons maple syrup
- 1 cup cooked mashed pumpkin
- ½ teaspoon ground cinnamon
- ½ cup fresh dates, pitted and finely chopped
- 1½ cups soy milk

Preheat the oven to 350°F.

Rinse the millet well and pat dry with a dish towel. Put the drained grain into a heavy-based saucepan with 1 cup water, cover with a lid and bring to the boil.

As soon as it reaches boiling point, turn the heat down as low as possible and cook over a gentle heat for 15 to 20 minutes. When it is ready, small steam holes should appear on the surface. Take the pot off the heat and leave to stand.

Put the kudzu (or arrowroot or cornstarch) in a bowl with the pear juice concentrate and maple syrup and mix to a paste. Add the pumpkin, cinnamon and dates and mix together well. Add the millet and then gradually stir in the soy milk until smooth. Pour the mixture into a 4 cup capacity 8½ inch ovenproof baking dish and bake for 40 to 50 minutes, or until the top is quite golden.

Apple and quince crumble

A fruit crumble remains the definitive dessert, delicious and very easy to prepare. Be generous with your fruit—choose a deep dish, fill with fruit, leaving just enough room for the crumble mix.

You can use other fruit in a crumble: alone (apple or peach) or mixed together (apple and blackberry, strawberry and rhubarb). Hard fruit (such as apples and quince) will need to be lightly stewed beforehand. Soft fruit (berries or stone fruit) only need to be sliced or put straight in the dish. Peaches work beautifully, as do rhubarb and raspberries.

SERVES 4 TO 6

1 to 2 quinces, peeled, cored and sliced
½ vanilla bean, split lengthways
1 tablespoon honey
4 Granny Smith apples, peeled, cored and sliced
zest of ½ a lemon

CRUMBLE
½ cup rolled (flaked) oats (or ½ cup oatmeal)
½ cup unbleached all-purpose spelt flour
½ cup lightly packed soft brown sugar
¼ cup shredded coconut
1 teaspoon ground cinnamon
5 to 7 tablespoons unsalted butter (the more you use, the softer the crumble mix will be)
½ cup walnuts, chopped

VEGAN AND WHEAT-FREE CRUMBLE ALTERNATIVE
¾ cup barley flour
¾ cup oatmeal
¾ cup shredded coconut

1 teaspoon ground cinnamon
¼ cup maple syrup
¼ cup almond oil
½ cup walnuts

almond custard cream (see page 252) (or cream or ice cream), to serve

Put the quince in a saucepan with ½ cup of water, the vanilla bean and the honey, cover with a lid and cook over a very gentle heat for 50 minutes to 1 hour. Check occasionally and add more water if it is running low. Check for taste, adding a little extra honey if needed (remember, there is sugar in the topping).

Meanwhile, put the apples in a separate saucepan with the zest from half a lemon. Add 2 tablespoons of water, cover with a lid and cook for 10 minutes or until just tender.

Preheat the oven to 350°F. Put the apples and quinces in a 7-inch square by 2-inch deep ovenproof baking dish. Meanwhile, using a food processor, pulse together the crumble (or vegan and wheat-free crumble alternative) ingredients, except the walnuts. It should combine to resemble chunky breadcrumbs. Add the walnuts and pulse through until just broken up. Sprinkle the mixture on top of the fruit. Bake for 30 minutes, or until the crumble topping is very lightly browned.

Serve with almond custard cream, fresh whipped cream or ice cream.

You can replace the walnuts in the crumble topping with flaked or sliced almonds. This is particularly delicious with summer crumbles.

Sweet pastries, tarts and pies

There is something about a pie, warm from the oven, which is comforting to the soul. Baked with the very best of ingredients, pies can be immensely satisfying foods.

Fat and pastry

Pastry is traditionally made with saturated fat (butter or lard), which gives it a soft, flaky and light finish. When incorporated into the flour the fat melts, and as the gluten in the flour sets around it, this creates the flake. It is possible to make pastry with oil. Olive oil works best for savory pastry and solid coconut butter/oil for dessert pastries. Both are stable fats in the presence of heat. The bottom line is, the more fat you use, the flakier the pastry will be.

Rich shortcrust pastry

This makes enough pastry to line a 9½ x 1¼ inch tart pan. If you are making a pie (with a bottom and a top of pastry), double the quantity. This recipe is best made with unbleached all-purpose wheat or spelt flour, but can be made with whole wheat or atta (see page 319), or even a percentage of them, using 1 to 2 teaspoons more liquid.

Roll between 2 sheets of baking paper into a 12 inch diameter circle. As the pastry becomes bigger, it will stick to the paper. Lift the paper off, sprinkle with flour, and then roll again. Gently turn the whole thing over (paper and all) and then repeat with the paper underneath, if you don't do this, the pastry will just stick to the paper and won't get any bigger.

MAKES 12 OUNCES

5½ tablespoons unsalted butter, softened
¼ cup raw (or golden superfine) sugar
1 egg yolk
½ teaspoon natural vanilla extract
1¼ cups unbleached all-purpose flour (wheat or spelt)
1 to 1½ tablespoons ice-cold water

Beat the butter and sugar until creamy. Add the egg yolk and vanilla extract and beat until well combined. Add the flour and water, and beat gently until it begins to come together. It should be firm, but not hard, soft, but not moist. Press the dough into a ball, and flatten. Cover well and rest in the fridge for approximately 20 minutes. The dough is now ready to use.

Coconut oil pastry

DAIRY FREE / VEGAN

This makes enough pastry to line a 9½ x 1¼ inch tart pan. If you are making a pie (with a bottom and a top of pastry), double the quantity. Coconut oil behaves in a very similar fashion to butter when making pastry, taking up space in the pastry, melting and thus contributing to flakiness and mouthfeel. It will, however, have a coconut taste. It is best served warm, as pastry made with coconut oil will toughen as it cools.

Coconut oil pastry is easy to roll—it 'greases' the rolling pin and is unlikely to stick. You may also need a small amount of flour to dust the rolling area and pin. These pastries are, however, difficult to move and cannot be folded. To move, use one hand and a knife to gently lift it into position.

MAKES 13½ OUNCES

¾ cup atta flour (or whole wheat spelt) (see page 319)
¾ cup unbleached all-purpose flour (wheat or spelt)
3 teaspoons raw (or golden superfine) sugar

¼ teaspoon baking powder
½ cup coconut oil, solid and preferably frozen
½ teaspoon natural vanilla extract
2 to 3 ounces ice-cold water

Method 1 by hand
Mix together the flours, sugar and baking powder in a bowl.

This pastry is very fragile, and it is good to slightly chill the pastry before lining the pan, or cutting.

Grate the frozen or well-chilled solid coconut oil into the mixture. Add the vanilla extract and gradually add the water, using a blunt knife to mix together. Add extra water if necessary. Press together with your fingertips.

Method 2 with a food processor
Put the flours, sugar and baking powder in the food processor. Add the coconut oil to the bowl. Pulse a few times until you have a crumbly consistency. Add the vanilla and water. Pulse, adding extra water as necessary, until the mixture comes together. Cover well and rest in the fridge for approximately 20 minutes. The dough is now ready to use.

Almond pastry

DAIRY FREE / GLUTEN FREE / VEGAN

With a texture similar to shortbread and a fragrant taste from maple syrup and vanilla, this is a very flexible and delicious pastry, great for small tart shells. It can be made ahead of time and stored in a sealed container for up to 2 days.

TO MAKE 16 TART SHELLS

1 cup ground almonds
1½ cups brown rice flour
½ cup maple syrup
¼ cup almond oil
1 teaspoon natural vanilla extract
1 to 1½ tablespoons ice-cold water

Put the ground almonds and brown rice flour in a bowl, and mix together. Whisk together the maple syrup, oil, vanilla extract and 1 tablespoon of water. Add to the dry ingredients and mix together with a fork. This mix should not have a dry, sandy texture and you may need to add a little more water to make it moist. Cover well and rest in the fridge for approximately 20 minutes. The dough is now ready to use. This pastry is not suitable for rolling. It should be pressed into the pan.

Wheat- and dairy-free pastry

DAIRY FREE / WHEAT FREE / VEGAN

This is a very simple, quick to make crust—ideal for tart work.

TO LINE A 9½ X 1¼ INCH TART PAN (OR MAKE 16 TART SHELLS)

1½ cups oatmeal
½ cup shredded (or ½ cup desiccated) coconut
½ cup macadamia nuts (or almonds)
2½ tablespoons almond oil (or 3 tablespoons melted coconut oil)
1½ tablespoons maple syrup (1 tablespoon extra, if required)

Using a food processor, lightly process the oatmeal, coconut and nuts until the nuts are just broken. Add the almond oil and syrup and pulse until combined. Check for consistency—it should stick together well when pressed together. The dough is now ready to use. This pastry is not suitable for rolling. It should be pressed into the pan.

Baking your pastry, tart or pie

The best results for tarts and pies will always come from very cold pastry going into a hot oven. This sets the fat and provides a better flake, and lighter pastry. Tarts should preferably be baked blind (see below), while pies with drier fillings (such as fruit pies) can be placed in the fridge to firm before going in the oven.

Lining the pan

To line the pan, first you need to roll the pastry. Roll out the pastry, then carefully fold the pastry back over and around the rolling pin and lift it gently from the surface. Unroll the pastry over the pan and ease it into the pan, pressing to fit the side. Roll the pin across the top to cut off the excess dough.

Baking blind

Partly cooking pastry helps to seal it, and thus avoid seepage. It also helps to ensure a crisp and well-cooked bottom pastry. This process is called 'baking blind.' To do it, carefully place a sheet of baking paper over the pastry-lined tart pan. Fill with raw beans or pastry weights. Chill well.

Preheat the oven to 400°F.

Bake the tart shell for 10 minutes, then lower the heat to 350°F. When the pastry begins to color around the edge, remove the weights and the paper. It is now partly blind baked. For a fully cooked shell, return to the oven (minus the paper and weights) and continue to cook until lightly golden.

TIPS FOR BAKING PASTRY

- The dish is also important for successful pastry cooking. Metal and enamel will distribute the heat rapidly to the raw pastry, enabling the gluten to set, before the butter has fully melted, while ceramic will diffuse the heat, which can result in tart pastry being a little soggy.
- To achieve a glazed pastry use either egg white, or egg mixed with a little water. With fruit pies, pastry can be sprinkled with sugar and cinnamon.
- Pies and tarts are cooked when the pastry is glistening and lightly browned, with flakes evident. Leave in the oven for a little longer (approximately 5 minutes) beyond this point to allow the pastry on the side and on the bottom to finish. They should then be allowed to sit for approximately 10 minutes, allowing them to settle before cutting.

Rustic peach and blueberry tart

DAIRY FREE / VEGAN

This is a lovely simple dessert—a free-form pie with lots of fruit. If you are wanting to reduce your fat, this is the way to do it—more fruit, less pastry.

SERVES 6 TO 8

- 1 quantity coconut oil pastry (see page 261) (or shortcrust pastry (see page 208) made with 1½ sticks butter and 1½ tablespoons of raw sugar)
- 4 to 5 medium peaches
- 7 to 9 ounces blueberries
- 1½ to 3 tablespoons raw sugar (or maple syrup) (or to taste)
- 2½ tablespoons arrowroot
- 1 teaspoon natural vanilla extract

Preheat the oven to 400°F.

Roll out the pastry and place the dough on a tray. Put the tray into the fridge to chill slightly while you prepare the filling.

Meanwhile, peel the peaches, cut into slices about ½ inch thick and put into a large bowl with the berries. Add the sugar or maple syrup, arrowroot and vanilla and mix through. Set aside.

Remove the pastry from the fridge and peel off the top sheet of paper. Either arrange the prepared fruit in an attractive pattern over the pastry, or simply pile it into the middle, leaving a border of approximately 2½ inches. Fold the pastry border over the fruit, peeling it from the paper underneath as you go. Sprinkle with a little extra sugar if desired. If required, trim the sides of the baking paper to fit the tray.

Bake for 15 minutes, then reduce the heat to 350°F for about 35 minutes, or until the pastry is lightly golden and the juices are bubbling.

VARIATION

Finely chopped nuts (especially walnuts) make a delicious addition. Sprinkle them over the tart before baking.

Apricot pie

When stone fruits come into season, this is the thing to do—go and buy lots, make a pie, sit outside in the evening and eat it with good vanilla ice cream.

SERVES 6

melted butter (or almond oil), for greasing
2 quantities rich shortcrust pastry (see page 261) (or 2 quantities shortcrust pastry (see page 208) each made with 1½ sticks butter and 1½ tablespoons of raw sugar)
3 pounds, 5 ounces apricots
3 to 6 teaspoons raw sugar (or maple syrup), to taste
2 tablespoons arrowroot (or kudzu powder or cornstarch)
almond custard cream (see page 252) (or cream or ice cream), to serve

Preheat the oven to 400°F. Brush a 9½ x 1¼ inch tart pan with a little melted butter.

Roll out half the pastry and line the pan, trimming the pastry to approximately 1¼ inch above the edge of the pan. Put in the fridge for at least 20 minutes to chill. Cover the remaining pastry and put in the fridge.

Meanwhile, wash the apricots, cut into halves or quarters (depending on size) and put in a mixing bowl. Add the sugar or maple syrup and arrowroot and toss together.

Remove the lined tart pan from the fridge and transfer the apricot mixture into it and even it out. Roll out the remaining pastry to a 10-inch circle, carefully cover the pie and gently press the edges to seal. Cut a small slit in the top to allow steam to escape. Immediately put the pie into the oven and cook for 45 minutes. Reduce the heat to 350°F and cook for another 45 minutes, or until the top is golden. Leave in the oven for a little longer (approximately 5 minutes) beyond this point to allow the pastry on the side and on the bottom to finish cooking. Sit for approximately 10 minutes, allowing it to settle before cutting. Serve with almond custard cream, fresh whipped cream or ice cream.

Passionfruit bavarois

DAIRY FREE / WHEAT FREE / VEGAN

These pastries taste great—light, yet filling, with an intense passionfruit flavor. A bit of a labor of love, as the passionfruit pulp must be strained to gain the delicious juice, but well worth the effort. Allow a couple of hours to make these as the various stages take time to set. They can be kept for a day in the fridge.

MAKES 6 BAVAROIS

½ quantity wheat- and dairy-free pastry (see page 263) (or almond pastry, see page 262)
20 passionfruit, halved
1¼ tablespoons agar flakes (or ¾ teaspoon powder) (see page 302)
3 tablespoons raw sugar
½ cup blanched almonds
¼ cup cornstarch
2 teaspoons natural vanilla extract
1½ tablespoons maple syrup
½ cup coconut milk

PASSIONFRUIT AGAR GLAZE

3 ounces passionfruit pulp, with or without seeds) (you'll need 3 to 4 passionfruit)
1 teaspoon raw sugar (or to taste)
1½ teaspoons agar flakes (or ¼ teaspoon powder) (see page 302)

Raw sugar is used here as the sweetener—a small amount will sweeten without adding any flavor.

Put the blanched almonds and 1¾ cups water in blender. Blend well. Peg 4 layers of cheesecloth onto a pitcher or bowl and pour the almond mix through and strain. Squeeze out the remaining milk from the cheesecloth. This should make 1½ cups of almond milk.

Put the cornstarch in a small saucepan. Add the vanilla and maple syrup. Slowly add 1½ cups of the almond milk, stirring with a whisk or wooden spoon until a thin paste is formed.

Put the saucepan over a low heat, and slowly bring the mixture to a boil, stirring constantly. The mixture needs to bubble, ensuring the cornstarch is cooked out, but only just. As soon as it begins to bubble, remove from the heat. Pour into a bowl, allow to cool, cover and refrigerate until cold.

Preheat the oven to 350°F. Line a baking tray with baking paper and place 6 small (3 x 1¼ inch) individual pastry rings on this. Cut 6 strips of baking paper (1½ to 8 inches) and line the interior sides of the rings. Divide the pastry into 6 even portions (about the size of a golf ball) and press each one into a ring, making a base (only). The pastry should be approximately ¼ inch thick. Put in the oven for 15 minutes or until lightly golden. Allow to cool before filling.

Scoop the passionfruit pulp into a sieve, sitting over a bowl. Press and mix through with a large spoon, allowing the juice to drip through to the bowl. This should make 1 cup of juice. Put the passionfruit juice and agar in a saucepan and allow to sit for 10 minutes. Add the sugar and bring to a very gentle simmer, reduce the heat to very low (a heat diffuser is useful here), cook for 10 to 15 minutes for flakes (or until dissolved) or 8 to 10 minutes for powder. Stir frequently to stop the agar sticking to the bottom. Allow to cool slightly.

Spoon the cold almond mixture into a food processor and add the coconut milk. Blend for 5 minutes, until very smooth. Add the slightly cooled passionfruit mixture and continue to blend until well incorporated. Pour or spoon this between the 6 rings. Place in the fridge for 30 to 40 minutes, or until set.

To make the glaze, put the passionfruit pulp, 1 ounce of water, sugar and agar flakes (or powder) in a small saucepan. Stir together and simmer over a gentle heat so barely a blip breaks the surface for 10 to 15 minutes for flakes, or until they have dissolved, or 8 to 10 minutes for powder. Stir frequently with a whisk or spoon to prevent the mixture from sticking to the bottom or boiling too hard and reducing. Allow to cool slightly, then spoon (rather than pour) onto the set passionfruit bavarois, approximately ¼ inch thick. Return to the fridge and set. To remove the completed bavarois from the mold, gently ease off the ring and peel off baking paper.

Fruit and almond tartlets

DAIRY FREE / GLUTEN FREE / VEGAN

These tartlets are delicious, light and beautiful for hot summer days.

MAKES 8 TARTLETS

almond oil (or melted butter), for greasing
½ quantity almond pastry (see page 262) (or wheat- and dairy-free pastry, see pages 263)
1 quantity almond cream (see page 250) (or fresh whipped cream with a drop of natural vanilla extract)
4 strawberries (or 8 raspberries, or 8 blueberries), cut in a fan shape
½ to 1 banana
½ mango
1 kiwi fruit, peeled and very thinly sliced

PASSIONFRUIT AGAR GLAZE

3 ounces passionfruit pulp with or without seeds (you'll need 3 to 4 passionfruit)
1 teaspoon raw sugar (or to taste)
1½ teaspoons agar flakes (or ¼ teaspoon powder) (see page 302)

Preheat the oven to 350°F. Brush eight 2¾ x ¾ inch tart pans with a melted almond oil and line with strips of baking paper (about 3¼ x ½ inch long) these will enable you to successfully pull the tart shell out, after it has baked).

Divide the pastry mixture into 8 even portions and then press into the pan to line. Bake in a moderate oven for 10 minutes, or until light golden. Remove from the oven, allow to cool for 2 minutes, then very gently loosen (not remove) the shells by lifting the edges of the baking paper strips. Allow to cool completely before removing.

Put the passionfruit pulp, sugar and agar flakes (or powder) and 1 ounce of water in a small saucepan. Stir together and bring very gently to the boil, then simmer for 10 to 15 minutes for flakes, or until they have dissolved, or 8 to 10 minutes for powder. Stir frequently with a whisk or spoon to prevent the mixture from sticking to the bottom or boiling too hard and reducing.

Slice the mango and banana into thin attractive pieces. Spoon approximately 1 tablespoon of almond cream into each shell, then arrange fruit on top of the cream. Spoon or brush the glaze over, and put in the fridge to set.

Glazes are useful to seal and protect the top of a tart and to add another layer of flavor. This is an extremely versatile and useful glaze, and is a great way to add the finishing touch to a cake or pie.

Mango and lime tart

WHEAT FREE

This is the most perfect tart to have on a really hot summer day. Light, delicious and full of flavor without any richness. Best eaten the day it is made.

SERVES 6 TO 8

melted butter (or almond oil), for greasing
1 quantity wheat- and dairy-free pastry (see page 263)
1½ tablespoons agar flakes (or 1 teaspoon powder) (see page 302)
1½ cups soy milk (or almond milk),
plus another ¼ cup
2 mangoes
zest of 1 lime
¼ cup lime juice
3 teaspoons kudzu powder (or cornstarch or arrowroot)
¼ to ½ cup maple syrup, to taste
mango slices, to decorate (optional)
fresh whipped cream (or almond cream, see page 250), to serve

Preheat the oven to 350°F. Brush a 9½ x 1¼ inch loose-based round tart pan with a little melted butter. Press the pastry into the pan and bake for 20 to 30 minutes, or until lightly golden. Leave the pastry to cool in the pan.

Meanwhile, combine the agar and the 1½ cups milk in a small saucepan. Stir together and bring very gently to the boil, then simmer for 10 to 15 minutes for flakes, or until they have dissolved, or 8 to 10 minutes for powder. Stir frequently with a whisk or spoon to prevent the mixture from sticking to the bottom or boiling too hard and reducing.

Put the mango flesh, lime zest and juice in a blender and process until smooth.

When the agar mixture is ready, combine the kudzu powder with the remaining ¼ cup of soy milk. Add this to the saucepan and cook, stirring constantly, until just boiled. Remove from the heat and add to the blender together with the maple syrup, to taste. Blend to combine, adding more maple syrup if desired. Pour into the baked, cooled tart shell still in its tart pan.

Allow to cool and set for at least an hour, then remove from the pan, leaving it on the base. Decorate with mango slices if desired and serve either by itself or with almond cream.

VARIATION

To turn the filling into a mousse, blend it once it has set, then spoon into a serving bowl.

Crème pie

DAIRY FREE / WHEAT FREE / VEGAN

With only a small amount of cornstarch to bind and hold, this is a delicate 'cheese-cake'. It needs to be baked in the dish from which it is served. It is essential to make this the day before you wish to serve it as it needs to set in the fridge overnight, and be perfectly cool before you top it.

SERVES 6 TO 8

BASE

¼ cup whole almonds

½ cup golden raisins

1½ tablespoons almond oil

¾ cup rolled oats

¼ cup oatmeal

FILLING

1 pound silken tofu

2 tablespoons cornstarch

¾ cup coconut milk

⅓ cup maple syrup

3 teaspoons natural vanilla extract

1 teaspoon lemon zest

1 tablespoon lemon juice

BERRY GLAZE

9 ounces raspberries (or strawberries)

1 to 3 tablespoons raw sugar

3 teaspoons agar flakes (or ½ teaspoon powder) (see page 302)

Preheat the oven to 235°F. Using a food processor, grind the almonds until quite fine. Add the rest of the base ingredients and process for 5 minutes, until the mixture sticks together. Press the mixture into a 9½ x 1½ inch ovenproof dish (preferably ceramic), but not up the sides.

Put all the filling ingredients in a food processor and blend for 5 minutes until thoroughly combined. Pour over the base and bake for 1 hour, until the top is lightly colored and just set but the middle still has a wobble. Cracking indicates it is beginning to overcook. Allow to cool then cover and place in the fridge overnight before topping and glazing.

To make the glaze, gently boil the berries and about ½ cup of water in a small saucepan with the lid on, for 8 to 10 minutes. Strain the mixture through a sieve (discarding the pulp)—you should end up with about 1 cup of liquid.

Pour this glaze liquid into a small saucepan, together with 1 tablespoon of sugar and the agar. Stir together and bring very gently to the boil, then simmer for 15 to 20 minutes for flakes, or until they have dissolved, or 8 to 10 minutes for powder. Stir frequently with a whisk or spoon to prevent the mixture from sticking to the bottom or boiling too hard and reducing. Check for taste during the cooking process, adding more sugar if required. Let the glaze cool a little, then spoon over the cold pie.

VARIATION

Fruit on top of the finished pie also adds extra flavor, but it should only be placed decoratively around the edges, where the pie is sturdiest.

Raspberry tart

DAIRY FREE / WHEAT FREE

This is a good tart to make any time of year. Here, the tart is topped with almond cream and when cut has the most beautiful appearance—deep raspberry inside with the pale almond cream on top.

SERVES 6 TO 8

melted almond oil (or butter), for greasing
1 quantity wheat- and dairy-free pastry (see page 263)
12 ounces raspberries (fresh or frozen (defrosted)) (plus extra, to decorate)
1½ tablespoons agar flakes (or 1 teaspoon powder) (see page 302)
1½ cups soy milk (or almond milk)
(plus another ¼ cup)
3 teaspoons cornstarch (or kudzu powder or arrowroot)
¼ to ½ cup maple syrup, to taste

almond cream (see page 250) (or whipped cream), to top
whole raspberries, to decorate

Preheat the oven to 350°F. Brush a 9½ x 1¼ inch loose-based round tart pan with a little almond oil. Press the mixture into the pan and bake for 20 to 30 minutes, or until lightly golden. Leave the pastry shell to cool in the pan.

Meanwhile, put the rasberries (and any juice) in a sieve with a bowl underneath. Press the berries through with a spoon, to remove the pips. You should end up with 1 cup of purée.

In a small saucepan combine the agar and 1½ cups of milk. Stir together and bring very gently to the boil, then simmer over a very gentle heat for 15 to 20 minutes for flakes, or until they have dissolved, or 8 to 10 minutes for powder. Stir frequently with a whisk or spoon to prevent the mixture from sticking to the bottom or boiling too hard and reducing.

When the agar mixture is ready, mix the cornstarch with the remaining ¼ cup soy milk. Add this to the saucepan and cook, stirring constantly until just boiled. Remove from the heat and put in a blender, along with the raspberry purée and maple syrup to taste. Pour into the baked tart shell. Allow to cool and set. Remove from the pan but leave on the base.

Once set, gently spread with a layer of fresh whipped cream or almond cream, decorated with whole raspberries around the edges.

Cakes and muffins

At its most basic, baking cakes and muffins involves a combination of wet and dry ingredients—something to sweeten, something to bind, something to flavor and something to moisten. Baking with wholefoods does involve a few tricks and a new level of understanding, but once you learn and apply the rules you can be assured of success.

Adding moisture and flavor

The best way to understand the role of moisture in wholefood baking is to understand the role that fat plays. Fat is one way to add moisture to a cake or cookie; it softens and smooths out whole grain flours and adds flavor. The less fat that is used, the greater the need for other ways to incorporate moisture and flavor into the finished cake.

Cakes with a low-fat content are noticeably different, although they can be equally delicious. Cakes use a grain medium and grains (particularly whole wheat) are best softened and tenderized with fat (butter, oil or eggs). Low-fat cakes are best eaten the day they are cooked, but many will still be delicious as they age.

Fruit also adds moisture to a cake, and is especially important when you are making a low-fat cake. When finely chopped, stewed or grated fruit takes up space in the cake batter, its soft moist fiber getting in between the harsher fibers of whole grain flours, making it less dense. When added raw, it oozes juice to the cake or muffin as it cooks, helping to moisten and flavor. When chopped into fairly large dice, it gives moistness in the mouth. The best fruits for moistening are stewed apple, mashed or roughly chopped banana, raw berries and chopped ripe fruit (apple, pear and stone fruits); pumpkin also works well.

As a rule, the more whole wheat flour (any grain) used, the more important it becomes to consider the addition of moistness. As well as including fruit, it is also important to consider how much liquid to add. This liquid can be in the form of milk (dairy, almond, rice or soy), even fruit juice (not concentrate) or water. Once the batter has come together, it's best to let it sit for a couple of minutes; it will thicken as it absorbs the liquid and you can then add more liquid if necessary. Whole wheat grains absorb more moisture than a simple unbleached, starchy, white flour and the finished batter needs to be slighty wetter than normal. Too wet, however, and the finished cake will rise and collapse a little; too stiff and the cake will be dry.

See glossary for types of flour.

Leavening

In traditional baking, there are three main ways to raise and thus lighten a cake: through steam (as the moisture expands it raises the mixture); with creamed or whipped butter and eggs (by trapping air); and the use of baking powder to produce a chemical reaction on mixing with moisture and heat, creating carbon dioxide to lift the cake.

Baking powders with no salt or aluminium are healthier and 'fast acting.' The chemical reaction begins at a lower temperature than other baking powders and contact with moisture. They need less stirring and must be put in the oven to cook as soon as possible after mixing. All recipes in this book use such a baking powder.

All baking powders use an alkaline, but there are different options. Many commercial baking powders use sodium bicarbonate as the alkaline, whereas better brands use potassium bicarbonate. Potassium bicarbonate creates less carbon dioxide to lift the cake than sodium bicarbonate and is preferred.

For the acid, most commercial baking powders use sodium aluminium sulphate or a phosphate aerator (also called sodium aluminium phosphate). Baking powders with these products have a noticeably bitter taste in the mouth (not to mention aluminium in the body). The healthier blends use calcium phosphate as the acid.

Another option to increase leavening is to add a touch of an acid liquid such as buttermilk; soy milk with the addition of lemon; or yogurt to boost the reaction when baking powder is present.

Whole wheat (any grain) flours are heavy and thought must be given to how the cake will rise. Many commercial 'healthy cakes' made with whole wheat grains have large amounts of baking powder in them, with a resulting bitter aftertaste. Instead, use baking powder in half the normal amount and depend on other methods to make the cake rise, primarily with raw fruit. When cut into small portions, fruit takes up room in the batter, and creates a type of inner scaffolding. By the time the fruit starts to cook and soften (and reduce in size) the batter has begun to set, thereby keeping the original dimensions. When the cake is cooked, this creates a small, soft piece of fruit with a beautiful air pocket around it. The only fruit that does not perform well in this respect is very wet fruit, such as berries. Berries are best included mixed with another, sturdier fruit. Fairly sturdy dry fruit (such as apple, pear and rhubarb) is best finely diced, while wet fruit (such as apricots, peaches and mangos) is best cut into larger portions as they will reduce considerably in size when cooked.

A note on self-raising flour

Self-raising flour is simply the addition of baking powder to an unbleached or whole wheat flour. More often than not, too much is added and the flour is overly aggressive in its raising action, especially if made with sodium bicarbonate and sodium aluminium sulphate or phosphate, with a corresponding strong taste. When using self-raising flour, I generally use half the quantity with another type of plain flour, and depend on other methods to raise and lighten the cake. You can make a 'self-raising' flour yourself, by simply adding baking powder to a plain flour, such as spelt. The suggested amount of baking powder is 2½ teaspoons per 1 cup of flour.

Any time you see 'egg replacer' used in a recipe you can replace it with eggs if you choose: 1 tablespoon egg replacer (and the suggested water) is equivalent to 1 medium egg.

Eggs

Eggs are traditionally used for leavening, adding moisture in the form of fat and liquid and binding a batter together. Generally, the more eggs used, the lighter the finished product will be.

It is possible to avoid using eggs (they are a common source of food allergies). Extra attention will need to be given to moisture and the results will be heavier and slightly flatter, but still lovely. Egg replacers are very handy and give extra leavening while helping to 'stick' a cake together. They do not contain fat, so this must be taken into account and other ingredients added to give moisture.

How to tell when the cake is cooked

Cakes made with large amounts of fruit and whole wheat grains are much more dense than traditional cakes, and some can take a long time to cook. Never hurry a cake (that is, raise the temperature)—cakes cook best at moderate temperatures. Large cakes should be cooked at a lower temperature still.

Learning to tell when a cake is cooked is something that takes a little experience, with cooking times being used as guidelines only. Traditional cakes made with large amounts of fat tend to be glossy when cooked; as you reduce the amount of fat you can expect a reduction in sheen. Generally, the finished color or tone of the top of the cake should be uniform. In low- and very-low-fat cakes this will appear as a drying out of color—uncooked batter looks wetter. In gluten free cakes, this drying out is also accompanied by a noticeable sandiness in appearance. Use a cake tester in the center of the cake. It should come out clean, and the cake should pull away from the side of the pan ever so slightly. When you touch the center of the cake with your finger, it should be slightly springy. As the cake cooks, it may crack. The crack should be evident in the center of the cake as well as the edges. The heavier the cake, the smaller and lighter these cracks will be.

To prepare the cake pan, either line the pan with baking paper or grease (with butter or almond oil) and coat with flour. After covering the greased surface with flour, shake it off into the bin, giving the pan a little tap. This method is especially good for decorative cake pans.

Storage

Because of the high quantities of whole grains and fruit in the following recipes, many of these cakes will get moldy quite quickly. During the cool winter months, they can sit at room temperature for a couple of days, but as the weather warms they must be refrigerated after one day.

Muffins

Muffins are the perfect way to practice wholefood baking. They are fabulous to keep in the freezer; with just a quick heat in the oven they are a ready-made snack.

There are no hard and fast rules about which fruit to add, but it is important to make the muffins interesting. A selection of fruits offers much deeper complexities of flavor than one type of fruit on its own. Moist fruit (such as berries) needs to be partnered with a firmer fruit (such as apple or banana) to provide structure (internal scaffolding) to the muffin.

When using very wet and fragile berries, such as blueberries and raspberries, hold these back to add at the very last moment.

FRUIT COMBINATIONS

All fruit should combine to equal approximately 14 ounces (wholefruit) and can be used in the following two recipes.

BLUEBERRY AND BANANA

1¼ cups blueberries

2 medium bananas, cut into slices ½ inch thick

RASPBERRY AND MANGO

1½ cups raspberries

1 large mango, peeled and roughly diced into 1 inch pieces

BLUEBERRY AND APPLE

1¼ cups blueberries

1 large apple, peeled and chopped into ½ to 1 inch pieces

MANGO, BANANA, LIME ZEST, MACADAMIA AND COCONUT

1 small mango, peeled and roughly diced into 1 inch pieces

1 large banana, cut into slices ½ inch thick

1 teaspoon grated lime zest

½ cup macadamia nuts, roughly chopped

¼ cup shredded coconut

STRAWBERRY AND BANANA

1 cup strawberries, chopped

2 medium bananas, sliced ½ inch thick

APRICOT AND PEACH

3 small apricots, cut into quarters

3 small peaches, peeled, cut into large chunks

PLUMS WITH CINNAMON

3 small plums, cut into quarters

½ teaspoon cinnamon

BANANA AND DATE

2 large bananas, cut into slices ½ inch thick

½ cup fresh dates, seed removed, flesh cut into small pieces

PUMPKIN, PRUNE AND PEAR

1 cup mashed precooked pumpkin

10 prunes, seeded and roughly diced

1 large pear, cut into ½ inch dice

Toppings on muffins add further flavor to the muffin. For the best results, match the flavors to complement the fruit used (see cinnamon topping, see below, and almond/macadamia topping, see page 282).

Simple muffin recipe

MAKES 8 MUFFINS

1 cup unbleached all-purpose flour (wheat or spelt)

1 cup whole wheat flour (wheat, spelt or oatmeal)

2½ teaspoons baking powder

½ cup raw sugar

1 quantity of your choice of fruit combinations (see previous page)

1 teaspoon natural vanilla extract

4½ to 5½ tablespoons unsalted butter, melted

¾ to 1¼ cups whole milk

CINNAMON TOPPING

½ cup roughly chopped walnuts (or pecans)

1 teaspoon ground cinnamon

2 tablespoons desiccated coconut

1 to 2 tablespoons unrefined brown sugar

Preheat the oven to 350°F. Lightly grease an eight-hole muffin pan.

Put the flour, baking powder and sugar into a bowl and and mix together well to break up the flours. Add the fruit (except berries) and stir gently through to distribute evenly. Add the vanilla, butter and ¾ cup of milk, adding extra milk if required (especially if using drier fruit, such as apple). Set aside for a few minutes to allow the batter to absorb the moisture, then add the rest of the milk if necessary. The batter should look slightly wetter than its traditional counterpart, and move smoothly and freely over the spoon as you mix, but not runny. A batter that is not moist enough will tend to be clumpy with little free-flowing movement as you stir. You will also need to take into account the fruit used in the batter—fruit that is inherently wet (such as stone fruit and berries) will ooze juice into the batter as it cooks. Gently fold through berries now, if using.

Meanwhile, combine the topping ingredients. Spoon the batter into the prepared muffin pans, sprinkle with the topping and bake for 35 to 40 minutes, or until golden. Cool for 5 minutes in the pans, then remove and cool on wire racks.

Gluten-free muffins

DAIRY FREE / GLUTEN FREE / VEGAN

MAKES 6 MUFFINS

1½ cups brown rice flour
¼ cup amaranth flour
¼ cup ground almonds
3 teaspoons baking powder
1 quantity of your choice of fruit combinations (see pages 280-1)
⅓ cup almond oil
½ cup maple syrup
1 teaspoon natural vanilla extract
1½ tablespoons egg replacer mixed with ½ cup water (or 2 eggs)
¼ to ½ cup malt-free soy milk

ALMOND/MACADAMIA TOPPING
½ cup slivered almonds (or macadamia nuts), roughly chopped
2 tablespoons shredded coconut

Preheat the oven to 350°F. Lightly grease a six-hole muffin pan.

Put the rice, amaranth flour, ground almonds and baking powder in a bowl and mix together well to break up the flours. Add the fruit (except berries) stir gently through to distribute evenly. In a separate bowl, combine the almond oil, maple syrup, vanilla extract, egg replacer and ¼ cup soy milk and add to the dry ingredients. Mix through, then let sit for 5 minutes, and add extra soy milk if necessary. (It is especially important this be a moist mix as the flours are all quite heavy.) Gently fold through berries now, if using.

Meanwhile, combine the topping ingredients.

Spoon the batter into the prepared muffin pans, sprinkle with the topping and bake for 35 to 45 minutes, until golden. Cool for 5 minutes in the pans, then remove and cool on wire racks.

Cakes

Real, good quality cakes can play a wonderful role in a wholesome, balanced diet. Made with whole, real ingredients, they provide nourishment not only for the body, but more importantly, for the soul.

Sponge cake with lemon butter and blueberries

GLUTEN FREE

A sponge cake is a light, fluffy cake and it can be the basis for a delicious afternoon tea or dessert. Making it in a large pan gives you a thinner cake with more surface area—perfect for topping with this light lemon butter and passionfruit.

MAKES 1 (11¼ X 7 INCH OR 9½ INCH) CAKE

LEMON BUTTER

2 large lemons

3 eggs, lightly beaten

7 tablespoons unsalted butter

5½ ounces raw sugar

SPONGE CAKE

4 eggs, separated

½ cup superfine sugar

1 cup cornstarch (or arrowroot), well sifted

1 teaspoon unsalted butter, melted and still warm

1 teaspoon natural vanilla extract

2 passionfruit

9 ounces blueberries

confectioners' sugar (optional), to dust

1 quantity almond cream (see page 250), cold

¼ cup coconut milk

2 passionfruit, top top

9 ounces blueberries

Preheat the oven to 350°F. Lightly grease an 11¼ x 7 inch or 9½ inch round cake pan and line the base and sides with baking paper.

To make the lemon butter, finely grate the zest, then juice the lemons. Strain the juice into a bowl. Combine all the ingredients in a heavy-based saucepan.Whisk together and continue whisking over a gentle heat, until the mixture has thickened. You may find it easier to tell when it is ready with a wooden spoon—when it coats the back of the spoon, it is ready. Do not allow it to boil, or it will curdle. Continue to stir when it is taken off the stove to cool it down. Once cool, cover and place in the fridge until cold—it should be nice and thick.

To make the cake, use electric beaters on high speed to beat the egg whites until stiff, then slowly add the sugar and continue to beat until sugar is dissolved—about 30 seconds. Reduce the speed to medium, add the egg yolks and mix until just combined.

Gently fold in the sifted cornstarch. Add the melted butter and vanilla, folding through very gently until just incorporated. Pour or spoon into lined pan and bake for 20 to 25 minutes (or 30 to 35 minutes for a 9½ inch round cake) until golden and springy to the touch. Turn oven off, and leave the cake in the oven with the door open slightly. Allow to cool completely before turning out onto a serving plate.

Spoon the cold and set almond cream mixture into a food processor and add the coconut milk and ¼ cup of water. Blend for 5 minutes, until very smooth. If the mixture is too thick, add a little more coconut or almond milk—the finished consistency is that of whipped cream.

In a separate bowl gently whisk together 1 cup each of the lemon butter and the almond cream (or change the percentages to your liking).

Gently spread the light lemon butter over the cake, cut the passionfruit and drizzle the pulp over the icing and, finally, sprinkle with the blueberries. If desired, dust with a little confectioners' sugar.

If making a 9½ inch cake, cut the cake in half and spread with half of the lemon butter. Drizzle over half of the passionfruit pulp and scatter with ⅓ of the blueberries. Replace the top and spread with the remaining lemon butter, scatter over the remaining blueberries and dust with confectioners' sugar, if liked.

Another delicious way to serve this cake is to top it with cream (whipped cream or almond cream for a dairy-free option) and fresh fruit (bananas, berries, and passionfruit), sprinkled with a little confectioners' sugar. It also makes an excellent trifle base.

Spring cake

DAIRY FREE / VEGAN

This is a vegan version of a pound cake. Intensely fragrant with vanilla, almond meal is used to add extra moistness and break up the flour. Because it doesn't have any eggs to help bind it together, it is important to treat this cake gently. It is a beautiful cake to celebrate spring or a special occasion.

MAKES 1 (8½ INCH) CAKE

ROSE GERANIUM ALMOND CREAM

½ cup blanched almonds
4 unsprayed rose geranium leaves, roughly cut
3 tablespoons cornstarch
2 teaspoons natural vanilla extract
¼ cup maple syrup
¼ cup coconut milk

SPRING CAKE

2½ cups unbleached all-purpose flour (wheat or spelt)

1 tablespoon baking powder

1½ cups ground almonds

1 cup milk (soy or rice)

½ cup almond oil

1 cup maple syrup

1½ tablespoons natural vanilla extract

4 teaspoons apple cider vinegar

TOPPINGS

2 cups raspberries

1½ to 2 tablespoons raw sugar (or superfine sugar)

9 to 10½ ounces strawberries

Preheat the oven to 325°F. Lightly grease an 8½ inch cake pan and line the base and sides with baking paper.

Put the blanched almonds and 1¾ cups of water in a blender. Blend well. Peg 4 layers of cheesecloth onto a pitcher or bowl and pour the almond mix through. Squeeze out the remaining milk from the cheesecloth. This should make 1½ cups of almond milk. Set aside. Pour ½ cup more water through the remains and squeeze this out. This weaker almond milk is used to thin the cream once it has set.

Pour 1½ cups of almond milk into a saucepan, add the rose geranium leaves and heat to 98°F. Remove from the heat and cool for 15 minutes (in summer, let this cool in the fridge).

To make the cake, sift the flour and baking powder into a bowl. Add the ground almonds and whisk together. Pour ¾ cup of soy milk into a bowl and add the almond oil, maple syrup, vanilla extract and apple cider vinegar. Add to the dry ingredients. Let sit for 5 minutes. Gradually, add the remaining ¼ cup soy milk to bring to consistency. As this batter has no fruit to provide moisture, it should be quite a wet mixture.

Pour the batter into the prepared cake pan and bake for 1 hour and 10 minutes, or until the center is cooked. Leave to cool in the pan before removing.

While the cake is cooking, continue to make the cream. Measure the cornstarch directly into a saucepan, add the vanilla and maple syrup. Remove the geranium leaves from the almond mlk and slowly begin to add the almond milk to the pan, stirring with a whisk or wooden spoon until a thin paste is formed.

Put the saucepan over a low flame and slowly bring the mixture to the boil, stirring constantly. The mixture needs to bubble, ensuring the cornstarch is cooked out, but only just. As soon as it begins to bubble, remove from the heat. Pour into a bowl, allow to cool, cover and refrigerate until cold.

This cake can be hard to move once cut. It is helpful to use a large knife (and your hands) to support the layer of cake as you move it.

Spoon the mixture into a food processor and add the coconut milk and the remaining almond milk. Blend for 5 minutes, until very smooth. Place in fridge until ready to use.

Put the raspberries and sugar in a small saucepan and cook over a very gentle heat (this will allow the berries to sweat out their juices, without burning) until of jam-like consistency. Stir frequently. Check for taste, adding more sugar if necessary.

When the cake is cool, cut it in half horizontally, removing the top layer and setting it aside. Gently remove the bottom layer to a cake plate. Spread with the raspberry 'jam' and top with half the rose geranium almond cream. Gently lift and place the top layer on. Spread with the remaining rose geranium almond cream. Cut the strawberries into quarters, leaving a small portion of their green leaves intact. Spread the remaining rose geranium almond cream on top of the cake. Arrange the strawberries round the edge of the cake, with their green leaves facing outwards.

VARIATIONS

This cake can be used in a variety of ways:

- Sliced horizontally (2 or 3 layers), filled with lemon butter lightened with almond cream, drizzled with passionfruit pulp and topped with thin slices of mango.
- Sliced, and served with fruit (fresh, baked, grilled or poached) and almond cream or fresh whipped cream.
- As cupcakes, cut in half and filled with almond cream and berries.
- As a base for trifle.

Banana cake

Here banana is used to moisten and flavor and dried fruit to add sweetness to this low-fat cake. If using soy milk, increase the amount of butter to 6 tablespoons. It is best eaten the day it is made, but still delicious the next couple of days—warm from the oven is especially good.

It is essential to take into account the fat content of the milk you choose, when considering moisture in a cake. Banana cake made with a non-homogenized, whole dairy milk will be more moist than one made with soy milk, which is extremely low in fat.

MAKES 1 LOAF

1 cup whole wheat flour (wheat or spelt)
1 cup unbleached all-purpose flour (wheat or spelt)
2 1/2 teaspoons baking powder
1 teaspoon ground cinnamon
1/2 teaspoon mixed spice
1/2 cup golden raisins
1/2 cup roughly chopped walnuts
1/2 cup fresh dates, seeded and chopped
3 very ripe bananas, roughly mashed with a fork (about 10 1/2 ounces)
1 to 2 bananas (extra), cut into 1/4 to 3/4 inch slices
5 tablespoons unsalted butter, melted
1/2 cup yogurt
1/2 to 3/4 cup milk (dairy or soy)

Preheat the oven to 350°F. Lightly grease a 4 cup capacity loaf pan and line the base and sides with baking paper.

Put the whole wheat flour in a bowl and sift in the unbleached flour and baking powder. Add the cinnamon, mixed spice, raisins, walnuts and dates and mix through so that the fruit is evenly distributed. Add the mashed bananas and all the other ingredients and mix gently through. (You may need to add an extra tablespoon or 2 of milk, so that the batter moves well over the spoon as you mix it.) Place into the loaf pan and bake for 50 to 70 minutes, or until golden and cooked in the center. Leave to cool for 15 minutes, then turn onto a cake rack.

Carrot cake

You wouldn't think there would be a need for another carrot cake recipe, but unfortunately few of them make the grade. Here, unrefined dark brown sugar lends a subtle richness of flavor, with extra sweetness coming from pineapple and raisins.

MAKES 1 (9½ INCH) CAKE

1 cup unbleached all-purpose flour (wheat or spelt)
1 cup whole wheat flour (wheat or spelt)
2½ teaspoons baking powder
1 cup dark muscovado (or molasses sugar)
½ cup shredded or desiccated coconut
1 teaspoon cinnamon
1 teaspoon mixed spice
¼ teaspoon freshly grated nutmeg
1 cup chopped walnuts
1 cup golden raisins
4 cups grated carrot
3 to 4 rings canned pineapple, roughly chopped
¼ cup pineapple juice/syrup (from the can)
½ cup almond oil
3 eggs, lightly beaten
1 teaspoon natural vanilla extract
¼ cup finely chopped walnuts, to serve

CREAM CHEESE FROSTING
1 cup cream cheese, softened
9 tablespoons unsalted butter, softened
2 teaspoons grated lemon zest
2 teaspoons natural vanilla extract
maple syrup (or confectioners' sugar), to taste

Preheat the oven to 350°F. Lightly grease a 9½ inch spring-form cake pan and line the base and sides with baking paper.

Put the flour, baking powder, sugar, coconut, spices, walnuts and raisins in a large bowl and mix together lightly. Add the remaining ingredients, then mix together well. Turn into the cake pan, gently spread out and bake for approximately 1 hour and 15 minutes, or until the center is cooked when tested with a cake skewer, covering with foil if the top starts to brown too quickly. Leave the cake to cool for 15 minutes in the pan, then remove and cool on a wire rack.

Meanwhile, to make the frosting, beat together the cream cheese, butter, lemon zest, vanilla and sweetener until light and creamy. Maple syrup will thin out the frosting. If using confectioners' sugar, you may need to add a little warm water to bring to a softer consistency.

Once the cake has cooled, spread the frosting evenly over the top and sprinkle with the chopped walnuts to serve.

VARIATION

For a dairy-free topping, use almond cream (page 250) rather than the cream cheese frosting.

Apple cake

WHEAT FREE

With a robust flavor coming from the oatmeal and barley, this cake remains an all-time favorite. Fabulous served warm as a dessert with fresh cream.

MAKES 1 (9½ INCH) CAKE

4 to 5 medium apples (preferably Granny Smith)
1 lemon, grated zest and juice
1 cup oatmeal
1 cup barley flour
2 teaspoons baking powder
7 ounces raw sugar
3 eggs
8½ tablespoons unsalted butter, melted
3½ ounces milk (dairy or soy)
1 teaspoon natural vanilla extract
1 to 2 teaspoons cinnamon
½ cup walnuts, roughly chopped

Preheat the oven to 315°F. Lightly grease a 9½ inch spring-form cake pan and line the base and sides with baking paper.

Peel, core, quarter and finely slice the apples. Toss in a bowl with the lemon zest and lemon juice and set aside. In a separate bowl, combine the oatmeal, barley flour and baking powder and use a whisk to mix together.

Using electric beaters, whisk together the sugar and eggs until thick and creamy. Slowly pour in the cooled, melted butter and the flour mixture. Beat or whisk gently until the flour is incorporated, and let sit for 5 to 10 minutes. Gradually, add the milk (you may not need it all) and the vanilla. The batter should be quite moist with the consistency of a thick pancake batter.

Pour or ladle one-third of the cake batter into the pan and top with one-third of the apple mix, discarding the juice. Repeat twice so that all the batter and apples are used up and you finishend up with a layer of apple. Sprinkle with the cinnamon and walnuts. Bake for 1 hour and 20 minutes, or until the center is cooked. Leave the cake to cool for 15 minutes in the pan, then remove and cool on a wire rack.

Blueberry teacake

DAIRY FREE / GLUTEN FREE

This is a beautiful cake—fragrant, moist with berries and with a soft texture. The flour mixture is made with ground almonds and brown rice flour—the two best mediums for successful gluten-free baking. Soy flour is added in a small amount to soften, with cornstarch to bind. Here it is made with blueberries, but strawberries work just as well. If you are using frozen blueberries, incorporate them frozen.

MAKES 1 (8 INCH) CAKE

1½ cups almond meal
1 cup brown rice flour
½ cup cornstarch
½ cup soy flour
1½ teaspoons baking powder
½ cup almond oil (plus 1 ounce, extra)
1 cup maple syrup (plus extra, for topping)
3 teaspoons natural vanilla extract
1½ teaspoons apple cider vinegar
⅓ cup malt-free soy milk

10½ ounces fresh (or frozen) blueberries
¼ cup flaked almonds, to decorate
1¾ to 2½ ounces berries (extra), for top (optional)

Preheat the oven to 350°F. Lightly grease an 8 inch spring-form cake pan and line the base and sides with baking paper.

Combine the first five ingredients in a bowl (excluding the flaked almonds) and whisk through well, breaking up any lumps as you go. Mix the wet ingredients together in a seperate bowl. Add the wet ingredients to the dry, and mix to incorporate. Allow the mixture to sit for 5 to 8 minutes. Gently fold in the blueberries, place the mixture in the prepared cake pan and sprinkle over the flaked almonds. Bake for 1 hour and 20 minutes, or until the center is cooked and a skewer comes out clean. Leave the cake to cool for 15 minutes in the pan, then remove and cool on a wire rack.

VARIATION

For a special occasion, it's really great to top this with a blueberry syrup (omitting the flaked almonds). To do this, place the additional berries in a saucepan with a little maple syrup to sweeten (to taste). Cook over a gentle heat, reducing the liquid to a thick syrup. (Too much liquid will wet, rather than glaze, the cake.) Pour berries over the cake.

Plum teacake

Rich with plums that ooze their fragrant red juices as they cook, this is the perfect summer cake. With only 1 cup of sugar and the tartness of plums, this cake is not sickly sweet, but refreshing and beautifully moist. This cake is best made using electric beaters—the butter and sugar must be well creamed and eggs must be added one at a time. Because this cake has a large amount of butter, the batter can be less 'wet' than other cakes made with whole wheat flour.

MAKES 1 (9½ INCH) CAKE

1 cup unbleached all-purpose flour (wheat or spelt)
2 teaspoons baking powder

- 1 cup almond meal
- 1¼ cups whole wheat flour (wheat or spelt)
- ½ pound unsalted butter, at room temperature
- 1 cup raw sugar
- 3 eggs
- 3 teaspoons natural vanilla extract
- ¼ cup milk (if needed)
- 15 plums (blood, maraposa or ruby blood)
- ½ cup slivered almonds
- ½ teaspoon ground cinnamon

Preheat the oven to 350°F. Lightly grease a 9½ inch spring-form cake pan and line the base and sides with baking paper.

Sift the unbleached flour and the baking powder into a bowl. Add the almond meal and whole wheat flour, whisk together and set aside.

Using electric beaters, cream the butter and sugar for 5 minutes, until light and fluffy. Add the eggs, one at a time, beating after each addition until creamy. Add vanilla, then gently mix in the flour mixture. If the mixture looks clumpy (because the flour is soaking up moisture), then add milk as needed. Spoon the batter into the cake pan.

Cut the plums into halves (or quarters if large), discarding the stones and press into the cake batter. The plums will reduce as they cook, so try to fit in as many as you can. Sprinkle with slivered almonds and cinnamon. Bake for 1 to 1½ hours, or until the center is cooked and a skewer comes out clean. Leave the cake to cool for 15 minutes in the pan, then remove and cool on a wire rack.

Celebration fruit cake

DAIRY FREE / VEGAN

A beautifully moist fruit cake, using miso to add depth of flavor and perfect for celebrations such as Christmas, weddings and christenings. As it contains a lot of wet fruit (stewed apple) it tends to get moldy fairly quickly in warm weather. It is best made close to the time you require it, and kept in the fridge or a cool spot.

MAKES 1 (9 INCH) CAKE

1 cup golden raisins
1 cup seedless raisins, roughly chopped
1 cup currants
1 cup dates, roughly chopped
6 dried figs, roughly chopped
1 teaspoon grated ginger
3 cups water
3 teaspoons genmai miso
½ cup pear juice concentrate (or maple syrup)
3 teaspoons natural vanilla extract
1½ tablespoons almond oil
3 apples, peeled, cored and chopped
3 cups whole wheat flour (wheat or spelt)
1 tablespoon baking powder
1 teaspoon mixed spice
1 teaspoon ground cinnamon
¼ teaspoon freshly grated nutmeg
1 cup brazil nuts, roughly chopped
1 cup walnuts or pecans, roughly chopped
20 to 30 raw or blanched almonds, to decorate
2 to 3 tablespoons brandy (optional)

Preheat the oven to 325°F. Lightly grease a 9 inch cake pan and line the base and sides with baking paper.

Place the golden raisins, raisins, currants, dates, figs, ginger and water in a saucepan and bring to the boil. Immediately turn off the heat and allow to cool. Once cool, add the miso, pear juice concentrate, vanilla extract and almond oil. Mix gently together.

Meanwhile, put the apple in a small saucepan with 1 to 2 tablespoons of water. Stew over a gentle heat until the apples are very soft. Strain through a sieve to remove any excess liquid.

Put the flour, baking powder and spices in a bowl and mix together with a whisk to combine. Add the brazil nuts and walnuts and give a brief stir. Add the cooked fruit mixture and stewed apple to the dry ingredients. Mix well. Spoon into the pan and press the almonds onto the top in the desired pattern. Bake for 3½ hours, or until cooked and a skewer comes out clean. Once the cake has been cooking for about 20 to 30 minutes cover the top with foil to prevent it from burning. As soon as the cake comes out of the oven, pour over the brandy, if using. Allow to cool for 10 minutes, then turn onto a wire rack to cool.

Chocolate beet cake

DAIRY FREE / VEGAN

This is a rich cake, designed to be served in small portions as a celebration cake. It keeps well, but the frosting (being extremely low in fat) does not. You can successfully use 3 eggs instead of the egg replacer.

MAKES 1 (9½ INCH) CAKE

3 medium beets
3 cups unbleached all-purpose flour (wheat or spelt)
1 cup cocoa powder
3 teaspoons baking powder
2 cups raw sugar
1½ cups almond oil
½ cup milk (soy or rice)
1½ tablespoons natural vanilla extract
1¼ tablespoons egg replacer, beaten with ⅔ cup water (or 3 eggs)

CHOCOLATE ICING
3½ ounces dark chocolate, roughly broken
10½ ounces silken tofu
3 teaspoons natural vanilla extract
2 tablespoons and 1 teaspoon maple syrup

Wash the unpeeled beets, then boil or steam for 30 minutes, or until tender. Leave to cool, then remove the skins and purée in a food processor. You should have about 2 cups of beet purée.

Preheat the oven to 325°F. Lightly grease a 9½ inch spring-form cake pan and line the base and sides with baking paper.

Sift the flour, cocoa powder and baking powder into a bowl. Add the sugar and whisk gently to combine. In a separate bowl, blend the almond oil, milk, beet purée, vanilla and egg replacer and mix together until smooth. Add the wet ingredients to the dry and stir gently until combined. Pour into the prepared cake pan and bake for 1 hour and 30 minutes to 1 hour and 50 minutes, or until the center is cooked and a skewer comes out clean. Allow to cool for 10 minutes, then turn onto a wire rack to cool.

The frosting can also be served as a simple mousse. Divide between six small ramekins, molds, or espresso cups and chill until serving.

To make the frosting, put the broken-up chocolate pieces in a heat-proof bowl sitting over a saucepan of barely simmering water and gently heat until melted. Put all the ingredients in a food processor or blender and blend until it forms a smooth consistency and color. Spoon into a bowl and allow to cool and set completely before using.

Cover the cake with the chocolate frosting. Serve with fresh raspberries, whipped cream, almond cream (see page 250) or vanilla anglaise (see page 253).

Oaty fruit cookies

DAIRY FREE /WHEAT FREE / VEGAN

These are handy to put in lunch boxes and great to snack on. The oatmeal is used to help stick everything together, without becoming too gummy. Kneading and squeezing the mixture together is important, and contributes greatly to the cookies sticking together.

MAKES 10 (2½ INCH) COOKIES

3 cups rolled (flaked) oats
¾ cup oatmeal
¼ cup toasted sesame seeds
¼ cup desiccated coconut
½ cup dried apricots, finely chopped
½ cup golden raisins, finely chopped
1½ tablespoons egg replacer mixed with ¼ cup water (or 2 eggs)
½ cup almond oil
½ cup honey

Preheat the oven to 350°F. Line a baking tray with baking paper.

Place all the dry ingredients in a bowl and mix together. Add the wet ingredients and knead all the ingredients together with your hands, squeezing the mixture together. This will help ensure the moisture comes into contact with the oatmeal.

Shape about 3 tablepoons of the mix into a golfball-sized ball, place on the baking tray and press into a circle shape, about 2 inches in diameter and ½ inch thick. Continue to shape the rest of the mix and place on the tray. Bake for 10 to 15 minutes, or until light golden. Cool completely before moving.

If you find these cookies too sticky to shape, wash your hands and keep them slightly wet.

Date and ginger cookies

DAIRY FREE / WHEAT FREE / VEGAN

- ¾ cup dried dates, finely chopped
- 3 cups rolled (flaked) oats
- ¾ cup oatmeal
- ½ cup walnuts, finely chopped
- ½ cup glacé ginger, finely chopped
- 1½ tablespoons egg replacer mixed with ¼ cup water (or 2 eggs)
- ½ cup almond oil
- ½ cup honey

Preheat the oven to 350°F. Line a baking tray with baking paper.

Soak the dates in ¼ cup of boiling water for 10 minutes, then mash with a fork.

Combine the oats, oatmeal, walnuts and glacé ginger in a bowl. Add the mashed dates and all the wet ingredients. Knead together with your hands, until well combined.

Shape about 3 tablespoons of the mix into a golfball-sized ball, place on to the baking sheet and press into a circle shape 2 inches in diameter and ½ inch thick. Continue to shape the rest of the mix and place on the tray. Bake for 10 to 15 minutes, or until light golden. Cool completely before moving.

the wholefood pantry

Glossary

Don't be put off by some of these ingredients if you haven't heard of them before and think that they are difficult to find—they're not. All of these ingredients can be found in healthfood/natural food stores and many can also be found in the natural foods section of your local supermarket.

Seasonings and standards

These are the tools you will need to enhance and brighten flavor, and to help bring out the best in a dish.

Black pepper

Pepper is high in volatile oils that will quickly disappear once exposed to air—it should therefore be freshly ground just before using. Freshly ground black pepper has a distinctive lemon smell to it that is quite delicious.

Eggs

Eggs are traditionally used to add moisture in the form of fat and liquid and to bind ingredients together. Generally, the more eggs used, the lighter the finished product will be.

Herbamare

This is a sea salt product that has been infused with biodynamic vegetables, herbs and kelp. It is a rich source of nutrients and tastes delicious. It is especially handy for adding flavor where subtlety is required; for example, in béchamel sauce.

Herbs

Fundamental for adding flavor, herbs are a cooking essential. Fresh will deliver a brighter and lighter flavor, while dried will give more concentrated, deeper and stronger flavor.

Kelpamare

Kelpamare is a fermented stock base product, made from the juices of fresh vegetables, herbs and enriched with kelp. It is a good source of iodine. The smallest amount will ground and enrich (both flavor and nourishment) savory dishes. It can be diluted into a stock.

Mirin

This is a sweet and subtle wine, fermented from rice. It works well to bring ingredients together, and has an ability to soften harshness of taste, and harmonize discordant flavors. It is indispensable when using lentils, counterbalancing their astringency beautifully. True (unprocessed) mirin is fermented, producing enzymes and lactic acid bacteria traditionally valued for good health. It does, however, have an alcohol content of approximately 12 per cent (and organic mirin higher still).

Nuts

These are useful in so many ways—to add extra fat to cakes and cookies, to reduce the tendency of flour to stick together and to provide flavor.

Sea salt

Either plain or flavored, sea salt in its natural state is a soft grey color, coarse and often damp, but extremely rich in minerals and trace elements.

Shoyu and tamari

These are soy sauces fermented in the traditional way. Tamari is available in wheat-free and salt-reduced varieties and is an invaluable tool to enhance and highlight flavor. Shoyu has a noticeably stronger fermented taste and contains wheat. When the weather is hot, these are best kept in the fridge.

Spices

These can be fresh commercial ground spices, but for superior flavor, freshly roast and grind them yourself. To do this, roast over a low heat—without adding any extra oil. Stir or shake lightly until they are lightly colored and become fragrant, being careful not to burn them, and then grind.

Tahini

This is a paste made from sesame seeds and is a rich source of calcium. It can be used as a spread instead of butter, or mixed into a dressing, a rich source of calcium. Buy good quality organic tahini, preferably those that have had their hulls removed.

Whey

When milk sours, lacto-fermentation takes place and the end result is a separation of the protein containing curds and the extremely valuable, watery whey. It is used when soaking grains.

Sea vegetables commonly come in dried form and expand when rehydrated—so it's good to remember when buying them that a little goes a long way. To rehydrate, cover them well with cold water and stand for approximately 15 to 30 minutes. Strain and squeeze out the excess liquid and use.

Sea vegetables

Sea vegetables (or seaweed) are an extremely concentrated source of nutrients. They are rich sources of protein, vitamin A, vitamin B group, vitamin C, iron, iodine, trace minerals and calcium.

Agar (agar-agar)

This is a nutrient-rich, high-fiber, no-calorie gelling agent made from seaweed. It comes in flakes, powder and bars. Agar will set at room temperature and can be boiled and reheated without losing its gelling ability. To achieve a good, but not too solid jelly, the basic equation is 1 tablespoon agar flakes or ½ teaspoon powder to 1 cup liquid. Agar will not set in distilled and wine vinegars or food with large amounts of oxalic acid (such as chocolate, rhubarb or spinach).

Arame
Rich in calcium and iodine, arame is a thin, noodle-like sea vegetable. Traditionally used to treat high blood pressure, breast and uterine fibroids, and to normalize menopausal symptoms. It is popular for promoting good, wrinkle-free skin. It can be added to salads and stir-fries and is excellent in soups.

Kelp
Rich in calcium, potassium, magnesium and iron, kelp is great for adding dry to soups and stews, or soaked and added to stir-fries.

Kombu
Containing glutamic acid, the safe and natural form of MSG, this is a wonder helper in the kitchen. It enriches and boosts the flavor of stocks, soups, stews and grains and tenderizes beans. Kombu is a high-protein sea vegetable, containing iodine, carotenes, the B, C, D and E vitamins, calcium, magnesium, potassium, silica, iron, zinc and germanium.

Nori
This sea vegetable is rich in carotenes, calcium, iodine, iron, phosphorous and protein. Nori sheets are available pre-toasted and ready to eat. Most famous as the nori roll, they are also great to crumble or cut into strips and add to soups (particularly miso), salads or even a bowl of steamed vegetables and brown rice. They are however, very fragile and must be sealed well once the packet has been opened—air and moisture make them very difficult to roll.

Wakame
A lovely sea vegetable—when rehydrated it is a beautiful green leaf with a mild flavor. It is a good choice for salads and stir-fries—incredibly rich in calcium with high levels of B and C vitamins.

Soy

These are the most common foodstuffs and names you will come across in regard to soy products.

Isoflavones

Plant-based estrogens, often referred to as phyto-estrogens. The best known isoflavone is genistein.

Miso

A fermented paste, miso is traditionally made from soy beans and salt, but often with added grains. Koji (*Aspergillus orzae* culture) is added to cooked soy beans with salt and left to ferment. The longer this fermentation takes place, the stronger the flavor. Miso is a source of vitamin B12 and is an excellent alkalinizer. Unpasteurized miso is a rich source of live *lactobacillus*.

Miso comes in a wide variety of flavors and colors. Two good misos are genmai (brown rice miso) and shiro (white rice miso). Pasteurized genmai is useful for adding flavor and depth to soups and stews, and unpasteurized genmai miso is great as a spread or for miso soup. Shiro miso works well in dressings and dips—to soften and bring flavors together.

Natto miso

Strongly flavored, natto is made from cooked soy beans and fermented with kombu, barley and often ginger. It has a rough texture and is used as a condiment.

Shoyu and tamari

See page 302 for information on shoyu and tamari.

Soy milk

See page 311 for information on soy milk.

Tofu

See chapter on 'soy' for more information on tofu.

Tempeh

See chapter 4 'soy' soy for more information on tempeh.

Textured vegetable protein

This is a highly refined, unfermented product used to replace beef. Not at all recommended.

Sweeteners

Sugar is a primary fuel for the body, but nature goes to a lot of trouble to make sure it is released into the body slowly. Sugar is generally encased and held within more complex forms, and it is released slowly as that food is broken down. When refined and separated from the valuable minerals and fiber, this pure (bleached) sucrose is like high-octane fuel to the body. It burns rapidly, overstimulating the pancreas to release insulin and leaching minerals (calcium in particular) from the bones. White, raw and brown sugar are basically highly refined sugar cane juice, with colors and, in the case of light and dark brown sugars, some of the molasses added back to the refined white sugar.

There are sugar products made from minimally processed organic sugar cane. After the cane is harvested, it is pressed to squeeze out the cane juice, which is then clarified, filtered and evaporated to remove excess water. The resulting syrup is then crystallized, and is rich with molasses flavor and the vitamins, minerals and trace elements that are naturally found in the sugar cane plant. This is often referred to as rapadura sugar, and is a high-quality whole sweetener. Sucanat is a similar product that has recently become far more refined. Both have a low to medium sweetening power with a marked molasses flavor. There are other types of 'unrefined' sugars available, and these include:

- organic raw sugar: often overly sweet, but a good choice when you want to use a very small amount with no interference of flavor.
- sifted cane sugar: an evaporated cane juice (like rapadura and sucanat) that is washed rather than bleached to remove much of the molasses flavor, leaving a more wholesome, but lighter tasting end product.
- demerara: a darker raw sugar that provides sweetness without a distinctive flavor.
- light muscovado: this is similar to a light brown sugar.
- dark muscovado: this is similar to a dark brown sugar.
- molasses sugar: similar to a dark muscovado, and rich in iron.
- superfine sugar and confectioners' sugar: with a subtle sweetness and golden hue.

Amasake (amazake)

With a very subtle sweetening power, amasake is a fermented rice product. Approximately 1½ to 2 tablespoons of amasake equals 1 tablespoon of sugar. It varies in cost and taste, but has a noticeably fermented taste.

Apple juice concentrate

Used to add an earthy sweetness to dishes, apple juice concentrate is an especially good counterpart for tomato. It is also good for sweetening chutney.

Barley malt and rice malt

These are the least sweet, and closest to a wholefood sweetener. They contain a high percentage of complex sugars, which take longer to digest than highly refined, simple sugars. In sauces, syrups and soft desserts they work well; however, they provide a chewy/brittle toffee texture in baking. They work well in combination with maple syrup. Rice malt is the more mildly flavored of the two.

Dried and fresh fruit

Often overlooked as tools to sweeten, fruit is a powerful medium to deliver natural sugars. Dates are the easiest way to use dried fruit to sweeten, but golden raisins and raisins are also excellent.

Maple syrup

The concentrated sap of maple trees, maple syrup is a wonderful sweetening agent. Rich in trace minerals, it imparts a beautiful taste to food. Organic maple syrup is very sweet, and only requires a small amount for a lot of sweetening power. It will, however, impart golden tones of color to the finished product.

Pear juice concentrate

This is best used in small amounts to balance a savory dish, rather than larger amounts to sweeten cakes and desserts. This has more sweetening power than apple juice concentrate, with a beautiful, fruity fullness. It is a good counterpart to the highly astringent family of lentils, particularly brown. It is also good for curries and dal where the fruity flavor is a positive contribution.

Raw honey

Much sweeter than sugar, honey contains sucrose and fructose. It is excellent used as a sweet topping but not for baking cakes as it will result in a chewy result. Look for raw honey—unfiltered, unprocessed, unrefined and unheated, which will still have its enzymes intact.

Stevia

Stevia rebaudiana is a plant native to Paraguay, where its leaves have been used as a sweetener for centuries and as a remedy for diabetes. It is available as a liquid, a white powder (where the sweetening components are separated) and in a more whole form, where the leaves are ground into a fine powder. Stevia is intensely sweet—too much and you will end up with a very bitter result. It is excellent in sweetening fruit desserts, but not as good in baked goods.

Vanilla bean, natural vanilla extract and essence

Vanilla is of enormous value for flavoring cakes and desserts. The seeds from the vanilla bean add a subtle flavor and are excellent when you don't want the color of extract to influence the finished product. To extract the seeds, simply cut down the length of the vanilla bean. Using a blunt knife, run it along the inside of the bean, scraping out the small black seeds. If using a natural vanilla extract or essence, it is important to buy good quality.

Good vanilla extract is just vanilla extractives and alchohol, inferior ones contain corn syrup, glycerin, fructose, propylene glycol and preservatives. True vanilla extract will give a truer and more beautiful flavor.

Oils

There are many good oils available, organically grown and cold pressed, full of nutritional goodness.

Almond oil

Cold pressed and refined with clay, rather than chemicals or heat, this is a good choice for cake and dessert work. It is naturally light colored, with a sweet taste.

Coconut oil

Sometimes called coconut butter, look for unrefined coconut oil, which in the cooler months will be solid at room temperature. A saturated and extremely stable fat, this is also a good choice for frying or heating (as in shallow or deep frying). Also an excellent choice for dessert and cookie work.

Flaxseed oil

This has a nutty flavor and is an excellent choice for dressing. It is high in Omega 3 fatty acid, and is an extremely fragile (unsaturated) oil that must be kept in the fridge. This oil should only ever be bought in a dark bottle from a fridge and should not be heated.

Macadamia nut oil

With a delicate flavor, this oil is good on an Asian or fruity salad.

Olive oil

A versatile and stable oil, olive oil is a cooking essential. Preferably use extra virgin olive oil and, when using raw (such as in a salad) where the taste of the oil is paramount, use unfiltered extra virgin oil.

Peanut oil

Both straight peanut oil and roasted peanut oil are available. They are great for Asian-inspired dressings. Peanuts, however, are a common cause of food allergies, and this needs to be taken into account before using.

Sesame oil

Unrefined sesame oil is a pure sesame oil, beautiful for Asian-influenced dressings. It can also be used for light heating (such as sautéing) and is a better option than peanut oil, which is not as stable to heat.

Roasted sesame oil is very strongly flavored oil—a little goes a long way. It comes with a variety of names; some brands even call it 'pure sesame oil'—if it is dark colored, it is roasted.

Safflower oil

This is one of the more highly unsaturated oils and thus very prone to rancidity. Only use a high oleic safflower oil, which is more stable than straight safflower oil.

Sunflower oil

A true organic sunflower oil has an extremely assertive taste. Only choose a high oleic sunflower oil.

Walnut oil

This oil is also high in omega 3 essential fatty acid, with a delicious taste. It partners beautifully with beet, parsnip, pear and apple. It is an extremely fragile (unsaturated) oil that must be kept in the fridge. This oil should only be bought in a can from a fridge, as it can easily become rancid.

Vinegar and other acids

True vinegar, traditionally produced, is the product of long fermentation over many months. Unpasteurized and unfiltered, it can be a rich source of many nutrients, and is very different to many, instantly produced, vinegars on the market today. Buy vinegar in glass—it is a solvent and will break down the polycarbons in plastic.

Apple cider vinegar

Unfiltered apple cider vinegar (a naturally fermented vinegar made from apples) is a health-promoting vinegar, and an extremely rich source of potassium. It is the best choice for making chutneys and pickling.

Brown rice vinegar

This vinegar is a perfect choice for Asian-inspired dressings and matches well with sesame oil. It works well with sushi nori in combinations with the rice and mirin. It is also good for pickling

Balsamic vinegar

This is a sweet low-acid vinegar with depth and richness of flavor. It is a good choice for Mediterranean-inspired salads including root vegetables.

Lemon

This is a classic acid to use with extra virgin olive oil in a dressing.

Lime

A little lime juice used with brown rice vinegar is a great combination for Thai-style salads.

Umeboshi
Technically not a vinegar, but the pickling salts from the umeboshi plum process, which drips down as they pickle. This is an excellent choice for use in a salad dressing, with great fruit flavor.

Wine vinegar
These are made from white or red wine, sherry or Champagne, each has something to offer. Champagne vinegar has a delicate, sharp and light flavor, while sherry is assertive and highly acidic. White wine mixes well with herbs while red will anchor a hearty salad.

Milk

Milk provides color, moisture, flavor and, in some cases, fat. It is important to consider the particular taste of the milk, and in baking it is essential to take into account the fat content of the milk you choose.

Almond milk
With a beautiful, sweet taste, this is a good choice for desserts. It is important to note, however, that homemade almond milk is far superior to that which is commercially available.

Coconut milk and coconut cream
Stir well before using. Avoid low-fat options as they tend to have additives and stablilizers. The coconut flavor can influence the taste of the dish, so it is good to use it in combination with other milk, such as rice milk.

Dairy milk (whole, non-homogenized)
With a high fat content, this milk adds wonderful flavor and texture to desserts and baked goods.

Rice milk
There are advantages and disadvantages to using rice milk. It is a sweet milk (very handy for desserts and cakes), however it is quite watery and lacking in fat. The sweetness should be taken into account in relation to other ingredients when using

and its watery nature thickened and made creamy with coconut milk. Adding coconut milk will also add some fat to the milk mix, making it more usable in cakes and desserts.

Soy milk

This is 'milk' made from unfermented, soaked and cooked soy beans. Many of the cheaper soy milks are made from soy protein isolate (SPI), with additions of highly refined oil and sugar. Keep in mind that the quality (and therefore the flavor) of the soy milk will be reflected in the end result. Care must be taken for gluten-free cooking, as most soy milks use barley malt, which is a gluten grain. Choose soy milk that is malt free. Soy milk is low in fat and this needs to be taken into account.

Be selective when buying soy milk, as many are a highly processed soy product, with large amounts of refined oil and white sugar. They also often have a strong taste that will influence the flavor of the finished product.

Beans and legumes

Adzuki beans

Considered the king of beans in Japan and extremely nourishing for the kidneys, adzuki are also much easier to digest than other beans.

Black lentils

Also called caviar or beluga lentils, they are less common than other varieties. They can be interchanged with green or brown lentils in recipes.

Black beans

Deeply flavored and delicious, these beans are particularly good in Mexican dishes. Be careful when soaking, as they can stain.

Black-eyed peas (black-eyed beans, cowpeas)

Often sold as beans, but none the less a pea. They are great in soups, stews and dips, and excellent in salads. A favorite.

Borlotti (cranberry) beans

Borlotti are great for stews and they mash well for dips. When fresh, they take approximately 30 minutes to cook.

Brown lentils

These are larger than a green lentil, with a strong, deep, astringent taste. They hold their shape well, but can easily be puréed.

Cannellini beans

This is a white bean with a soft, mellow flavor. Be careful not to overcook, as they can lose their shape.

Channa dal

These must be pre-soaked. Related to the chickpea family, black (also called brown) channa and split channa (yellow channa) are available.

Chickpeas

Technically peas, chickpeas are most often categorized as a bean due to their long cooking time. They are excellent for dips, stews and salads, and work well with curry flavors.

Fava beans

A good bean for Italian and other Mediterranean dishes, these vary greatly in size. As they cook their skins loosen—and must be removed for best flavor.

Great northern beans

White beans, larger than navy beans, with a beautiful creamy flesh.

Green lentils

These are small, hold their shape well and can be used in place of brown lentils. The best known are 'Puy lentils.'

Green split peas

These are quite sweet and an excellent addition to vegetable soups—providing flavor and body. Yellow are not as sweet, but excellent for soups, dips and dal.

Kidney beans

One of the harder beans to digest, kidney beans work best in dishes that cook for a long time. They have a deep strong flavor.

Lima (butter) beans

This is a delicate and delicious bean. Be careful not to overcook—they tend to crumble and disintegrate easily. Baby limas are also available, and are delicious in salads.

Mung (moong) bean

Probably the most widely known of the dal family, these are small and yellow and cook quickly. They are an easy to digest and nourishing legume.

Navy beans

Creamy textured and sweet, these are the classic for baked beans.

Pinto beans

Pintos are excellent for any Mexican dish. They are sweet and lightly flavored.

Red lentils (masoor, mansoor or mussouri dal)

These are small lentils that break down easily when cooked. Best used in soups—they can also add flavor and help to thicken dals and pâté bases.

Soy beans

Soy beans have little flavor and are rarely served in their natural form. They contain large amounts of protein and nourishment and are used to make tofu and tempeh.

Toor (toovar) dal

Often known as pigeon peas, this dal is also particularly easy to digest. They are often sold with a covering of castor oil for protection against insects—simply wash this off before use.

Urad (urid) dal

Rich in protein, small and greyish in color, these are sometimes found with the skin intact.

Whole red lentils (brown masoor)

These are sold with their skins on, and resemble a small brown lentil, but inside are characteristically red. The skins are quite astringent and need counterbalancing to soften the taste.

Grains

Barley

Barley is a high-starch grain—and wonderful for use in winter soups. As the soup cooks, the barley starch helps to thicken it, while providing flavor, texture and creaminess. For this reason, it is also a good alternative to rice for a winter risotto. The most commonly used barley has two hard inedible husks. Thus, most barley is milled to some degree to make it edible.

The barley used in these recipes is good quality hulled/whole brown grain. Organic growers generally refer to it as pearled, although technically it should be hulled or whole.

Pearled barley

Good, organic or biodynamic pearled barley has had the outer husks removed, but the germ and bran left intact and is brownish in appearance, while supermarket-bought pearled barley removes all but the inner white grain and is highly refined.

Barley flakes or rolled barley

This is barley that has been steamed, rolled and flattened so that it cooks more quickly.

Barley meal

Hulled and broken down into very small pieces, this barley requires only a short cooking time (excellent for porridge).

Naked barley

This is an old variety, no longer popular due to its low yield. It naturally occurs with little husk, so when available it is less refined than pearled barley.

Buckwheat (gluten free)

Technically, buckwheat is not a grain at all, but rather a fruit related to the rhubarb family. Historically, it is a staple peasant food, most noteably in the cold climates of Russia. When other crops failed, buckwheat was a grain that could be relied on, able to grow in the poorest soil. It has a distinctive nutty taste and an earthy quality that works well with root vegetables, onions and mushrooms.

Buckwheat is high in protein (particularly lysine), is a rich source of the B vitamins and a major source of bioflavinoid, rutin, which is good for the heart and circulation). Soba (buckwheat) has long been treasured as a health food in Japan.

Buckwheat groats (kasha)
Technically buckwheat is called *groats* when unroasted, and *kasha* when roasted. When unroasted they are a pale, almost light green and tan color, with a bland flavor that requires dry roasting to develop flavor.

Cracked buckwheat
Most cracked buckwheat is made from unroasted groats, broken down into smaller pieces. It can be used for porridge.

Soba noodles
Made from buckwheat flour, soba noodles are absolutely delicious in Asian inspired noodle bowls, stir-fries or salads. Be selective when buying, however, as many soba noodles available use half wheat flour.

Corn (gluten free)
Corn is one of the most loved grains around the world. 'Corne' was the Old English word for the predominate grain of the land; thus when the English landed in the New World (the Americas), and saw the abundance of maize growing, they named it ' Indian corne.' There are many varieties of corn products and unfortunately they are often called by different names in different stores.

Corn on the cob (sweet corn or green corn)
Grown for use as a vegetable, this truly is a 'sweet corn.' Good sweet corn has to be fresh; once picked, it begins to convert its sugars into starch.

Even corn bought fresh from the markets will be at least a day old and this period of time is enough for a marked reduction in flavor. There are however, new strains of sweet corn being developed (such as silver queen) that slow down this conversion, so it pays to ask what kind of corn you are buying.

Polenta (cornmeal)
Made from a hard corn, this is either a coarsely or finely ground meal. In many cases the skin and germ are removed to extend shelf life. Search and ask for polenta that is made from corn with the germ intact (this should be stored in the fridge to avoid spoilage). In some cookbooks this is often referred to as cornmeal, in others it is called polenta.

Mealie meal
This is a whole polenta (skin and germ intact)—a white corn that has been ground into a meal. Cool storage conditions are crucial to avoid spoilage.

Cornmeal

Softer than polenta, this is a mix of a finer-ground polenta and corn flour. It makes good soft polenta or porridge but is too soft for sturdier work.

Blue or red corn

This blue- or red-colored corn is usually ground into flour and used for tortillas. The blue is higher in the amino acid, lysine, and has a fabulous flavor.

Popcorn

With an especially hard endosperm, these are corn kernels that 'pop' when heated.

Millet (gluten free)

Millet is vastly underrated, but it is a superb, gluten-free grain. It has an equal-to-higher protein level than wheat, is high in phosphorous and B vitamins and very high in iron. Millet (hulled) has a lovely buttery, sweet taste. It responds particularly well to dry roasting before cooking.

Whole millet

This has the husk still intact and birds love it. It is difficult for humans to digest, but is good for sprouting. To use whole millet it should be ground and will take approximately 1 hour to cook.

Hulled millet

This is easier to digest than whole millet.

Millet flakes

These are the rolled (flattened) whole millet grains.

Oats

Oats are higher in unsaturated fats than other grains, and are usually thought of as a winter grain. This higher fat content provides energy for warming, and hence their place in many cold-climate cultures, such as Scotland.

Oat groats/Oat kernels

These are whole oats from which only the inedible outer hull has been removed.

Rolled oats (or oat flakes)

Probably the most common form of oats, these are oat groats/kernels that have been steamed and flattened. If you see rolled oats referred to as 'stabilized,' this means that they have been steamed to make rolling easier.

Steel cut oats (Scottish)

These are oat groats/kernels that have been cut into small pieces.

Whole oats

This has the outer husk still intact and is generally sold for sprouting.

Oats are generally used more often in sweet foods rather than savory, and with good reason. The higher fat content of oats works to adds moistness to scones, cookies, desserts and cakes. Biodynamic oats have been noted to carry some vitamin B12, and their ability to positively effect good (HDL) cholesterol levels in the body is also documented.

Quinoa (gluten free)

Quinoa is a recent addition to the Western world and not technically a grain, but a member of the *Chenopodium* plant family. Greatly revered and called 'the mother grain' by the ancient Incas, quinoa boasts the highest amount of protein among all grains and is exceptionally high in B vitamins and calcium. It is a rich source vitamin E and contains the amino acid, lysine. It is coated with saponin, a natural insecticide, and must be washed well before using.

It is a wonderfully versatile grain with a delicate flavor, which requires only a short amount of cooking time. Traditionally, all quinoa is pre-soaked or (at least) well rinsed, and when it is cooked a tiny, white spiral appears, encircling the grain. Flakes, pasta and flour quinoa are all commercially available.

Rice (gluten free)

For many people with allergies, rice and millet are the most easily tolerated grains. Generally speaking, brown rice has a nuttier, stronger flavor, and is more nutritious than white rice.

Arborio

An ideal rice for making risotto, it is covered in a soft starch that dissolves during cooking, contributing to the creaminess that is so essential. This rice should never be rinsed. Other varieties include carnaroli and vialone.

Basmati

This a beautifully flavored long-grain rice. Nutty, yet sweet, this works well with curry and coconut flavors. Brown basmati is also available, but is less common.

Jasmine

This is another fragrant long-grain rice. Originally from Thailand, it has a sweet and smooth taste.

Brown

With the bran and germ intact, brown rice comes in long- and short-grain varieties. Short-grain rice is generally stickier and is the best choice for desserts, sushi and rice balls where the stickiness is an advantage. Long grain tends to remain separate and is preferable for savory dishes such as fried rice, pilafs or served on its own. Brown rice flour can be used as porridge, and is the essential flour for gluten-free baking.

Sticky (glutinous)

This can be both long- and short-grained, with a high starch content a little like arborio. It comes in black, white and even red; it is used for 'mochi' and is the essential ingredient for sticky rice puddings.

Wild

Technically, this is not actually rice, but an aquatic grass seed. Nutritionally speaking, wild rice has more B vitamins and protein than other rice, with a very assertive flavor. It is best used in combination with brown rice, to soften the taste. Wild rice generally takes 1 hour to cook, with a ratio of 3 cups liquid to 1 cup wild rice. Allow it to sit and steam with the lid on after cooking for 10 minutes.

Wheat, spelt and kamut

Perhaps the most prevalent cereal grain grown and consumed in the world today, wheat is one of the world's most valuable currencies. Because it is so important, it is usually highly protected, and is thus generally treated with a good deal of herbicides, pesticides and fungicides, both in its growing and storing stages. It is this enormous exposure to chemicals that contributes to its being one of the most allergenic substances for people.

Spelt and kamut are precursors to what we know as wheat today, and contain a more digestible form of gluten. Spelt flour is particularly wonderful, because you can use it in place of wheat flour for just about everything, with fabulous results.

Wheat is usually referred to as hard or soft; the harder it is, the higher the gluten content. The high gluten content in hard wheat is essential for successful bread making, while the softer wheat, with lower gluten levels, is useful in cakes and pastries.

Bulgar

These are wheat berries that have been cooked (usually steamed) then dried and cracked. Because of this, it takes a very short time to be ready for use, just needing reconstituting with a liquid.

Bulgar is best used in combination with other flavors, rather than just cooked and served on its own (as for rice). It is a particularly good choice for a pilaf, adds texture and body to stews and soups and works well in patties. Probably its most famous role is in tabouleh.

Bulgar is an assertive-tasting grain and responds well to strong flavors, both in spices and vegetables. It marries best with Middle Eastern flavors, such as fresh cilantro or ground coriander, parsley, mint, allspice, cinnamon, cumin and pine nuts.

Couscous

This was the fast food wonder of the 1990s and is made from precooked, and then dried, semolina (the coarsely ground endosperm of hard wheat). Couscous, like anything else, varies in quality. Good, organic couscous is slightly darker in color and nuttier in flavor and is readily available.

Wheat, rye or spelt berries

These are the whole grain wheat or rye or spelt with only the husk removed. They can be labeled groats or wheat berries—make sure the husks are removed. Chewy and sturdy, they make a great addition to salads and soups.

Flours and thickeners

Arrowroot (gluten free)

Similar in appearance to cornstarch, arrowroot comes from the root of a tropical plant that grows on tidal flats, absorbing sea minerals and calcium. It can be used as a thickening agent for sauces, but is not as effective as cornstarch.

Atta flour

This is a whole wheat flour that has been sifted to remove some of the heavier bran, it is, so to speak, a light whole wheat flour.

Barley flour
Used in small portions, this is a good alternative to wheat and readily available.

Brown rice flour (gluten free)
This is the foundation of gluten-free baking; its advantage is a smooth and mellow flavor.

Buckwheat flour (gluten free)
This is a beautiful-tasting flour, but one that is best used in combination with other flours, either brown rice or wheat. Buckwheat flour will absorb large amounts of liquid and become quite viscous when left to sit.

Cornstarch (gluten free)
Check the packet when you buy cornstarch as it is often actually made from wheat.

An extremely fine ground starch, cornstarch is used as a thickening agent and is particularly useful where some structure is required in the finished product, as opposed to a sauce. It is also used in small portions as a flour, to aid binding.

Kudzu (kuzu) (gluten free)
In cooking, kudzu is a powder used to thicken, as you would use arrowroot or cornstarch, made from the starch of the kudzu plant. It is well known in Japan and China for its medicinal qualities, where it is traditionally used to treat digestive problems such as upset stomach and to sooth the nerves.

When used to thicken sauces it imparts a beautiful, clear sheen to the finished sauce. It will also set soft desserts. Kudzu must be completely dissolved first, and then gently brought to the boil, stirring constantly. Approximately 2 teaspoons will set 1 cup of liquid to sauce consistency, while 2 to 2½ tablespoons will set to a soft pudding consistency. Kudzu is usually bought in solid form, to measure, simply grind it up using either the end of the rolling pin in a bowl, or a pestle and mortar.

Corn flour
Made from 'flour corn,' this looks like a fine whole grain flour, and is a beautiful, pale yellow color.

Masa harina
This is a corn flour treated with lime and is used to make authentic corn tortillas.

Millet flour (gluten free)
Available in meal and flour, meal is ground from whole millet and the flour from hulled. Millet flour has a strongly astringent taste and is best used in partnership with other flours.

Commercally packaged gluten-free flour is generally made from potato flour, tapioca flour and other very refined starches and gums. It works by gumming things together and tends to do the same thing in your stomach.

Oatmeal, oatflour and rolled oats
With their high fat content, these are excellent alternatives to wheat, with a beautiful, mild taste. Oatmeal refers to the oat kernel, ground to a flour and is the preferred medium, excellent for binding ingredients. It is available as coarse, medium and fine grinds—fine is the best for baking. Oatflour is very similar to fine oatmeal. Rolled oats have been steamed and rolled and, even when ground, do not perform as well as oatmeal.

Potato flour (gluten free)
This is made from dried potato, finely ground, and has a consistency similar to cornstarch. It is very difficult to use and achieve anything but a gluey consistency.

Quinoa and amaranth flour (gluten free)
These flours are best used in very small quantities mixed with brown rice flour and a little almond meal to cut their very assertive flavors.

Rye flour
This is heavy in texture and taste and, therefore unsuited in cake or dessert work.

Soy flour (gluten free)
Ground from organic full-fat soy beans, it has a noticeably bitter taste and should only be used in small ratios with other flours.

Spelt
Also known as *dinkle* or *farro*, this is an ancient relative of modern wheat. It behaves almost identically to wheat flour, but has a much lower gluten content. Many people allergic to wheat flour find they can successfully eat spelt. It is available in whole wheat or unbleached plain.

Wheat flour

This is the traditional baking medium, available in whole wheat, unbleached and atta. Whole wheat refers to whole grain which has been ground. It can be ground by stone or mill; stone-milled is preferable as the process generates little heat, thus preserving the good quality fats in the germ. Unbleached flour is just the starchy inside and the least nutritious. Atta refers to whole wheat flour that has been sifted to remove some of the bran (a light whole wheat, so to speak). Most wheat flour available is made from hard wheat with a fairly high protein count, which results in heavier and drier cakes. Soft wheat (low protein count) flour is harder to come by, and is referred to as cake or pastry flour.

Index

D

E

F

G

H

T

U

V

Bibliography

Bertolli, Paul. *Cooking By Hand*. Clarkson Potter Publishers, 2003.

Colbin, Annemarie. *Food and Healing*. Ballentine Books, 1986.

Colbin, Annemarie. *Food and our Bones*. Penguin Books, 1998.

Enig, Mary. *Know Your Fats*. Bethesda Press, 2000.

Fallon, Sally. *Nourishing Traditions*. ProMotion Publishing, 1999.

Lewis, Edna. *In Pursuit of Flavour*. Knopf, 1988.

Madison, Deborah. *Vegetarian Cooking for Everyone*. Broadway Books, 1997.

Madison, Deborah. *The Savory Way*. Bantam Books, 1990.